Trafficking Subjects

Trafficking Subjects

The Politics of Mobility in Nineteenth-Century America

Mark Simpson

University of Minnesota Press
Minneapolis
London

An earlier version of chapter 1 was published as "Nat Turner at the Limits of Travel," *Cultural Critique* 37 (fall 1997). Parts of chapter 4 appeared in different form as "Travel's Disciplines," *Canadian Review of American Studies* 26, no. 2 (spring 1996): 83–115; reprinted with permission of University of Toronto Press Incorporated.

Published by the University of Minnesota Press
111 Third Avenue South, Suite 290
Minneapolis, MN 55401-2520
http://www.upress.umn.edu

Library of Congress Cataloging-in-Publication Data

Simpson, Mark, 1967-.
Trafficking subjects : the politics of mobility in nineteenth-century America / Mark Simpson.
p. cm.
Includes bibliographical references and index.
ISBN 0-8166-4162-5 (acid-free paper) — ISBN 0-8166-4163-3 (pbk. : acid-free paper)
1. United States—Social life and customs—19th century. 2. United States—Social conditions—19th century. 3. United States—Economic conditions—19th century. 4. Social mobility—United States—History—19th century. 5. Travel—Social aspects—United States—History—19th century. 6. Freedom of movement—United States—History—19th century. 7. Social mobility—United States—Historiography. 8. Social mobility in literature. 9. Travel—Social aspects—United States—Historiography. 10. Travel in literature. I. Title.
E161.S48 2004
304.8'0973'09034—dc22 2004015728

Printed in the United States of America on acid-free paper

The University of Minnesota is an equal-opportunity educator and employer.

12 11 10 09 08 07 06 05 10 9 8 7 6 5 4 3 2 1

In memory of
Margaret Ann Simpson

Contents

Acknowledgments

For me, the pages in this book read like secret maps that chart distances covered, pathways followed, contacts made, intimacies enjoyed, and debts incurred.

I am lucky to have such remarkable teachers to thank. At Alberta, Shirley Neuman and Ian MacLaren transformed my sense of reading. At Duke, Cathy Davidson, Ted Davidson, and Toril Moi asked questions that continue to provoke and inspire. Special thanks go to Janice Radway, who supervised the thesis from which this book developed. She taught me sustaining lessons about intellectual risk and trust. I cherish her incisive, exacting, generous commitment to my work. She is the best mentor anyone could have.

A number of friends, students, and colleagues have enlivened this project over the years. Early on, Jon Beller, James Cornelius, Dan Itzkovitz, Eva-Lynn Jagoe, Katie Kent, Scott Lucas, Diane McKay, Brian Neelon, Gus Stadler, Neferti Tadiar, David Thomson, Scott Trafton, and Ben Weaver tested my ideas with energy and verve. More recently, I have enjoyed insight, advice, and encouragement from Gamal Abdel-Shehid, Rachel Adams, Karyn Ball, Rosemary Banks, Glenn Burger, Mark Driscoll, Mo Engel, Judy Garber, Gary Kelly, Julie Rak, Stephen Slemon, Imre Szeman, Duncan Turner, Matthew Wispinski, and Teresa Zackodnik. During my time at Alberta, the four chairs of the English department, Pat Demers, Garrett Epp, Jim Mulvihill, and especially Jo-Ann Wallace, have offered invaluable support for my research as for my career. Christine Bold, Bill Brown, Mike Epp, Ian MacLaren, Nicole Shukin, Peter Sinnema, Pauline Wakeham, and Priscilla Walton have read versions of the manuscript in whole or in part, helping with their generous responses to improve its arguments exponentially. For well over a decade, Michael Lahey has brought vitality to the play of ideas, giving me new and unexpected ways to think about the products of culture. And for even longer, Heather Zwicker has been a sparkling interlocutor, my closest intellectual comrade.

My family has been a constant source of inspiration and support through this project's extended development. Memories of my grandfather George Hardy's great stories of great travels have, I now realize, textured my book from the start. Jean Mill always asked after the book's progress with interest and affection, as did my Edmonton cousins and, further afield, Helen and Barbara Dickinson. Frank Kroll wisely reminded me to enjoy some pause within the rush of things. My father, Jim Simpson, helped to sustain me materially as well as emotionally, with deep intellectual engagement and unwavering faith. Except for his support and his example, I could not have begun, much less completed, this project.

I feel tremendously fortunate to have an editor as gifted and supportive as Richard Morrison. His belief in my project and his expert guidance through the publication process have made the impossible seem possible after all. Thanks as well to the rest of the University of Minnesota Press staff—especially Pieter Martin and Andrea Kleinhuber for their editorial assistance, Daniel Leary and Mike Stoffel for their production assistance, Mary Poggione for her marketing expertise, and Paula Friedman, my incomparable copy editor. Two anonymous readers supplied rigorous commentary that challenged me to make my arguments stronger. A grant from the Social Sciences and Humanities Research Council of Canada brought the teaching release necessary to finish the manuscript.

Well before I undertook to question travel as a concept, I learned from my parents to love traveling. They have given me numerous routes to explore and countless memories to embrace. So too has Leslea Kroll, whose passion and wit, intelligence and care, nourished me in writing this book. Her spirited restlessness guides me in all things. She is my nerve and transport, the one who moves me, the one with whom I always want to move.

Introduction

For a Politics of Mobility

> For it does seem that mobility, and control over mobility, both reflects and reinforces power.
>
> —*Doreen Massey, "A Global Sense of Place"*

Simon Pokagon's visit to Chicago's White City on 9 October 1893 was not an uncomplicated one. He was hardly the typical tourist: a tribal leader of the Michigan Potawatomi (the last remainder in the region of an Algonquin people forcibly removed to the Plains from their traditional lands around the Great Lakes), Pokagon had been invited to participate in the Chicago Day celebrations at the World's Columbian Exposition by ringing the Columbian Liberty Bell and addressing the assembled dignitaries. Unrefusable, the invitation was nonetheless more insult than honor, the belated, begrudging inclusion of a man whose father had, some sixty years earlier, ceded in treaty the land on which the fairgrounds stood.[1]

Pokagon's words that day rang with dispiriting urgency. He proclaimed the inevitability of Native erasure in America: "Our children *must* learn that they owe no allegiance to any clan or power on earth except the United States. They must learn to love the Stars and Stripes, and, at all times, to rejoice that they are American citizens."[2] Although often recalled to cement Pokagon's reputation as an assimilationist cipher, his speech does point to the impossibility of the situation he faced—and so to the kind of crisis inevitably attending American Indian performance at the World's Columbian.[3] From the start, the fair had turned aboriginality to profit while consistently avoiding any official Native participation. Its spectacles reified First Peoples, fixing them in roles supplied by an exoticizing, commodified ethnography. And this strategically limited incorporation served pedagogy as well as commerce: the educative design conceived and articulated by the fair's organizers could not do without aboriginal difference.[4]

Nearly two years before the fair's opening, in September 1891, Frederick Ward Putnam, newly appointed head of the fair's Department of Ethnology and Archaeology, had articulated in graphic terms the lesson at issue. According to Putnam, the exposition, undertaken to showcase the "remarkable character" of national and continental development in the four centuries since Columbus's discovery of America, would fail in its purpose without exhibiting, as a point of "comparison" against which to measure developmental progress, "the native peoples of America."[5] "These peoples," Putnam had observed, "as great nations, have about vanished into history, and now is the last opportunity for the world to see them and to realize what their condition, their life, their customs, their arts were four centuries ago. The great object lesson then will not be completed without their being present. Without them, the Exposition will have no base."[6] Thus the grim inevitability, yet also the brutal paradox, of Simon Pokagon's performance on Chicago Day: given the suspect honor of ringing in the end-time of American Indians, of announcing, by means of liberty's peal, the requisite freedom of his race to vanish, he was asked to mark by his presence the near absence of his kind, to embody certain disappearance and exemplify looming invisibility.

Some months before Chicago Day, Pokagon—outraged by the use of Natives as mute objects not vocal subjects in the fair's 1 May opening ceremony—wrote "The Red Man's Rebuke," a stinging critique of Columbian history, printed on birch bark and circulated at the fair. Where, in his October speech, Pokagon chose, for whatever reason, to capitulate to the fatal logic of native disappearance (as to the static immobility of the assimilationist role), in the circulating souvenir pamphlet he refused simply to concede the hegemonic self-evidence of such erasure.[7] Declaring to "the pale-faced race that has usurped our lands and homes" that American Indians "have no spirit to celebrate with you the great Columbian Fair now being held in this Chicago city, the wonder of the world," since to do so would be "to celebrate our own funeral, the discovery of America," Pokagon commands reckoning through remembrance: "do not forget that this success" (the success of cumulative cultural achievement celebrated at the fair) "has been at the sacrifice of *our* homes and a once happy race."[8] Sacrifice, in the history he tells, corresponds not least to the nineteenth-century revolution in transport—"the present network of railroads, and the monstrous engines with their fire, smoke, and hissing steam, with cars attached, as they go sweeping through the land"—all uncannily mirroring the elder's vision, in tribal lore, of a "vast spider web spread out over the land from the Atlantic Ocean toward the setting sun . . . made of rods of iron" along which rush "monstrous spiders . . . clad in brass . . . [h]issing from their nostrils . . . fire and smoke."[9] Rail signifies as it facilitates the repeated betrayal of native "confidence," betrayal proving "that greed for gold was all the balance-wheel [whites] had" when driving natives "from the homes of [their] childhood and from the burial places of [their] kindred and friends, and scatter[ing them] far westward into desert places, where multitudes have died from homesickness, cold, and hunger, and are suffering and dying still for want of food and blankets."[10] What remains, for Pokagon in 1893, is a defensive anticipation: "We only stand with folded arms and watch and wait to see the future deal with us no better than the past. No cheer of sympathy is given us; but in answer to our complaints we are told the triumphal march of the Eastern race westward is by the unalterable decree of nature, termed by them 'the survival of the fittest.'"[11] Pokagon's intimation of the poverty of such an answer ("we are told," "termed by them") will serve to expose, and to undermine, the self-congratulatory white supremacism of the comparison that Putnam evidently aimed to advance through the inclusion of Native Americans in the fair's spectacle.[12]

Although, as Pokagon's pamphlet intimates, the whiteness of the White City cannot be comprehended without reference to the dynamics of racial discourse in the postbellum era, I choose to begin with the complex story of his Columbian offerings for a less readily obvious reason: its significance for issues of movement and mobility. Consider again some key terms from "The Red Man's Rebuke": by insisting that railway expansion and gold fever conspire to scatter native peoples far from their ancestral lands, and by doubting that the westward movement of white people represents "the unalterable decree of nature," Pokagon challenges his audience to understand mobility not as a naturally occurring phenomenon but much more rigorously as a mode of social contest decisive in the manufacture of subjectivity and the determination of belonging. At stake is what, in this project, I term *the politics of mobility,* the contestatory processes that produce different forms of movement, and that invest these forms with social value, cultural purchase, and discriminatory power.[13] Taking Pokagon's challenge seriously, in the pages that follow I endeavor to comprehend the politics of mobility at work in a number of scenes of traffic and transit across the U.S. nineteenth century—from slave revolt to neocolonial tourism, from imperial expedition to tramping protest, from fugitive escape to market circulation. Each scene bears, in distinct yet complementary ways, on what it can mean to become subject to America, in all the conflicted senses of that phrase.

The larger, messier problematic of Native American disappearance condensed and constellated within Pokagon's White City encounter gives one means by which to focus the conceptual dynamics at play in the politics of mobility. Although by 1893 assimilationism had supplanted segregationism as state protocol for managing Native peoples, the specter of the vanishing Indian continued to haunt social life and public discourse in the United States when Simon Pokagon traveled to Chicago. The concerted effort, by many white reformers and critics in the postbellum period, to supplant race with environment as the explanatory cause of aboriginal disappearance only underscores the sedimented status and capacious resiliency of the trope. What I want to stress here is the importance of this trope, its sedimentation, and its resiliency to the conduct, yet also to the veiling, of what I understand as an extended struggle over the determinations and unpredictabilities of movement. Again and again during the course of the nineteenth century, the prospect of aboriginal disappearance served to naturalize Native removal, resettlement, and containment as state policy, most spectacularly in legislative acts such as the passage of the Removal Bill in 1830 and in state-compelled migrations such as the Cherokee Trail of Tears in 1838–39, the Navajo "Long Walk" of 1864, and the Poncas removal in 1877, but every bit as decisively in the more incremental dislocations entailed by ongoing territorial appropriation. Removal and reservation politics are obviously geopolitics, bound up with contestatory dynamics of locale and movement, and determining, as they are determined by, racial, national, and imperial subjectivities. Ideologically, vanishing expresses in terms of spatio-temporal inevitability the historically contingent violence of territorial invasion, ingress, displacement. And through a brutalizing tautology, the trope of the vanishing Indian could serve at once to legitimate and mystify removal: by staving off (in the view of white politicians, bureaucrats, writers, and settlers) the dire threat of aboriginal disappearance, westward removal managed simultaneously to confirm the inevitability of such fate. Thus could social intervention—the effectively genocidal policies of Euroamerican imperial expansion—hide behind a fateful, fatal chronotope.[14] Such occluding mystification relied powerfully on the micropolitical manufacture and dissemination of aboriginal disappearance as hegemonic common sense in a broad range of nineteenth-century cultural forms, from poems and novels to travelogues and memoirs, from essays and lectures to theatrical performances and traveling exhibitions.[15] The point is precisely that modes of discursive representation and circulation played a key role in the contest over mobility conducted through American Indian removal: traffic in narratives of white–red contact legitimated material (while inscribing ideological) tactics of displacement. The power of such discursive traffic will bear out Gilles Deleuze's claim that "[t]he capacity of falsity to produce truth is what mediators are all about": the mediatory fiction of vanishing aboriginality disseminated in products of the culture industry was instrumental in advancing the material and ideological conditions needed for Native Americans to disappear by the thousands.[16] All the more ironic, then, that, throughout the nineteenth century, "vanishing Indians" populated the diverse textualities of U.S. culture with a proliferating abundance. Aboriginal peoples were never more present within hegemonic American culture than when disappearing.[17]

As Frederick Ward Putnam's insistence on the negative capacity of nearly vanished (yet paradoxically present) Indians to supply a "great object lesson" about white American progress will intimate, the World's Columbian Exposition called into high relief not just the trope of vanishing aboriginality but the politics of mobility at stake in this trope's continued circulation. A touristic destination of global significance, the fair worked to commemorate one narrative of mobility's power in the past (the myth of discovery framing Columbian exploration), not least by epitomizing a distinct but related manifestation of mobility's power in the present. Its exhibits capitalized on those modes of modern transit they celebrated, working, in a spectacular redundancy, to draw from afar a mass of visitors to marvel at the technologics enabling their arrival. As Curtis Hinsley argues, "traffic, exchange, and movement" occupied "the heart of the fair and of [its vision of] human progress. . . . Here one found an unmediated commerce among peoples. The flow of human traffic occupied the center of the picture."[18] To the extent that the fair made *progress* the overarching term for the dynamics of such traffic, it complemented the discourse of vanishing aboriginality it presumed by, once again, converting territorial contest into temporal common sense. The key terms *progress* (the destiny of Euroamericans) and *disappearance* (the fate of Indians) worked in tandem to veil, as natural and inevitable, the historicity and contingency of the processes by which particular forms of "traffic, exchange, and movement" came to dominate the Americas.[19]

"Travel," the concept most ubiquitous when naming modern human movement, will clearly fail to describe the full complexity of the dynamics I have been tracing here. And such failure only emphasizes the need to retool our critical vocabularies, at least if we want to articulate more precisely and incisively the mutually determining interimplication of the diverse forms of movement among which travel has tended to prevail. Hence the critical impetus of my project: by directing the emphasis of critique toward the problematic I call the politics of mobility, I mean to refuse travel's hegemony in favor of mobility's contest. To the extent that mobility can be said to constitute a *field*, then it will—to apply Pierre Bourdieu's more general theorization—necessarily take shape not just "as a field of *forces*, whose necessity is imposed on agents who are engaged in it," but also "as a field of *struggles* within which agents confront each other, with differentiated means and ends according to their position in the structure of the field of forces, thus contributing to conserving or transforming its structure."[20] At issue is how, at different moments in the U.S. nineteenth century, such forces and struggles work to shape and direct mobility's field—how mobility, as a process, a practice, and a social resource, comes in the instances I analyze to be distributed, invested, directed, and determined.

Travel's Limits

So conceived, my project does not concern travel in any obvious or conventional sense. It is not really about travel or travel writing, and it rejects the self-evidence of those categories (while respecting their material and generic histories and specificities). I seek instead to intervene within a number of ongoing debates in contemporary social and cultural theory about the material and ideological determinations of human movement, particularly as these bear on the making and breaking of subjectivities: local, national, and imperial; classed, racialized, and engendered.

Yet for reasons that will register the problems of critical vocabulary just outlined, travel as a key term punctuates these debates, overshadowing the analyses they advance. In disciplinary and transdisciplinary formations from poststructuralism to postcolonial theory to feminist theory to human geography to cultural studies, travel as a concept has proven theoretically and methodologically decisive. As geographers Neil Smith and Cindi Katz observe, "everyone seems to be 'travelling.'"[21] The very translatability of the concept, its apparent capacity to *do* what it *names*, will provide one way of understanding why travel has been so attractive to so many critics and theorists for so many reasons and toward so many ends. "Travel," that is, has tended to travel very well.[22]

Accordingly, the conceptual articulation of mobility as social contest will need to contend with travel's critical purchase. The term's attractiveness, I maintain, brings with it real risk for the practice of cultural critique. Travel's nearly irrepressible traveling in current critical debate marks its metaphorical appeal, an appeal symptomatic of the term's power yet also of its limitation as a critical concept. Pressed into circulation as a capacious signifier for distinct, even irreconcilable, experiences, relations, and events, travel comes to stray from its material determinations, gliding derealized in semiotic free flow.

In a demanding, nuanced example of the tendency I am describing, Georges Van Den Abbeele champions travel's metaphoricity by entitling his book *Travel as Metaphor from Montaigne to Rousseau*. For Van Den Abbeele, travel seems all but impossible to avoid, since "to call an existing order (whether epistemological, aesthetic, or political) into question by placing oneself 'outside' that order, by taking a 'critical distance' from it, is implicitly to invoke the metaphor of thought as travel."[23] Given such an understanding, "[t]ravel . . . becomes the metaphor of metaphor while the structure of the metaphor becomes the metaphor for the travel of meaning."[24] Although manifestly provocative, such theoretical pronouncements do manage to hive travel off from its historical and material articulation. Granted, at points Van Den Abbeele strives for historical framing, as in his association of commerce with travel: "Historically, the great economic and commercial powers have been those most successful at manipulating the means of travel, and vice versa. If there is a great investment in travel, it is perhaps because travel models the structure of investment itself, the *transfer* of assets that institutes an economy, be it political or libidinal, 'restricted' or 'general.'"[25] Yet note how, exactly at the moment of historical appeal, travel's metaphoricity reemerges, such that travel only *models* the structure of investment, rather than, in distinct ways at distinct moments to distinct ends, materializing historically particular investment structures, in a co-constitutive or mutually determining process.[26] The associative elasticity of travel as metaphor (or indeed as "the metaphor of metaphor") comes, I would argue, at the expense of its interpretive force. Much as Smith and Katz contend about spatial metaphors, the proliferating tropes of travel "are problematic in so far as they presume that [travel] is not."[27]

In what ways and to what ends, exactly, will the use of travel as metaphor enable social and cultural theorists to achieve the sort of "critical distance" that Van Den Abbeele invokes at the outset of his study? The answer, for him, seems to lie in conceptual dislocation and defamiliarization: "a displacement of whatever it is one understands by 'place.'"[28] At stake is the unhomeliness of travel as metaphor, an unhomeliness that pits the domesticating "economy of travel" against "the transgressive or critical possibilities" entailed by "an infinite or unbounded travel."[29] In Van Den Abbeele's understanding, "[t]his complex economics of travel rehearses once more the paradoxical play of entrapment and liberation evinced in critical thought."[30] Yet to associate domesticity with entrapment and travel with liberation is hardly to model "critical distance," let alone "transgressive or critical possibilities" of the sort that travel, as metaphor, supposedly promises to supply. On the contrary, as feminist theorists have taken great care to emphasize, this antinomy epitomizes conventional thought about location as about movement.[31] And the contradiction, in which Van Den Abbeele proves to be least critical and most conventional at the moment of his boldest theoretical claims, begins to indicate the limitations of a paradigm ill-suited to account for the material determinations and historical contingencies by which—to remain with the specific instance at hand—the conceptual or symbolic interchangeability of home with entrapment and travel with liberation has acquired and then maintained its status as cultural common sense.[32]

The larger point is neither to reject metaphor as a method of articulation in critical practice (as if that were possible) nor to diminish the signal importance of travel as a key term in the analysis of mobility's field. I do mean, though, to question the status of travel as a master trope subsuming not just all forms of movement but also strikingly distinct modes of social activity such as *theory* or *writing*. Despite the fact that the etymology of the term harks back to the Greek *theor* (from which *theory* likewise derives), etymology alone will not transcend the historical particularities and social relations within which travel as a concept and a practice has materialized.[33] My concern in this project has everything to do with such material conditions and constraints, a commitment inspired by Stuart Hall's axiom, "[m]aterial circumstances are the net of constraints, the 'conditions of existence' for practical thought and calculation about society," and resistant to what Smith and Katz term the "undifferentiated fusion" of materiality with metaphoricity.[34] Accordingly I situate my inquiry alongside the works of those critics and theorists—James Buzard, Inderpal Grewal, Bruce Harvey, Caren

Kaplan, Mary Louise Pratt, and Susan Stewart, most notably—who insist on the tensions that, at different historical moments and in different historical circumstances, attend mobility's practice (not to mention its invocation and circulation in critical discourse) so as to restore, at the forefront of critique, the materiality of mobility alongside its differential production and reproduction.[35]

The theoretical interventions of Grewal and Kaplan, in particular, inflect the argument I mean to develop here. Although distinct in focus, our projects share a common theoretical and methodological commitment to articulate the historical and material specificities and determinations of distinct yet interpenetrating modes of mobility. Grewal makes the case incisively at the outset of her study, contending much as I have that "the deployment of the term *travel* as a universal form of mobility... erases or conflates those mobilities that are not part of this Eurocentric, imperialist formation... [with the effect that] migration, immigration, deportation, indenture, and slavery are often erased by the universalizing of European [or, I would argue, more broadly first-world, bourgeois] travel."[36] Yet, as Kaplan argues, such universalizing erasure will at the same time falter over those historical traces it bears: "'travel,' as it is used in Euro-American criticism, cannot escape the historical legacies of capitalist development and accumulation, of imperialist expansion, and of inequities of numerous kinds."[37] Thus in Kaplan's formulation "[t]o question travel... is to inquire into the ideological function of metaphors in discourses of displacement."[38] Against the liberatory rhetoric often accompanying the invocation of travel as metaphor, these arguments critique the limitless extension of the concept in order to contest its ongoing circulation as little more than a dematerialized sign, a reified critical commodity.

Precisely because, as Kaplan contends, "travel is central to modernity, ... the critique of travel must be a fundamental priority in contemporary critical practices."[39] For both Grewal and Kaplan, such critique turns on intimate difference—on what, to use Kaplan's term, constitutes the "juxtaposition" not opposition of different forms of mobility.[40] One effect of this critical emphasis will be to foreground the often jarring asymmetries that, in distinct ways at distinct historical moments to distinct effects, attend the production and distribution of mobility as a social resource. Kaplan theorizes the dynamic I am describing in terms of "the *uneven* operations... that produce possibilities for some and delimit or obstruct opportunities for others."[41] These "uneven operations," though invoked by Kaplan to characterize "post-modernity," capture exactly the sense of differential tension I see in contests over mobility in nineteenth-century America—whether these entail slave revolt, as analyzed in chapter 1, or the uncertain trade in narratives of exploration and transit, as analyzed in chapter 2, or fugitive moves, as analyzed in chapter 3, or contingencies and crises within mobility's discipline, as analyzed in chapter 4.

The prospect of "uneven operations" invoked by Kaplan also recalls the recent retheorizations of space and subjectivity in the discourse of human geography. Attentive in diverse ways to what Neil Smith calls uneven development under capitalism, "the geography of politics and the politics of geography," these retheorizations reject the positivist understanding of the givenness of space, autonomous and static, for a nuanced conception of the interimplication of space with the social, in which spatial and social relations produce one another in dynamic fashion.[42] So conceived, spatiality and its problematic take on a substantially renewed significance with respect to the understanding of human mobility and subjectivity in their diverse manifestations: untenable as simply the setting or scene through which human subjects move, space instead helps to determine those subjectivities and mobilities that at the same time determine it. And as the feminist geographer Doreen Massey makes clear, this dynamic sense of the spatial will challenge the ways we imagine the relation of space to time. No longer, as a result of such understanding, the inert antithesis or ground to time's motive force, space must be conceived "in tension" with the temporal.[43] The implications, as Massey concludes, are decisive: "to insist on the inseparability of time and space" will serve "to say that the spatial is integral to the production of history, and thus to the possibility of politics, just as the temporal is to geography."[44] These retheorizations are key to my understanding of the question of space in the politics of mobility I analyze here—as for instance in the ideology of aboriginal vanishing with which I began, where the tendency to express territorial appropriation and dislocation (removal politics) in terms of temporal inevitability (the fate of vanishing Indians) served precisely to disarticulate space from time and to produce and so capitalize on the givenness of both: "the frontier" simply there, a given, in both senses, for Euroamerican whites; Indian disappearance a foregone conclusion, a given. Likewise, the nearly hegemonic understanding of spatial expansion as progress, as Manifest Destiny, will mark the givenness of these conceptions of both space and time—conceptions that serve, I would argue, to deny the historicity of the events they gloss (where historicity names not just the temporal over against the spatial but precisely the interimplication and co-constitution of time and space). Reading and critiquing the politics of mobility, those contestatory processes producing and investing mobility as a differential social resource, can by contrast draw such historicity into view.

Mobility in the Shadow of Capital

The sort of historical understanding I am proposing here necessarily locates mobility and its contests within capital's long shadow. The production and reproduction of mobility as a material and social resource in nineteenth-century America cannot be understood apart from the modulating flows that characterize the processes (and the transformations) of capitalism during the nineteenth century. As a concept and a rubric, *the politics of mobility* must draw political economy into play.

In a very broad sense, the operations of capitalism supply the conditions of possibility within which, during the historical period that concerns me here, contests over mobility as a material practice and a social resource unfold. Capitalism's social relations effectively produce mobility's field, determining the ways and means of movement as practice, as resource, as contest. Yet as Marx makes clear, these determinations are in important ways reciprocal: produced by capital, mobility—or, more accurately, mobility's *problematic*—goes a long way toward producing capital in its turn. These interrelated determinations prove as vexatious as necessary for capitalism, not just because the system requires immobility, capital's suspended investment, alongside mobility, capital's ceaseless flow,[45] but, more profoundly, because the process of circulation (most immediately expressive, in Marx's work, of mobility, and inextricable for him from the production process) brings with it a compelling contradiction: "Capital cannot . . . arise from circulation, and it is equally impossible for it to arise apart from circulation. It must have its origin both in circulation and not in circulation."[46] The contradiction at issue entails a problem for profit: the maximization of surplus value key to capital's reproduction cannot occur without the circulatory processes that tend to eat away at surplus value. As Marx explains in the *Grundrisse*, since "[c]apital exists as capital only in so far as it passes through the phases of circulation, the various moments of its transformation, in order to be able to begin the production process anew, . . . [therefore] these phases are themselves phases of its realization—but at the same time . . . of its *devaluation*."[47] Although he uses this insight to comprehend the historical tendency of capital to annihilate space with time—extending the dimensions of the market ever more globally while intensifying the speed of commodity circulation[48]—I would want to underscore, here, the tremendous power yet tremendous undecidability of mobility's dynamic for capital. Mobility, in other words, is deeply contested under capitalism: a source of contest structural to its operations, and concomitantly, I would argue, a key mode or medium of contest within its histories.

Thus understood, mobility will constitute a means of mediation decisive within modernity. In this deployment "mediation," defined by Régis Debray as "the dynamic combination of intermediary procedures and bodies that interpose themselves between a producing of signs and a producing of events," works two ways at once, serving as a descriptive term with which to characterize the material status and effect of mobility, and as a critical tool with which to analyze and critique the seeming naturalness of the division or indeed reification of material and social forms of movement under capital.[49] "[A] positive process of social reality," in Raymond Williams's sense, mobility is mediatory in that it determines and produces those destinations, those derivations, those spaces by which it is determined and produced, working to mediate among an array of discrete, even dissimilar forms and discourses of movement, locale, and subjectivity.[50] The point, I should stress, is not at all to discount or erode meaningful material differences between mobility's distinct manifestations and articulations: as Fredric Jameson reminds us, "the distinguishing of two phenomena from each other, their structural separation, the affirmation that they are not the same, and that in quite specific and determinate ways, is *also* a form of mediation."[51] To the extent that mobility is not so much a common condition as a social and material resource crucial to the production and reproduction (the "uneven development") of national, racial, engendered, classed subjectivities, it becomes the locus of contest. Reading mobility's mediations across the decades under study can illuminate in what ways and to what ends the intimate differences among distinct concepts and practices of mobility—travel, transport, placement, displacement, fugitivity, migration, immigration, removal, traffic, circulation, and so on—have come to materialize; it can likewise show how those intimate differences bear on identification and disidentification, subjectivity and subjection, interpellation and its resistance. And this analytic method has the decisive advantage of underscoring the interimplication, at the level of material practice, between forms of mobility and their account—the inextricability, that is, of "the *medium* as a device or system of representation" and "*mediation* as the actual use or disposal of resources."[52] Hence my attention, throughout this study, to print discourse, the prime medium or technology during the 1800s for the symbolic articulation of mobile practices, and also my effort to comprehend material movement, social mobility, and commercial circulation together. The point is historical and material, not merely notional or thematic, since under capitalism the values attached to mobility's discourse prove impossible to disarticulate from the values attached to mobility's practice (a point elaborated in chapter 2).[53] Contests over the production and reproduction of mobility, that is, inflect and interpenetrate the production and circulation of mobility's accounts. At stake is not least what Debray calls "the 'becoming-material' forces of symbolic forms."[54]

By advancing an understanding of mobility in terms of mediation and contest, I mean, among other things, to historicize and critique the traveling ideal that, emphasizing individuation, freedom, leisure, solitude, refinement, taste, reflection, discernment, sensibility, and disinterested detachment, treats as universal, as the common condition and capacity of all persons, what are in fact the dispositions, privileges, and values (the habitus, to use Pierre Bourdieu's term) of a particular social class under capitalism. Historically, such travel has tended to serve an importantly pedagogic function, teaching even as it presumes an "ideology of natural taste" of the sort Bourdieu theorizes—an ideology that, "like all the ideological strategies generated in the everyday class struggle, . . . *naturalizes* real differences, converting differences in the mode of acquisition of culture into differences of nature."[55] This tutelage bears decisively on the production and reproduction of forms of social power—actual capital, to be sure, but also what Bourdieu calls symbolic capital ("economic or political capital that is disavowed, misrecognized and thereby recognized, hence legitimate, a 'credit' which, under certain conditions, and always in the long run, guarantees 'economic' profits") and, with it, the capacity to exercise symbolic violence ("the violence which extorts submission, which is not perceived as such, based on 'collective expectations' or socially inculcated beliefs").[56] So conceived, travel in its hegemonic manifestation trains subjects to acquire what Bourdieu calls "the power to impose the legitimate vision of the social world, or, more precisely, . . . the recognition, accumulated in the form of a symbolic capital of notoriety and respectability, which gives the authority to impose the legitimate knowledge of the *sense* of the social world, its present meaning and the direction in which it is going and should go."[57] Access to mobility as a material and social resource serves to reproduce its conditions of possibility, such that to travel for the purposes of cultural attainment or education will help to generate those forms of real and symbolic capital that, in turn, maintain or increase access to material and also social forms of mobility. The freedom and privilege to travel determine, as they are determined by, resources in social mobility. And the differentiating work achieved through travel as a mode of social training occurs in crucial respects through material processes of incorporation—through, that is, the habitual mobilities of bodies themselves, such that the disinterested contemplation necessary to travel's tutelary work occurs not against the body but exactly through its launching into motion.[58]

I foreground this orthodoxy because historically it has done much to determine, but also to mystify, the politics of mobility at issue here. Yet I would stress that hegemonic belief can never really be total: uneven in its development, textured by gaps and seams, it must, in Terry Eagleton's phrase, "engage with counter-hegemonic forces in ways which prove partly constitutive of its rule."[59] Although (much like the account of removal politics with which I began) the case studies I undertake in the pages that follow often entail practices conceivable in terms of travel and travel writing, they tend to register the insufficiency of travel as an interpretive paradigm and as a form of cultural common sense. Unfolding in tension with travel as a hegemonic concept—intimate with it, yet intimately different from it—they invite forms of analysis that can refuse the givenness of travel's ideal so as to account for the material contingencies that, historically, shape mobility's contests.

Mobility and/as Progress in the American Nineteenth Century

In its aims (if not necessarily in its effects), the World's Columbian Exposition exemplified the educational, acculturating principles bound up with the traveling ideal. As Robert Rydell observes, "[t]he fair . . . served as an exercise in educating the nation on the concept of progress as a *willed* national activity toward a determined, utopian goal."[60] Conceived, as Progressive Era commentator Henry van Brunt put it, as "a university, open to all, where the courses of instruction cover all the arts and sciences, and are so ordered that to see is to learn," the fair promised to "furnish to our people an object lesson of a magnitude, scope, and significance such as has not been seen elsewhere," making them "for the first time . . . conscious of the duties, as yet unfulfilled, which they themselves owe to the civilization of the century."[61] Such aims intimate, to provocative effect, the crucial value of cultural training in service of the state. In their trenchant account of this dynamic, David Lloyd and Paul Thomas argue that the state, "at once an institution that derives from the people and one which expresses at a higher level the still developing essence of that people," ushers its subjects "towards the realization of their own essence and towards an ever greater approximation to universality" by the supplementary mediation that cultural education can provide.[62] Furnishing "an ethical training devoted to the 'educing' of the citizen from the human being" less, according to Lloyd and Thomas, through any content than through the representation of representation itself, culture thus constitutes "the very form of bourgeois ideology, proffering on the one hand a purely formal space of reconciliation through identification while on the other containing, in transmuted forms, the constant deferral of autonomy that is the inevitable consequence of a substitution of political for human emancipation."[63] The theoretical account supplied by Lloyd and Thomas speaks powerfully to the material and ideological operations of the Chicago Exposition: fashioning a curriculum of ethnographic spectacles that could capitalize on supposedly immutable differences in racial nature so as to affirm the progressive supremacy of American national life, the fair-as-university worked to represent representativeness and to educe representability, fostering among its homegrown visitors identification in national superiority while at the same time, through object lessons in unrealized duty, deferring their political and social autonomy. I would underscore the crucial importance of mobility to this process: as an exemplary display and a materialization of modern traffic, the fair served not least to inculcate in its visitors a belief in the inextricability of the material technologics of human movement from the ideological lessons of progress—to represent representability, that is, by mobilizing mobility.

In so doing, the World's Columbian Exposition epitomized, even as it celebrated, the longstanding tendency, inscribed again and again in the American nineteenth century, to articulate entangled ideologies of national identity and progress, using mobility as their prime sign or symptom. Treating mobility as the key to national temperament became habitual, even hegemonic, serving to bind together two traits supposedly intrinsic to "the American": the need to move (freedom as geographical expansiveness) and the need to rise (freedom as social uplift). At stake in such synonymity was, in a sense, nothing less than the promise of American democracy; as Amy Schrager Lang argues, the repeated "appeal to individual mobility" throughout the nineteenth century aimed at "excising the prospect of class conflict"—an appeal that, in its fantasy of classlessness, marks mobility as a key part of what Lang, so incisively, calls "the syntax of class."[64] Yet if ideologically the practice of conflating movement with national identity served very well to occlude, in claims for mobility's common condition, the fact of mobility as a differential means to power—to sustain yet conceal class difference in classlessness while naturalizing, as national essence, those projects analyzed by Wai-chee Dimock under the rubric "empire for liberty"—nevertheless in its ubiquitous circulation the orthodox clench of "travel" with "Americanness" could not break free from haunting contests over mobility as a material and social resource.

When, in the April 1896 issue of *Cosmopolitan*, Agnes Repplier conceded, rather defensively, that "Americans *do* roam," the statement invoked a cultural commonplace of longstanding familiarity.[65] Nearly eighty years earlier, and writing in advance of the histories of westward expansion and transport innovation that give, in the U.S. instance, one broad material substrate for mobility's symptom, the editor of the autumn 1829 issue of the *American Journal of Science* could likewise assert, as fact, that "[w]e are a nation of travellers."[66] Flying in the face of shifts in the technologies, practices, and determinations of mobility so profound that *movement* can only in the most generalizing sense be said to name the same endeavor in 1896 as in 1829, the apparent interchangeability of the contentions just quoted will mark, I suggest, less a particular meaning or content of America than a formal operation, one method by which inhabitants of the United States managed to name, to circulate, to represent their representability as American subjects. For a newly nationalizing people notoriously anxious about its professed lack of sedimented cultural history, one of the chief means *to* cultural distinction under modernity, travel's practice, could in a perfect tautology serve as the very sign or mode *of* cultural distinction. Once the inextricability of "mobility" and "American" was secure, a given form not a mutable content, then the very act of roaming would not merely achieve but affirm cultural and national distinction. Movement signaled the orthodox mode of being-in-the-world requisite to a nationalizing ideology in which, as Dimock contends, the nation "stood at once as the culmination of progress and end to progress, fulfillment of history and emancipation from history."[67] At least in terms of hegemonic articulation, becoming American through the strenuousness of mobility's exercise meant being American in the gloriousness of mobility's condition. Ideologically speaking, restlessness—ceaseless mobility—supplied one key to the American subject's vaunted exceptionalism.[68]

"The Americans on Their Travels," an essay by Robert Tomes published in *Harper's New Monthly Magazine* in June 1865, delineates to revealing effect the force, but also the complexity, of the hegemonic common sense I have been outlining. For Tomes, what Amy Kaplan calls "promiscuous mobility" constitutes the very core of American being and belonging.[69] He presupposes this view from the start: "The American is a migratory animal.

He changes places with such facility that he never seems so much at home as when leaving it."[70] So conceived, the restless habit constitutes the intrinsic mode of American habitation; the animal's "migratory" instinct gives the mobile measure of the citizen. The apparent paradox of a being at home in movement serves, in fact, to flag national subjectivity since, for Tomes, to live and be at home in America, to *belong* as subject and citizen, requires transit: "The Americans are necessarily great travelers. Such is the spaciousness of their country that they can not perform many of the ordinary duties of life without a great deal of locomotion."[71] Here space corrects the cultural deficiency that a supposed want of history entails, as the geographical surround of national life affords ample room to practice national identity. The circumstance has ensured a perfect harmony between technological extension and national demand:

> The facilities for travel are in proportion to the American necessity for practicing it. With miles of railroad and length of navigable river more than those of all the rest of the world together, a citizen of our vast republic passes with ease and rapidity from the Lakes to the Gulf of Mexico, or from the Atlantic to the Pacific. Thus readily moving over a great continent, within the limits of his own country, he becomes almost unconscious of space, and so habituated to travel that he thinks no more of counting the hundreds of miles of his frequent journeys, by railway and steamer, than the steps of his daily walk.[72]

The effect of such habituation is implicitly democratic, tending to level the distinctions between types of journeys. Yet at the same time, and more worryingly, the mobile habit holds risky potential for the *loss* of national spirit, as the same unconsciousness of homeland space that characterizes Americans renders them vulnerable to foreign influence:

> The American is conscious enough of the grandeur, in the aggregate, of his vast and bounteous land, and exults even to satiety in its qualities. He, however, is not disposed to analyze its characteristics, and observe minutely its particular elements of interest. He cares not a fig for the sublime, the beautiful, and picturesque, if they are only seen by him in his own country. . . . A mountain at home is less visible than a mole-hill abroad.[73]

Here Tomes underscores the risk, to the "migratory animal," of restlessness: indifferent to home's glory, the American jeopardizes national character through the mobile practice intrinsic to it, manufacturing aesthetic pleasure and profit from trivial foreign material. Thus the habit that defines home likewise threatens its integrity. No longer straightforwardly fundamental, here mobility threatens the national temper it works to define. Against such threat, Tomes advocates an intimate familiarity with the home said to produce in its subjects the locomotive itch: "The best preparation for a journey abroad is a knowledge of home. Every man, supposing that he does not wish to *denationalize* himself, should, before he travels, become familiar with his own country."[74] Never more at home than in departure—the perfect justification for national expansion—Americans must nevertheless know the home that, by quitting, they extend; otherwise, in the absence of home-bound tutelage, the migratory instinct that nationalizes them threatens, paradoxically enough, to effect denationalization. Thus in Tomes's account the inevitability of American expansion, such that excursive adventure will always constitute the dimensions of home, requires a nativist intimacy and insinuates a nativist anxiety that, together, begin to limn the ideological complex Amy Kaplan calls Manifest (or traveling) Domesticity.[75]

The stakes at issue in Tomes's vision of domesticating restlessness take on a significantly different cast when we begin to consider those excluded by normative concepts of nativity, nationality, belonging, and mobility in the nineteenth-century United States. Simon Pokagon's grim reminder, at the outset of "The Red Man's Rebuke," of the loss of aboriginal homes and lifeways with the advent of imperial exploration certainly convolutes the orthodox overlay of roaming with home as synonymous signs of "the American." The very restlessness that, in 1835, Alexis de Tocqueville took for the symptom of American modernity held the capacity to restrict as much as sanction physical movement and social mobility—a fact exemplified, for Tocqueville, by those countless workers (northern as well as southern, free as well as enslaved) who, "in the midst of universal movement," were by the material conditions of their labor "rendered . . . stationary."[76] In her celebrated memoir, Harriet Jacobs shows just how fraught, and how unpredictable, the interrelation between movement and stasis could be when she details her fugitive strategy—seven years of self-confinement, of tactical *immobility* directed against slavery's imprisoning, immobilizing regime.

> I hardly expect that the reader will credit me, when I affirm that I lived in that little dismal hole, almost deprived of light and air, and with no space to move my limbs, for nearly seven years. But it is a fact; and to me a sad one, even now; for my body still suffers from the effects of that long imprisonment, to say nothing of my soul.[77]

Clearly antithetical to travel's common sense, Jacobs's strategy will exemplify the difficulty and, I would argue, underscore the urgency of comprehending mobility in its contested field. Hence the need to recognize, in the very hegemony that holds mobility to be a flatly common condition in America, the power of mobility as a differential resource—to trace those lines of force that connect mobilities and immobilities in contestatory formation—and hence, too, the need to address the ways and means by which the politics of mobility bear on subjectivity's manufacture. The work of such analysis is precisely the aim of the case studies that follow.

Analyzing Mobility's Contest

I develop my understanding of mobility as social contest in nineteenth-century America over the course of four chapters that, in their broad contours, proceed more or less chronologically from the early 1830s to the first years of the twentieth century. Although in some sense only a critical convenience, my decision to analyze the politics of mobility within these historical coordinates speaks as well to my sense that they frame a decisive, albeit ragged, trajectory in the American genealogy of mobility's contest: just as the moment around 1830 initiates what Ronald Takaki understands as a "celebration" of technological traffic and transport as signs of the progress and nationalism of a "people . . . in constant motion, socially and geographically," so it marks, with the federal passage of the Removal Act, a departure of sorts in the aims and practices of imperial intervention, aims and practices that, while effectively continental in scope until the globalizing interventions at century's end, unfolded (as both Bruce Harvey and Amy Kaplan have expertly shown) in intimate tension with transnational itineraries.[78] Yet although I find myself compelled by Harvey's contention that much work remains to be done in analyzing travel writing that concerns the experience of U.S. national subjects in locales beyond the spheres of U.S. influence, I maintain that such analysis will require, as its necessary complement, a much better understanding than we yet have of the ways and means by which, within the American scene, contests over mobility as a social resource help to legitimate some material and discursive practices (whether continental or global in scope) at the expense of all others.[79] These dynamics constitute the politics of mobility—and, to the extent that they admit national description, they tend in my view to invite critical consideration at what Kaplan, following Lora Romero, names "the 'home fronts' of imperial culture."[80] Hence my decision to organize my project around an archive of materials confined almost exclusively to the geographical space of the United States.

Chapter 1, "Nat Turner's Restlessness," takes up the Southampton slave revolt of 1831 as a material (and particularly volatile) instance of contest within mobility's field. Reading for a restlessness irreducible to the conception of American national subjectivity already orthodox in antebellum public discourse, I find within a cluster of historical materials documenting this revolt manifold signs of struggle over the terms and ends of human movement. Central here is the text of Nat Turner's confession, prepared for publication by Thomas Gray: against its disciplinary will to fixity I argue that the indeterminate character of the text itself—especially with respect to the dissonant play of accusing and accused voices within in it, and to the contradictory effects of confessional discourse for the enslaved—only compounds the volatility of insurgent movement under slavery. The implications, I suggest, are discursive as well as material, in ways that can illuminate the problems of rumor haunting Gray's pamphlet as it ventures to market.

In chapter 2, "Abandoned to Circulation," I shift my generic focus from legal discourse, as exemplified by the *Confessions*, to fictionalized travel narrative. Yet by this shift I aim to extend and elaborate the analysis of human movement and discursive traffic undertaken in chapter 1. I focus on two antebellum texts, Edgar Allan Poe's *The Narrative of Arthur Gordon Pym of Nantucket* and Herman Meville's *The Confidence-Man*, comparably absorbed with what I call dramas of uncertain circulation: the contingencies that help to determine the commercial power and potential of narratives of travel in the emergent capitalist publishing industry. For Poe, I argue, the commercial indifference of discursive difference in a book market dominated by plagiarism and piracy erupts again and again through his spoof on exploratory travel; for Melville, comparable problems of differentiation only serve to fuel the crises of confidence that haunt less exotic, more routine forms of transit and traffic. In both instances, investment in fictions of mobility brings with it taxing costs.

Where mobility entails open revolt in chapter 1, and exploratory extremes and transitory routines in chapter 2, in chapter 3, "Secret Circuits, Fugitive Moves," it constitutes a habitually illicit practice. Again the generic focus shifts, this time falling on historiographical, biographical, and autobiographical texts: accounts of the Underground Railroad by Levi Coffin, Ebber Pettit, and William Still; Henry Bibb's fugitive narrative *Narrative of the Life and Adventures of Henry Bibb*; Sarah Edmonds's Civil War memoir *Nurse and Spy in the Union Army*; and Harriet Tubman's two memoirs, as inscribed by Sarah Bedford. My framing concern has to do with the interimplication of movement with secrecy, such that crises of motion in the years surrounding the Civil War effectively become crises of knowledge. So understood, the texts in question help to illuminate problems in national belonging as they determine and are determined by contested forms of mobility.

Chapter 4, "Mobility's Disciplines," moves well into the postbellum period, focusing on a constellation of materials produced at the fin de siècle—Stephen Crane's Mexican travel dispatches and Jack London's tramp writings and novel *Martin Eden*—framed by the discourse on manners supplied by etiquette manuals from the period. I theorize a concept called *disciplinary pace* to account for the striking concern, across this disparate range of texts, over the interrelation of motion with stasis and, concomitantly, over the technologics of motion control. At a social moment characterized by the increasing ubiquity of mass transport yet also shaken by social and industrial conflict (as exemplified most spectacularly by the great strikes of the century's final decades), the vocabularies of disciplinary pace aim to manage volatile mobilities by deploying so as to capitalize on strategic forms of frozen motion. Yet, judging from the materials I read in chapter 4, the power of stasis as a means of regulating mobility is finally insufficient to settle or indeed fix its energies. As a result, I conclude, such attempts at regulation only underscore mobility's crises in the period—its contingency, its unpredictability, its accidentalism. Linking this final chapter to an epilogue on mobility's contest in the contemporary, globalizing moment, more generally the issue of mobility's volatile power yields the most urgent lessons of this project. For if, in the U.S. nineteenth century, struggles over mobility typically distribute it as a differential resource, privileging some citizens (white, male, bourgeois) at the expense of their social others, nevertheless unpredictabilities do haunt this dynamic. Strains of excess texture the politics of mobility, intimating the contingency of modern transit and traffic—not to mention the illogic of the capitalist system they so often serve. Thus, even when normative or regulatory, mobility's histories will figure forth, in those traces of contest they must contain, the conditions of possibility for their undoing.

1
Nat Turner's Restlessness

> The cruelties of property and privilege are always more ferocious than the revenges of poverty and oppression.
>
> —*C. L. R. James*, The Black Jacobins

> Five hundred black men, divided into guerilla bands, and working their way through the mountain Ranges of Virginia, Kentucky, Tennessee, Arkansas, and the swamps of the Atlantic Coast, can do more to destroy slavery than five-thousand Regulars. It only wants men determined to do or die. White men had this spirit at Harpers Ferry on that memorable October morn. We want Nat Turner—not speeches; Denmark Vesey—not resolutions; John Brown—not meetings.
>
> —*George Lawrence Jr.*, The Weekly Anglo-African

"We want Nat Turner": in 1861 the desire thus voiced bespoke the urgency alongside the legacy of violent resistance in America. Thirty years after the slave uprising led by Turner had been brutally suppressed, for many abolitionists and activists in the United States his name, like those of his revolutionary counterparts Denmark Vesey and John Brown, continued to circulate with nearly talismanic force. Although (to revise Lawrence's formulation) in *doing* Turner had died, the restlessness charging the revolt he inspired could not so readily be quelled.[1]

To frame in this way the story of Nat Turner's revolt is already to insinuate its dissonant intimacy with the normative discourse on American mobility outlined in my introduction. The key term is restlessness: invoked again and again by nineteenth-century commentators to name a recognizably universal American temper, restlessness, when used to characterize the complex, volatile energies surrounding the Southampton rebellion and its aftermath, undergoes a decisive shift in meaning. For since slave status ruled out national membership, Turner's restlessness was categorically *not* American restlessness, yet it worked to supplement (to add to, yet substitute for, and so displace) the commonplace forms of subjectivity and the orthodox forms of mobility that, under slavery, Turner could never enjoy.[2] Channeled into the acts of violent uprising, such restlessness will, when read in retrospect, give a material instance and a symptom of mobility as social contest. Reading for restlessness thus becomes this chapter's project.

Restlessness and Repression, Southampton County ca. 1831

Inspired by what he took to be a series of signs from God, on 21 August 1831 Nat Turner led seven of his fellow slaves in revolt against their masters. Others quickly joined the rebellious company, which at its largest numbered nearly sixty. Over the next two days they killed between fifty-seven and sixty-four whites. Confronted on 22 August and again on 23 August by white militiamen, the group dissolved. Unlike many of his compatriots, Turner avoided immediate arrest, remaining until his capture on 30 October in hiding and on the run, yet never straying far from the Travis house where the uprising started. The rebels' trials began on 31 August, and their executions soon after, on 4 September—although, significantly, many of the capital sentences were commuted in favor of transportation out of state. When captured, Turner was held in the Southampton county jail through his trial on 5 November until his execution, by hanging, on the eleventh of that month. At some point between 1 November and 3 November, he is presumed to have given his confession to the lawyer (and nominal author of the *Confessions*) Thomas R. Gray. According to one source, Turner's "body, after death, was given over to the surgeons for dissection"; according to another, following "tradition, souvenir purses were made of his skin."[3]

Although the events of the Southampton revolt of 1831 thus admit ready summary, their larger social significance proves more difficult to grasp. Turner's uprising makes for messy history, not least because the chief historical source, the *Confessions*, is (in ways analyzed below) such a provocatively indeterminate text. Leery of the will to historical comprehensiveness and fixity, I mean here to undertake an exactingly *partial* reading of the rebellion, hoping to get at its volatility by emphasizing the movement, and the mobility, that insurgency required. I maintain that, in this context, revolt and mobility cannot be disarticulated—that in important ways the first holds no meaning without the second. My aim is thus to locate in Nat Turner's rebellion a political practice that contests enslavement not least by troubling the disciplinary distribution of mobility as a material and social resource.[4]

Traces of human movement shoot through the historical record of the Southampton revolt. We might begin by noting the repeated dislocations, ubiquitous in slave experience, instrumental to slavery's operations, that seem to have characterized Turner's existence. As Kenneth Greenberg observes, "[e]ven a simple recounting of Nat Turner's movement from owner to owner during the course of his life suggests the horror of repeated reshuffling of families and communities. No move was over a large distance, but each must have been experienced as a major disruption caused by circumstances beyond his control."[5] For many of slavery's critics, such apparently local and particularized occurrences served to instance a systemic injustice for which the nation itself bore full responsibility. As William Lloyd Garrison insisted in his early September 1831 account of the rebellion, "[t]he crime of [slavery's] oppression is national. The south is only the agent in this guilty traffic."[6] So conceived, the micropolitics of human movement from plantation to plantation cannot be separated from the macropolitics of mobility suffusing national conduct alongside slaveholding practice. Thus Turner's articulation (as reported by Thomas Gray) of the task assigned to him through divine revelation, to "slay my enemies with their own weapons," serves not merely to specify the axes and guns used by the rebels to kill local whites but more profoundly to intimate the considerable significance of mobility's control within slavery's larger arsenal.[7] Subject from childhood to the routinized yet terrorizing force of unwanted, irresistible movement, Turner the rebel undertook to seize mobility itself as his weapon—as the very engine of insurgency.

The state response to Turner's revolt only compounds the argument I am making here. In a letter to James Hamilton Jr., the governor of South Carolina, dated 19 November 1831, John Floyd, Virginia's governor, outlines at length the widely held view that the unchecked mobility of outside operatives inspired restlessness in Virginian slaves. "I am fully persuaded," Floyd observes, that "the spirit of insubordination which has, and still manifests itself in Virginia, had its origin among, and eminated from, the Yankee population, upon their *first* arrival amongst us, but most especially the Yankee pedlers and traders."[8] By this account, the inescapability of commerce under capitalism makes for problematic social relations under slavery: the "pedlers and traders" who help to facilitate the interface between the plantation economy and the larger market constitute a source of ideological contamination that complicates, and indeed compromises, their mercantile utility. And though Floyd quickly adds that "[t]he course [of such contamination] has been by no means a direct one," wending its way through religious instruction and literacy education, religious assembly and the circulation of "incendiary publications," the outcome is plain: "*the mass* were prepared by making them aspire to an equal station."[9] Hence the decisive significance of his intended response: "I shall in my annual message recommend that laws be passed—To confine the Slaves to the estates of their masters—prohibit negroes from preaching—absolutely to drive from this State all free negroes—and to substitute the surplus revenue in our Treasury annually for slaves, to work for a time upon our Rail Roads etc etc and these sent out of the country, preparatory, or rather as the first step to emancipation."[10] Thus envisioned, the refusal of "mass" equality requires a comprehensive, systematic politics of mobility, a determined reassertion of the state's power to control the terms and ends of human movement, to restrict or withhold the mobility of some and to demand and direct the mobility of others. Not surprisingly, the trial and punishment of the Southampton rebels had already inaugurated just such a politics: finding, in the commuted sentence of transportation, an artificially benevolent alternative to execution—an alternative that, in practice, constituted a corrective weapon, preserving the human commodity while entailing a kind of social death for the enslaved—Floyd and the Southampton judiciary broadcast slavery's crushing compassion so as to reinforce and revitalize the methods of slave circulation threatened by the recent insurgency.[11]

Such, I would contend, are the broad contours of the contest over mobility, the contest pressuring, animating, determining, and ultimately containing Nat Turner's revolt. Yet within the limits they describe, much remains to be learned about the force and reverberation of Turner's restlessness. Its impact is most immediate and insistent in the discursive artifacts generated in wake of the revolt—the text of his confession, obviously, but also contemporaneous accounts in the popular press. Accordingly, I now turn to consider this constellation of materials in detail.

Reading Restlessness in the *Confessions*

As a document prepared for public consumption, Thomas Gray's record of Nat Turner's confession works to perform a manifestly educational service. In his prefatory remarks Gray outlines something of his own compositional motives: "finding that Turner was willing to make a full and free confession of the origin, progress and consummation of the insurrectionary movements of the slaves of which he was the contriver and head I determined for the gratification of public curiosity to commit his statements to writing, and publish them, with little or no variation, from his own words" (40).[12] The result, in Gray's view, "reads like an awful, and it is hoped, a useful lesson, as to the operations of a mind like his, endeavoring to grapple with things beyond its reach. . . . It is calculated also to demonstrate the policy of our laws in restraint of this class of our population, and to induce all those entrusted with their execution, as well as our citizens generally, to see that they are strictly and rigidly enforced" (41). Heading off all concerns about coercion ("full and free confession") and manipulation ("with little or no variation, from his own words"), Gray claims to advance entirely impartial, even transparent insight into criminal aberrance ("the operations of a mind like his"), legal design ("the policy of our laws in restraint of this class"), and civic duty ("induce all . . . to see that they are strictly and rigidly enforced"). We might note, here, that by these terms the pamphlet's emphasis falls on *two kinds* of conduct: not just the deviance of the rebel, which needs comprehending, but also the vigilance of the citizen, which needs bracing. At stake is what I would call *trespass*, the "insurrectionary movements of the slaves" combined with Turner's restless psyche "endeavoring to grapple with things beyond its reach." Against the threat of such trespass, Gray's pamphlet undertakes to reassure its readers through lessons in communal, social, and racial fixity.

So understood, the text of the *Confessions* is clearly disciplinary in its force, striving not just to settle in retrospect the problem of rebellious motivation but also to restore and reproduce the proper terms of social relation among *all* Virginians. Yet, perhaps surprisingly, despite these disciplinary tendencies, the *Confessions* remains a powerfully indeterminate document, troubled precisely by the interpenetration of voices within it. Lacking all commonplace forms of social and political entitlement, let alone the elaborate, abstract authorial technologies crucial to what Richard Brodhead calls "literary access," nevertheless, in the process of confessing, Nat Turner begins to vex the space of authorship occupied by Thomas Gray.[13] As Eric Sundquist argues, the *Confessions* "defies our normal conceptions of authorship and narrative," manifesting instead "the entire phenomenology of slavery in which the dialectic of opposing wills was subject to continual borrowings and absorptions of power, alterations of ascendancy, and recognitions that the ontological planes of bondage and mastery could from time to time—in sudden flarings of resistance, escape, or deceit—become inverted."[14] And even though "[b]ecause their collaboration also resembles the collaboration of master and slave, the *Confessions* recapitulates the dynamics of bondage," this fact itself, according to Sundquist, "entails our reading Turner's text—like the 'text' of slavery itself—from more than the master's perspective and therefore with an eye to the slave's own intellectual and cultural power."[15] If Gray aims to diffuse and discipline Turner's revolutionary authority with a specifically authorial as well as legal agency, nevertheless the insurgent slave's responses supplement that undertaking. To see Gray's pamphlet in this way gives an instance of what Sundquist, following Orlando Patterson, terms the parasitical relationship of master and slave, and so a means to imagine the dissonance at issue in the scene of confessional production itself.

In Turner's case such dissonance complicates the common sense that, linking freedom and authorship, defines by contrast enslavement as the material and metaphysical inability to write. "[C]ontriver of the conspiracy" recorded in the *Confessions*, Turner likewise contrives to undermine the official act of authorship that would indict him (41). Turner's intervention holds to the way in which, with the terms of his confession and the rhetoric of its delivery, he troubles a discursive form in defiance of the allied institutions of slavery, law, authorship, and publication called upon by Gray, the court, and Virginian slaveholders to discipline his insurgence.

Here I should stress that I understand the sort of vexed collaboration at issue in light of the concept of "authorial personality" advanced by David Saunders and Ian Hunter in their essay "Lessons from the 'Literatory.'" For Saunders and Hunter, "the delineation and attribution of authorial personality is governed not by the logic of subject formation but by the historical emergence of particular cultural techniques and social institutions."[16] Thus, authorial personalities "are positive forms of social being attributed unevenly across individuals and institutions in a variety of ways and according to a variety of cultural, legal, technological, economic, and ethical imperatives. The expressive author represents a particular configuration of this shifting distribution."[17] The prospect of such "shifting distribution" bears to telling effect on the discursive interplay (or indeed contest) between Gray and

Turner so palpable in the *Confessions*. Although Gray embodies the commonplace form of expressive authorship, Turner comes, in spite of his vexed relation under slavery to "the logic of subject formation," however haltingly into what Saunders and Hunter call a positive form of social being through the "cultural techniques" of confession that, aimed at discipline, cannot do without his collaboration in the authoring of Gray's text.

Turner's first words indicate something of the force of his intervention. "Sir," he begins: "You have asked me to give a history of the motives which induced me to undertake the late insurrection, as you call it—To do so, I must go back to the days of my infancy, and even before I was born" (44). Although here as throughout the *Confessions* the basic question of informational accuracy and authenticity will complicate any analysis—are Turner's words rendered, on Gray's part, with little or with no variation?—nevertheless the emphasis on motive, narrative, naming, and interpretation remains telling. A history of motive, to judge from Turner's articulation, is (to risk redundancy) fully *historical*, involving frequencies more complex than the merely personal or experiential. By claiming as his context the moment "even before [he] was born," Turner meets the subjectifying hail of confessional narrative (why did you do what you did?) by intimating contentious claims to a larger history. The effect, I suggest, entangles world-time with the otherworldly: notorious for his claim of divine inspiration, Turner, by gesturing to knowledge of events before his birth, makes inextricable historical with visionary comprehension.

As important for understanding Turner's intervention is the way his opening statement finds in the disciplinary act of confessional narration the potential for dispute and contest. The phrase "as you call it" is crucial here: it marks the site of interpretive disagreement; it acknowledges the force and yet the insufficiency of legal naming; it insists on the discursive mediation that Gray, with his emphasis on Turner's "own words" presented as though "without comment," attempts to deny; it hints at the way Turner mimics, so as to challenge, a normative discourse; above all, it leaves ambiguous the point of its reference—does Turner dispute the use of the term "insurrection," or the claim that insurrection has ended (40, 41)? The first possibility will call attention to the imprecision and impropriety of the charge, since under Virginia law the enslaved cannot be charged with treason (see note 1). The second possibility will mean that, by itself, legal language cannot consign to the past a revolt still looming in the present—that in this case insurrectionary motive is not only historical, but has a pressing future. The tactic begins to suggest how confessional disclosure might reveal more than one meaning: disputing the semantic termination of rebellion, Turner enacts a rebellious interference within the confessional scene itself. Thus from the outset Turner injects a dissonant energy into the fixing, disciplinary apparatus of confession: the power of naming becomes explicit as the truth of names becomes partial; vocabularies, voices multiply, and Gray's exclusive, singular authority begins to erode. Already we can see Turner the accused criminal entangling the roles of native informant (satisfying ethnographic as well as sensationalizing curiosity) and antagonistic collaborator (shaping discourse, directing its energies, manipulating anxiety about rebellion's continuance). The effect bears out the text's discursive complexity while at the same time insinuating the threat most feared by white Virginia: Turner's apparently "fanatic[al]," "fiend-like" power (54).[18]

The problems of motive so prominent from the start of the pamphlet only intensify the problems of movement at issue in the substance of the confession itself. Judging from Gray's treatment, Turner's account of revolt proceeds by means of its itinerary: reflecting on his desire "to proceed to Jerusalem," he details the quite methodical progress of the rebels from plantation to plantation, "carry[ing] terror and devastation wherever we went"; then he tells of his much more haphazard flight—"pursued almost incessantly" from hiding place to hiding place following the rebellion's breakdown, and ultimately captured (52, 50, 53). Yet the meaning of such movement, as of its record within the text of the *Confessions*, is hardly untroubled: serving to punctuate the scenes of corporeal puncture, mobility comes to supplement rebellious violence, not so much incidental or intermediary to bloodshed as inextricable from it. Hence the orderly reconstruction of movement by means of itinerary only underscores a crisis of movement under slavery, in which an unlicensed, unpredictable slave mobility actually constitutes material and social violence.

To gauge the full force of such crisis as it resonates in the *Confessions*, we need to consider the power and privilege that, in the antebellum period, movement or travel would necessarily entail. Presupposing a degree of material integrity (investments in time as in money), movement as a social resource likewise presupposes a degree of subjective integrity—a measure of motive force, of selfhood, of will. Thus generic discourses of human movement, such as travel writing, have tended in the modern era to articulate mobility's practice not least in terms of self-extension. As Larzer Ziff contends, in characterizing this hegemonic tendency: "[a]way from the familiar surroundings that formed and sustain his sense of himself, the traveler becomes radically aware of where he ends and all else begins; his individuality is, as it were, thrust upon him, and as a result the written account of what he sees and does serves inevitably to affirm the self he has discovered in the process of moving among strangers."[19] So understood, the traveling habit presumes leisure and freedom alongside masculinity (note Ziff's use of gendered pronouns), and social agency alongside introspection and insight. Yet, I would stress, such presumptions are historically particular—normative in the moment around 1831 in ways that, even fifty years earlier, they had still to secure. The historical shift at issue will register not least in the generic conventions attending mobility's account; as Susan Stewart observes, "[b]etween the eighteenth and the nineteenth century, . . . a literature of exploration involving the cataloguing of curiosities surrendered to a literature of travel involving the transformation of a subject through first-hand experience."[20]

The terms of this privileged model of mobility take for granted even as they dramatize an elaboration, a *deepening*, of subjectivity, such that movement's defamiliarizations inspire in its human agents an increasing (sometimes shocking) familiarity and intimacy with intellect, sensibility, and desire. At its most schematic, the forms and terms of subjective realization map ontology onto geography, hinging the work of mobility on the relation of *in* and *away*—of interiority and exteriority, of incursive and excursive moves calibrating even as they cross territorial bodies and affective states.[21] As evinced over and over in the historical formation that Stewart calls the "literature of travel," movement out and away figures movement inward, *producing* that deep subjectivity it would seem to discover. Significantly, the emergent subject will, at least in the U.S. context, often cleave to what Lauren Berlant calls "national fantasy"—"his province of selfhood," in Wai-chee Dimock's phrase, "akin to a national polity."[22] Attesting in discourse to an expressive, "natural" relation between the character of the land and the character of the nation's subject, the traveler here consolidates what Dimock calls the "mutuality between self and nation . . . [that] constituted both the self and the nation in antebellum America."[23] At stake, as I suggested in my reading of Robert Tomes's essay in the introduction, is what Amy Kaplan calls an "idea of traveling domesticity": the paradigm secures the dimensions of a national allegory and, to the extent that this allegory invents a homeland, holds in tight relation travel and home, the project of departure and the scene of return.[24] As Bruce Greenfield contends, "[i]n nineteenth-century American narratives, journeys are on the verge of becoming one-way. . . . Early national narratives invite the nation to move with the narrator."[25]

This interrelation of mobility and subjectivity, travel and home, takes for granted, or indeed occludes, the material particularities (notably property ownership) that tend to invest historically particular concepts of home in the modern liberal tradition.[26] Here the possession bound up with home underwrites the self-possession attending the sort of interiority, of deep subjectivity, produced by the conceptual and ideological complex, the mobility regime, that I have been describing. Both possession and self-possession mark habits of intimate belonging unevenly available through the institutional and ideological structures in 1830s America. These habits bring with them resources of differentiation and control; they mark the political contingency of a paradigm that works to intricate travel and home in compensatory or mutually elaborating relation. Linking, as if natural, the ability and desire to leave home with the ability and desire to return there, this paradigm tends to fuse mobility with property, the right to move with the right to own. Thus, if in the period in question movement or travel comes to epitomize, as merely natural or commonplace, what Dimock calls the "mutuality between self and nation," practically and materially such mutuality required those more exclusive tests and measures of citizenship: whiteness, maleness, property.

I trust the significance of these issues for the problem of movement at stake in Nat Turner's *Confessions* is already clear, since the paradigm I have been discussing necessarily precludes any slave. Slaves could only be, and never own, property. The possession and self-possession bound up in the traveling habit of antebellum citizens were off-limits to them. Although slaves were everywhere tied to plantations or landed estates, and although they regularly managed to fashion the affective conditions and material space of a kind of home, nevertheless ideologically speaking they remained *homeless*, lacking both domestic and national entitlement. And it goes without saying that the brutal force of this dispossession involved both parts of the paradigm: not just the intimate, rooted forms of belonging that home's possession supplied, but the expansive, routed forms of belonging that mobility's exercise could secure.[27]

Here I would emphasize, however, the practical impossibility (not to mention the economic undesirability) of completely restricting slave movement. In a broad sense, the circulation of slaves was the motor of southern slavery. And given the varieties of local and regional labor that slaves supplied, their day-to-day mobility might be said to offer one index of economic performance and security. The workings of the plantation economy depended as much on routine movement by the enslaved as on the ritualized traffic orchestrated at the auction block. The need for such routine mobility marked a kind of calculated risk: to the extent that, as chattel, slaves were reduced, under plantation ideology, to merely part of the apparatus of domestic property, their everyday movements could create the conditions of possibility for a troublesome straying of domestic property away from its rightful place (that is, from its place at home). Thus, in limit-cases such as Turner's, the prospect of slave movement, carried to a troublesome extreme, undercuts the understanding that would intricate travel and home in compensatory relation. Even in envisioning the mobility required by revolt, Turner jeopardizes both the orthodox prospect of homeward return and the ideological project that, expanding through tropes of excursion the dimensions of home, renders travel a properly domestic activity. Lacking an ideologically recognizable subjectivity until after his confession, in his restlessness Turner moves as an illicit agent who confounds by exploiting the interdependence of property and mobility.

This movement, propelling him against the interdictions of the slave system, throws into vexed relief the matter of a slave's "homelessness," and cracks the binarism articulating mobility (and its extension) in terms of the property of home: in undertaking insurgent movement, Turner can neither presume an end-point of homeward return nor imagine the intimacies of home moving with him. Accordingly, his illicit mobility underscores potentially destabilizing effects in the *work* of motion under slavery, where that work can contest the situation and function, *as property*, of bodies as well as of terrain. In this case, the restless slave troubles the ideology that, in calibrating movement with home, always already presumes a supposedly natural set of property relations (property relations continually reinforced, and so belied as natural, through material and discursive forms of violence).

In the editorial frame to his pamphlet, Thomas Gray aims to restore a sense of communal and systemic order—of what we might, to invoke a current phrase, call "homeland security"—by fixing the rebel, and more especially the problem of his illicit movement, within the confession of his crime. Designed to fashion the image of regional stability through the exercise of legal narrative, while at the same time to create temporal, spatial, and juridical distance between the events of rebellion and the readers who consume them in retrospect, the confessional project thus purports to establish a barrier between knowledge of Turner's crimes and the crimes themselves. Yet the power of confession is complex, not least in its tendency to incite the formation of subjectivity. As Michel Foucault argues, in modernity "[t]he truthful confession [has been] inscribed at the heart of the procedures of individualization through power."[28] Confession invents, as though retrospectively, the workings of a deep subjectivity to which it gives coherence and narrative form. Through the process of unveiling (especially with respect to crime or sin), confession likewise promises development, bearing witness to an evolution, or indeed an elevation, of consciousness, spirit, belief. Yet as Stewart notes in *Crimes of Writing*, "the function of description in the confessional mode is not the replication of an 'outside,' an objective world unaffected by authorial consciousness, but *the invention of the speaking subject as the location of veracity*."[29] Thus the seemingly retrospective cast of confession is in fact prospective, in ways decisively political in significance.

For Foucault, the longstanding primacy of confession within cultural methods of "individualization by power" means that

> [t]he obligation to confess is now relayed through so many different points, is so deeply ingrained in us, that we no longer perceive it as the effect of a power that constrains us; on the contrary, it seems to us that truth, lodged in our most secret nature, "demands" only to surface; that if it fails to do so, this is because a constraint holds it in place, the violence of a power weighs it down, and it can finally be articulated only at the price of a kind of liberation. Confession frees, but power reduces one to silence; truth does not belong to the order of power, but shares an original affinity with freedom.[30]

Gray is able to marshal the habitual, reflexive force of this understanding of confession when in his pamphlet he insists that Turner gives his confession spontaneously, "without being questioned at all," and that the confession itself is full, free, and voluntary (44). Yet Turner's case clearly taxes this conventional view precisely by underscoring interimplicated problems of individuation or selfhood, on the one hand, and of volition on the other: as chattel, Turner by definition has neither self nor will; as confessing criminal, he cannot *not* hold both of these. The situation gives a compelling instance of the more general problematic analyzed by Saidiya Hartman: "[t]he slave was recognized as a reasoning subject who possessed intent and rationality solely in the context of criminal liability; ironically, the slave's will was acknowledged only as it was prohibited or punished."[31] The double bind requires, I would suggest, that we recognize Turner's dissonant relation to notions of full or voluntary speech or action. Such dissonance indicates not just the ideological constraints binding the enslaved but also, and crucially, the ways Turner's restlessness, in utterance as in action, render inadequate liberal presuppositions about fullness and will.[32] At the same time, because of what Sundquist terms the "taut suspension" calibrating matters of property and will, the restorative ambitions at stake in Gray's project (confirming crime while calming the fears of slaveholding and pro-slavery whites) must falter over confession's inflationary effects, effects creating the troublesome prospect of will in a body that, under slavery's ideology, could otherwise have none.

Effectively, Turner managed, by insinuating his voice to dissonant effect in the text of his confession, to pressure the discursive technology designed to restrict—or indeed to correct a failure to regulate—excessive, rebellious movement by the enslaved (a point that will underscore as it complicates the intimacy, with regard to subject formation, of criminal confession and historically particular forms of traveling discourse: both instrumental in producing subjectivity, travel in concert with the fiction of liberty, confession in concert with the fact of liberty's loss). Moreover, Turner's fraught relation to the text of his confession recollects the likewise fraught relation of any slave to the master's document (usually a chit or letter) that typically would set out the terms, paths, and limits of slave movement.[33] Violating the command of such written regulation, Turner's rebellious tour was not least a form of *textual* trespass, even as it threw into relief the tenuousness of the join between discursive regulation and material movement. In effect, by means of his restlessness he challenged the regimen binding slave motion to the sanction of written text. In leading the Southampton rebels Turner moved with disdain for the fixing inscriptions of slavery, thereby wrenching together questions of animate property and slave will, and troubling the ideological investment, on the part of the slaveholding class, in the fixity of property and the stability of subjectivity.

By detailing, yet thereby compounding, such textual trespass, the *Confessions* compromises its disciplinary project. Designed, as I have already suggested, to provide a barrier between readers and the events about which they read, Gray's pamphlet also serves as a threshold: its emphasis on bloodshed and especially on Turner's calculating fanaticism reanimates insurrectionary violence, jeopardizing precisely that sense of distance Gray aims to institute. Crucial, here, is the travel story Nat Turner tells early in his confession, before he gives the details of revolt: having run away from a new overseer, after thirty days he comes back, "to the astonishment of the negroes on the plantation," braced by a vision from God to direct his "wishes" and purpose "to the kingdom of Heaven" (46). The moment is key, since it marks the beginning of the process I would call Turner's divine *transport*, through which, by his own account, "from the first steps of righteousness until the last, [he] was made perfect" (47). Thus does the runaway's otherwise inexplicable return mark the start of a spiritual carrying-away, a shift in commitment and in tactic from fugitive flight to revolutionary restlessness. Such transport inspires the orchestration of uprising through material mobility: being moved by visions will, in Turner's case, impel insurrectionary movement. And by insisting so emphatically on Turner's visionary fanaticism, Gray's pamphlet counteracts its own fixing ambitions, managing instead to keep the uncanny promise of this kind of transport in motion.[34]

The problems I have been analyzing here bear not just on the immediate events compelling the text's production but likewise on the specter of geopolitical and geoeconomic calamity standing behind them. As Sundquist notes, since, in the early nineteenth century, slavery was most often "defined in hemispheric terms," so memory of the San Domingo revolution of 1791 offered "a prophetic simulacrum of events feared to lie on the horizon of American slavery."[35] Accordingly, the regional crisis of Turner's uprising must have animated far-flung anxieties about hemispheric apocalypse, taking the event's immediate, local audience on imaginative flights to foreign scenes conflated and confused by racist rage and panic. To the extent that, behind its specific itinerary, the *Confessions* contains a *model* of slave revolt, and to the extent that San Domingo signified the ubiquitous pretext for the possibility of such revolt, Gray's text effectively returns the prior knowledge of San Domingo home to Virginia, while simultaneously transporting readers to potential San Domingos all across the slave-holding hemisphere. Thus understood, the pamphlet, produced through an asymmetrical contest of voices, mimics to haunting effect the tendency of travel writing to collapse imaginatively and affectively those distances on which it ceaselessly remarks and insists.[36]

"Gossip Rumour, with Her Hundred Tongues"

This reading turns on an instability that, written into the text of Turner's confession, threatens the epistemological security afforded to whites by slavery's system. Precisely because of such instability, the *Confessions* troubles those forms of social and racial common sense on which slave-holding hegemony depended. Appropriately, then, Gray's pamphlet, against its own design, the project of its white author, and the overarching desire of Virginian jurisprudence, managed to animate those teeming, proliferative rumors it sought to kill.

From the start, the *Confessions* announces its aim to lay rumor's ghosts to rest. Appealing "TO THE PUBLIC," it begins by observing that "[t]he late insurrection in Southampton has greatly excited the public mind, and led to a thousand idle, exaggerated and mischievous reports" (40).[37] Evidently inflated, as the charge of exaggeration makes abundantly clear, these reports are nevertheless threatening enough to require an authoritative rebuttal capable not just of distinguishing truth from falsehood but also of reestablishing some orderly distance between them. At stake in such discriminatory differentiation is not least the well-being of Gray's readers, who in his view have endured much suffering as a result of rumor's circulation: "[p]ublic curiosity has been on the stretch to understand the origin and progress of this dreadful conspiracy, and the motives which influenced its diabolical actors" (40). Figuring interest's anguish—collective, yet oddly anonymous, depersonalized, disembodied—in terms of torture ("on the stretch"), Gray intimates that rumor can cause an epistemological torment commensurate with the sort of physical suffering inflicted by Turner and his Southampton compatriots. For Gray, the confessional project will dispel rumor so as to relieve the public from its agonies. His motives, I would stress, are complex: by insisting on the authority of his account, Gray undertakes to establish himself as a juridical medium, a dispassionate expert, and an inspired savior—healing the public (or indeed corporate) imaginary in ways impossible for the state to achieve with respect to the scores of dead slaveholders left in Turner's wake.

Gray's emphasis on the reparative force of his authority necessarily exists in supplement to, and in tension with, an array of comparably authoritative accounts circulating in the regional press. As early as 23 August, the Richmond *Constitutional Whig* sounds the alarm, attending at the outset of its first article on the revolt to the "[d]isagreeable rumors" that threaten to disturb Richmond's public life.[38] For the *Petersburg (VA) Intelligencer* of 26 August, the rumors are "so numerous and contradictory" that accurate reporting is flatly impossible; for Norfolk's *American Beacon* of the same date, "the many exaggerated statements with which gossip rumour, with her hundred tongues, has hourly abused the public conscience" demand in answer either "authentic information" or outright silence on the topic of the revolt.[39] Much like the rebels, rumor offers a volatile threat to personal safety (the reader "will scarcely be safe if he believes a fiftieth part of what he hears," warns the *Richmond Compiler* on 24 August).[40] If, by contrast, when seen in a certain way rumor can be said to perform a bracing, consolidating function within the public sphere ("rumors sufficient to keep alive the vigilance of the people," as Richmond's *Enquirer* for 2 September avers), nevertheless the very fact that rumor persists in remaining "afloat" (as the *Compiler* for 3 September puts it) and so circulating in suspended, unpredictable fashion, constitutes its perpetual threat—one bound up with its treacherous, nearly *treasonable* character.[41] As the anonymous author of perhaps the most influential newspaper account of the rebellion implies, rumor demands correction because it jeopardizes national stability: "there are so many rumors afloat, and so many misstatements in the public prints, that *a sacred duty to my country*, demands a correct view of this tragedy" (Richmond *Constitutional Whig*, 26 September).[42] Hence the urgent need for cure noted most forcefully in Gray's text: as if a virus, rumor assails and corrupts the body of nation.[43]

But of course something so abstract and elusive as communal peace of mind is not the only thing at stake in matters of national health. Wellness of country likewise depends on the animation of its limbs, its local and regional parts, which in turn depends significantly on the smooth operation of local and regional economies. In the Virginia of 1831, as in most of the South (and, in complex, distinct ways, much of the North), such smooth operation followed in particular from the perpetuation of slavery, the traffic in enslaved bodies, alongside the circulation of material commodities and discursive artifacts. With respect, then, to Turner's revolt and the intense public outcry it generated, the news/rumor complex necessarily composed a vital technology for the production, reproduction, and dissemination of value (and values) under slavery. Despite its apparently juridical, disinterested posture, Gray's text invested heavily in these more diffuse forms of commercial circulation inextricable from slavery's traffic—the pamphlet's claim, shown on the title page, to provide "an authentic account of the whole insurrection, with lists of the whites who were murdered, and of the negroes brought before the court of Southampton, and there sentenced, &c" amounting to a strategy to command a significant market share (38).[44] This recognition lends added force to Sundquist's claim that "[i]n bringing forth a text meant to answer the 'thousand idle, exaggerated and mischievous reports' caused by the revolt, and acting for 'the gratification of public curiosity,' Gray thus produced one as likely to cause alarm as to allay fears."[45] If what I am arguing is right, public fear and increased sales, interimplicated indexes of the desire to know and to reaffirm jeopardized knowledge, coalesced under the hovering sign of rumor.

In this way, rumor and its attendant fears constitute the dimensions of a public as well as the substance of publicity, and do so precisely according to signs of panic, stress, and fracture. That is, in this case rumor supplies the principle by (or, more particularly, against) which a community imagines itself. Necessarily, though, we must ask what happens to the idea of a *public* when rumor's circulation comes to constitute public discourse. As a powerful type of disembodied speech, lacking a traceable origin or author, rumor compels an unwonted social body predicated on and fascinated by its own distress. Such manufacture becomes especially telling as we remember that one of the effects of the uprising was to insist on the corporeality of slaveholders; butchery on such a scale necessarily drew attention to the limbs, the blood, the guts of social agents whose institutional legitimacy and cultural power ordinarily derived from an ideology of social disembodiment.[46] Thus one way to interpret the news media's declared commitment, in the wake of Turner's rebellion, to quell the disruptions of rumor is in terms of a desire to recalibrate the hegemonically proper relation between the body politic and its invisible or disembodied authorities: as Nat Turner quite literally, and rumor more abstractly, brought distressing forms of physical and social embodiment to the ruling classes (since, even if socially privileged, one must find one's body in the moment of its violation), so the news media's attempts to settle rumors concerning Turner's revolt sought to make such traumatic corporeality dissolve, or at least fade from view.

Here I would return to the insistence on authority in Gray's text, authority intimately bound up with the disciplinary aims of the confessional project. As I have already suggested, confession seeks in a case like Turner's to *re*subject the rebellious slave to the broader community of slaveholders and proslavery whites, making him or her a textual subject proper to (that is, owned by) a tacitly white, male, landed, literate community so as to restore some equilibrium of property and propriety within the public so recently terrorized by rebellious trespass.[47] In Gray's pamphlet, as I have argued, this disciplinary effort falters over both the inflationary capacity of confession and the dissonant effect of Turner's performance. What I want to emphasize, though, is the commercial dimension of textual authority: Gray's disciplinary ambition speaks not least to the marketplace, where an authoritative posture proves at once uniquely and repetitiously desirable. Even as each account of the Southampton revolt claims sole authority, people cannot get enough of authoritative claims. Knowledge means power not least to the extent that it means sales. Accordingly, Gray's commercial advantage will hinge on his ability to produce the goods: Turner's words, ostensibly advanced without prompting—where spontaneity implies guilt or sin alongside immediacy or unmediation—and published "with little or no variation."

Both the stability and the exclusivity of these goods depend on the authenticating, disciplinary mark of the copyright. For Gray, this mark represents a means to guarantee—that is, to *prefigure*—the trustworthiness of the account.[48] Much like the "certificate of the County Court of Southampton" affixed to the *Confessions* by the presiding justices, copyright makes legitimate (even before any act of reading) the confession as "a faithful record," providing yet one more "stamp" with which to impress upon the reader the "truth and sincerity" supposedly immanent in Turner's words (40). In this capacity, copyright aims to remove "doubts and conjectures from the public mind which otherwise must have remained" and moreover to sanction Gray's attempt to mobilize regional and also national sentiment against the destabilizing effects of rumor (42). As Gray maintains, "[i]f Nat's statements can be relied on" (a needless prevarication, given the copyright itself):

> the insurrection in this county was entirely local, and his designs confided but to a few, and these in his immediate vicinity. It was not instigated by motives of revenge or sudden anger, but the results of long deliberation, and a settled purpose of mind. The offspring of gloomy fanaticism, acting upon materials but too well prepared for such impressions. It will be long remembered in the annals of our country, and many a mother as she presses her infant darling to her bosom, will shudder at the recollection of Nat Turner, and his band of ferocious miscreants. (41–42)

At one level this passage works to head off lurking fears about unpredictable, undetectable, sudden violence. But the image of the shuddering mother with infant to bosom counteracts the sober reassurance with which the passage begins. It marks a clear attempt to capitalize on larger cultural investments in sentiment and sensation, and helps to confirm by example Sundquist's claim that Gray's "copyright immediately reminds us that we are reading a text placed before the public as a commercial venture . . . and casts an especially bright light" not just "on the slave's status as property and commodity" but also on Turner's capacity to jeopardize this status along with its attendant ideological relations (here naturalized through the sentimental tropes of mother and child).[49]

Just as forcibly, the matter of copyright lets us see the provocative relation that links the problem of slave movement to rumor's troublesome career. Rumor's restlessness threatens to upset the smooth workings of an economic regime where stories instead of bodies constitute the commodities exchanged in the marketplace. Thus it becomes imperative that texts, not unlike slaves, circulate only with their proper documentation.[50] Rumor's seeming parasitism in the literary marketplace demands that a story such as Turner's cease to move without its proper legal and textual constraints, that it submit to discipline and only travel along accepted paths of communication and consumption, that it change from a promiscuous discourse to "a faithful record" (40). To this end, we may infer, Gray copyrights his project, hoping that the discriminatory technology concentrated in the copyright's mark will reestablish the proper (and proprietorial) relations articulating fact and fiction, truth and rumor.

Yet, much like Turner's confessional performance, rumor starts out as a vocal form.[51] And because rumor consists in uncontrolled and uncontrollable talk, thereby working against the grain of printed text, its instabilities achieve a discursive value in excess of the disciplinary regulations of copyright. The achievement of such value hinges on the ways in which, as I suggested above, rumor proves profitable within a public articulated in part by rumor's circulation; in order to sell, Gray's pamphlet requires that rumor both desist and persist. This paradox is written into the climax of the text, where, in keeping with the rhetorical demands of sensational discourse, Gray pleads inarticulateness at the moment of his most ostentatious eloquence:

> I shall not attempt to describe the effect of his narrative, as told and commented on by himself, in the condemned hole of the prison. The calm, deliberate composure with which he spoke of his late deeds and intentions, the expression of his fiend-like face when excited by enthusiasm, still bearing the stains of the blood of helpless innocence about him; clothed with rags and covered with chains; yet daring to raise his manacled hands to heaven, with a spirit soaring above the attributes of man; I looked on him and my blood curdled in my veins. (54–55)

Supremely descriptive, speaking volumes, the phrase with which Gray rules out description marks the point at which terror becomes at once incomprehensible and marketable, unreproducible yet ready to package. At the same time, and in ways that only compound the problems of visionary transport analyzed above, Gray's insistence on Turner's spectral "soaring" supplies one means by which rumor may continue its career, hovering alongside the rebel's terrific spirit over the several printings of Gray's text.[52] For if Nat Turner is superhuman, or demoniacal, as Gray's terrified yet presumably authoritative claim here attests, then the rumors of his continued power even when jailed may prove all too true, confirmed by authority of the text that has until now labored to discredit such rumors. The bloodcurdling moment signals textual fascination but also textual crisis; as it undercuts Gray's hard work in prying apart truth from falsehood and sobriety from sensation, so it contributes to the textual instability inflecting relations of authenticity, authority, marketability, and rumor that copyright alone cannot hope to rectify. Accordingly, this moment suggests a means by which to understand the rumors of Nat Turner as an extension of his trespass and his restlessness. Rumor is, after all, an unceasingly restless form. As Avital Ronell warns, "[r]umors are in the air; they fly"—and so refuse to be pinned down.[53] Rumors hover, and haunt as they do so.

2

Abandoned to Circulation

> The immortality which money strove to achieve by setting itself negatively against circulation, by withdrawing from it, is achieved by capital, which preserves itself precisely by abandoning itself to circulation.
>
> —*Karl Marx,* Grundrisse

> Political economy came into being as a natural result of the expansion of trade, and with its appearance elementary, unscientific huckstering was replaced by a developed system of licensed fraud, an entire science of enrichment.
>
> —*Frederick Engels, "Outlines of a Critique of Political Economy"*

"The Atlantic Cable," published in 1868 by the Cherokee author John Rollin Ridge as a part of his collected *Poems*, dwells with an unbridled optimism on one of the key achievements of the mid-nineteenth century "information revolution," the union of "the Old and New World" in 1866 by means of transatlantic telegraphy. After a compound call to celebration—"Let Earth be glad! . . . Let all mankind rejoice!"—the first stanza asserts the power of the transatlantic cable, as "a courier for the thought," to conquer "time" and "space" and, in so doing, to affirm as it realizes the unity of "the human race." To underscore this power, Ridge rehearses a schematic history of the modes of communication and transport that precede telegraphy, a history beginning with the "skin-clad heralds" of a preliterate, prescientific past and moving through the eras of the "beasts," of the "oar-propelled" boats, of the "winged ships"—on which, in Ridge's suspect recasting of imperial conquest, "sea-divided nations nearer came, / Stood face to face, spake each other's name,/ In friendship grew, and learned the truth sublime, / That Man is Man in every age and clime!"—and, most recently, of "steam," through the "miracle" of which "distance . . . was shortened into days" and scientific innovation seemed to reach its apotheosis. Yet telegraphy, in Ridge's account, has eclipsed all such modes through the immediacy that electricity affords—"lightning's wondrous power," "mightier" because "subtler" than steam in manifestation. The credit, for Ridge, falls to "America," a "great, free land" suited, as though by destiny, to "give the lightning's voice to Liberty." And the achievement, gloriously enough, will bring an end to the very real forms of misery and bloodshed wrought by spurious differences and divisions between peoples: "For Nation unto Nation soon shall be / Together brought in knitted unity, / And man be bound to man by that strong chain, / Which, linking land to land, and main to main, / Shall vibrate to the voice of Peace, and be / A throbbing heartstring of Humanity!" So conceived, the transatlantic cable marks the start of "millenial" time.[1]

Implicit in "The Transatlantic Cable" is a claim for the power of poetry, advanced by a latent analogy between the electric capacity of the cable and the status of poetry as cultural current: both, in this reading, can harness "the lightning's wondrous power" to span and so transcend time and space—though Ridge's poem offers a low-voltage instance of such poetic power. Yet, whatever its aesthetic limitations, "The Atlantic Cable" demonstrates vividly the deep investment of its author in the ideology of progress key to American exceptionalism.[2] Written in the wake of the Civil War's scarifying carnage, the poem seems to relish its own obtuseness about the violent dynamics that, on the national as on the international stage, marked political struggles and social relations, not to mention the interrelated materialities of communication and transport in everyday life.

Such obtuseness becomes still more striking when we consider the violent impress of politics and mobility for the Cherokee during Ridge's lifetime. After all, the 1830s, the decade of his childhood and early adolescence, featured an increasingly aggressive federal program of removal, culminating in 1838 with the forced relocation of the Cherokee from Georgia to the Indian Territory along the Trail of Tears. The human cost of this imposed mobility was grim indeed: nearly fifteen hundred died in camps before the start of the removal, sixteen hundred died en route, and at least nine hundred more died through illness and hardship in the following year.[3]

For reasons having significantly to do with the role of his family in the removal, Ridge came to understand in distinctive ways its personal and communal costs. Both his father and grandfather were members of the Cherokee political elite who argued in favor of the necessity of relocation; on 29 December 1835, against the will of the majority Ross party, the Ridge-Boudinot faction secretly signed the Treaty of New Echota with Federal authorities, conceding the Cherokee nation's Georgia land in exchange for 13,800,000 acres in present-day Oklahoma and some $4,500,000 in annuities. The treaty facilitated the removal process that would begin two years later, on 6 June 1838, and would continue until 25 March 1839, when the final group arrived in the Indian Territory. The decision by the Ridge-Boudinot party to treat with Jackson's government was hardly unpressured, and will teach, in its determinations as in its outcomes, a much different lesson about encounters between nations than that offered in "The Atlantic Cable." In the 1830s (as in subsequent decades), white America tended to "give the lightning's voice" to betrayal, not liberty, where native peoples were concerned. Yet despite the overwhelming indications of federal rapacity and treachery given by the New Echota episode, "[t]o this day," as Cheryl Walker observes, "the voluntary compliance of the Treaty Party—who acted, from their point of view, out of a sense of necessity and in order to protect the lives of the people in an era of Indian massacres—is regarded with contempt by other Indians."[4] On 22 June 1839, members of the Ross party documented their contempt in blood. Disregarding an 1828 Cherokee law that criminalized murder, they answered the "treason" of New Echota "in terms of an older tradition of clan revenge" by killing three of the leaders of the Ridge-Boudinot party—Ridge's father (John Ridge), his grandfather Major Ridge, and Elias Boudinot.[5] Himself witness to his father's slaughter, Ridge, in documenting the Ross party's retribution, commemorates the eloquence for which his father had been celebrated, in terms that, by emphasizing the loss of speech in blood, intimate a crisis of communication in violence:

> I saw my father in the hands of assassins. He endeavored to speak to them, but they shouted and drowned his voice, for they were instructed not to listen to him for a moment, for fear they would be persuaded not to kill him. They dragged him to the yard, and prepared to murder him. Two men held him by the arms, and others by the body, while another stabbed him

> deliberately with a dirk twenty-nine times. . . . [After the stabbing, he] raised himself on his elbow and tried to speak, but the blood flowed into his mouth and prevented him. In a few moments more he died, without speaking that last word which he wished to say. Then succeeded a scene of agony the sight of which might make one regret that the human race had ever been created. It has darkened my mind with an eternal shadow. In a room prepared for the purpose, lay pale in death the man whose voice had been listened to with awe and admiration in the councils of his nation, and whose fame had passed to the remotest of the United States, the blood oozing through his winding sheet, and falling drop by drop on the floor. By his side sat my mother, with hands clasped, and in speechless agony. . . . There was yet another blow to be dealt. Major Ridge had started on a journey the day before. . . . A runner was sent with all possible speed to inform him of what had happened . . . [only to return] with the news that Major Ridge himself was killed. It is useless to lengthen description. It would fall short, far short of the theme.[6]

Affectively and conceptually as well as generically, here we are a long way from the almost utopian eclipse of violence through the power of human communication Ridge envisions in "The Atlantic Cable." In this account of familial catastrophe, reproduced in the preface to his collected poems of 1868, Ridge sets the failure of language to represent against the potential of language to persuade. The sentimental convention that indicates the insufficiency of words to mediate an emotionally charged reality underscores, with pointed irony, the threateningly immediate power of eloquent speech to undermine or transform political will. Human communication and violence are intimate, not opposed; chaotic powers of the tongue—shouts and cries—foster divisions among people by drowning out persuasive speech; the voice of peace gives way to the discourse of the blade.

In 1854, still haunted by the scene of his father's murder, Ridge would put this discourse of the blade to striking use, finding ways, in the sensation-novel he published that year, to make blood speak. Set in California's gold rush, *The Life and Adventures of Joaquín Murieta, the Celebrated California Bandit* reinscribes, on page after page, the viscerally expressive power of violence to communicate. The novel's protagonist, drawn in composite from several bandits active in the region, is a Mexican immigrant who is three times dispossessed of his land and his honor by "lawless and desperate men . . . [bearing] the name of Americans but [failing] to support the honor and dignity of that title."[7] The repeated injustice finally transforms Murieta into a bandit driven by the desire for revenge—and sets into motion a plot memorable for its unrelenting violence. "Their social justice was destruction":

scenes of dismemberment dominate the narrative, becoming ubiquitous in their reiteration, though no less spectacular for that metronomic ubiquity.[8] Key to their impact are the incalculable movements of Murieta himself. Possessed of an electric motility of being ("the lightning was not quicker and surer in the execution of a deadly errand") the bandit plays upon dynamics of presence and absence to effect, at least in the experience of those whom he terrorizes, the annihilation of time and space.[9] He embodies, in other words, a perversion of the principle of telegraphy celebrated by Ridge in "The Atlantic Cable," deploying the powers of an uncanny immediacy to spark social discord. And, in a compelling echo of the aftermath of the Southampton rebellion of 1831, the ensuing crisis is only compounded by the uncontrolled, uncontrollable circulation of rumor: as Ridge makes clear near the outset of the narrative, "rumors . . . rife of murder, robberies, and thefts" animate the region, causing "[c]onsternation [to spread] like fire—fear [to thrill] through the hearts of hundreds, and all [to dread] to travel the public roads."[10] Powerful *because* disembodied, untraceable to any source, such rumors delineate a public and the terms of public life through violence and crisis. Under rumor's rule, the spirit of community becomes the spirit of distrust; terror and suspicion serve as the principles of social organization, the stuff of fellow feeling. In Ridge's treatment, rumor, in all its volatile promiscuity, serves, ironically enough, to supply communal identity by pulling apart the social whole.

So understood, rumor limns the promise of sensational narrative. Intensifying as it plays on the notoriety of the "real" Murieta, rumor helps to set the stage for Ridge's attempt at bestselling fiction, since of course a community haunted by rumor must in theory constitute a more eager readership than a community secure in its safety. With his novel, Ridge looks to cultivate a sensational authority through which to manage (by fueling while quelling) the rumors that, after Murieta's death, have grown uncannily. Much like Thomas Gray before him, Ridge aims assiduously to link, under rumor's hovering sign, public fear and increased sales, twin measures of epistemological desire. In this fantasy only an authorial act such as *The Life and Adventures* can perform in intimate tension with rumor (and the fear it compels) to invent and increase market demand.

All the more significant, then, that Ridge's novel, a decisive commercial failure upon its publication in 1854, would five years later become something of a regional sensation when serialized in pirated form by the *California Police Gazette*. The vicissitudes of capitalist circulation demonstrated a cruel tendency toward violence that, if subject to periodic idealization (witness "The Atlantic Cable"), was much less readily overcome.

I begin with the particular tensions apparent in these examples from Ridge's literary output because they highlight the larger issues at stake in this chapter, issues having to do with the interimplication of physical movement, social mobility, and commercial circulation in the literary field at midcentury. Rumor, as countered by Thomas Gray in his transcript of Nat Turner's confession, and as invoked by Ridge in his narrative of Joaquín Murieta's career, provides a kind of limit-case for such interimplication, precisely because, by binding together the unpredictable, illegitimate movement of bodies and circulation of stories, it highlights the constitutive force of crises of motion and mobility within antebellum social formations. In what follows, I am less concerned with the trace of such crises in spurious, liminal discourse than with their significance for understanding the dominant, or indeed hegemonic, mechanisms of literary production in the antebellum era. The emphasis, in other words, falls less on discursive vagaries thematized as rumor than on material contingencies entailed by commercial publication, contingencies that could, as in Ridge's case, turn failure into bestseller through piracy.

My focus, in elaborating the details of my argument, falls on two texts that stage what I call dramas of uncertain circulation: Edgar Allan Poe's 1837 *The Narrative of Arthur Gordon Pym* and Herman Melville's 1857 *The Confidence-Man*. Both texts tell travel stories, Poe's concerning fantastic extremes of global exploration, Melville's concerning insidious aspects of regional transit. Moreover, both incorporate deeply felt anxieties about the material circulation of literary artifacts. In addressing them together, I mean not simply to connect, in some notional way, as merely thematic counterparts, physical movement and literary circulation. I mean to argue, more incisively, that the terms of commercial circulation for these novels had, in distinct ways but to comparable effect, everything to do with the marketability of travel stories in the middle decades of the nineteenth century. Particularly since information remains prime among those commodities that mobility makes available and that travel writing puts into widespread circulation, the commercial viability of travel stories will be difficult to separate from the commercial powers of traffic and transit. Accordingly, *in interimplication with* the material conditions of publishing as an industry, the material conditions of mobility as a way of distributing bodies and commodities work to set the terms by which novels reliant (as are *Pym* and *The Confidence-Man*) on the value and viability of travel stories will have the chance to move in the commercial sense—will succeed or fail in negotiating the circuits of capitalist exchange. As we shall see, in these dramas of uncertain circulation "travel" as traffic materializes the motions of capital.

Between Pleasure and Profit

In his March 1843 "Prospectus of *The Stylus*" Poe makes sure to emphasize near the outset interrelated issues of aesthetic worth, commercial value, and authorial control that preoccupied him throughout his literary career: "The late movements on the great question of International Copy-Right, are but an index of the universal *disgust* excited by what is quaintly termed the *cheap* literature of the day:—as if that which is utterly worthless in itself, can be cheap at any price under the sun."[11] Eight months earlier, in a private correspondence to the journalist and novelist Frederick W. Thomas dated 27 August 1842, he chooses to express his relation to the problem of international copyright in terms not of aesthetic revulsion but, instead, of shocking, sensational vulnerability. "Literature," he complains, "is at a sad discount. There is really nothing to be done in this way. Without an international copyright law, American authors may as well cut their throats."[12] Although the suicidal brutality of Poe's advice will shock—dramatizing, in eerie anticipation of Ridge, the loss of words in blood—this gory alternative to international copyright doubtless came easily to the writer of so many tales of human mutilation. Nevertheless, if in one sense the prospect of authorial throat cutting will indicate the elasticity, the promiscuity, of Poe's gothic vocabulary, in another it will limn the potential of gothic violence throughout Poe's work to figure deeply felt anxieties about the loss of authorial control. In this argument, the crises of self-possession and spectacles of dismemberment irrupting again and again in Poe's writings will signify, on one level at least, a gothicized recasting of the everyday materialities of authorship in the antebellum literary field.

A number of critics—most notably Jonathan Elmer, Meredith McGill, Michael Newberry, and Terence Whalen—have recently produced searching analyses of Poe's authorial persona and literary production and, in so doing, have effectively recast the framing concerns within which Poe criticism must proceed. Whalen, in particular, has in his *Edgar Allan Poe and the Masses* offered a superlative account of what he rightly terms the political economy of Poe's writing. The generative influence of the work of these critics on my own reading of Poe's *Pym* will quickly become apparent. What I want to emphasize, though, is that the specific issues of copyright and broader questions of political economy shown by Whalen and others to be crucial to any reading of Poe are themselves inextricably bound up with what I call dramas of uncertain circulation—precisely because these issues and questions hold such significance for the often complex ways literary artifacts circulate (what it means, as an author, to own or be owned in the antebellum marketplace having much to do with the material conditions determining and pressuring the movement of one's words). If the unregulated circulation of literature was, for Poe, effectively equivalent to authorial throat cutting, where better to take stock of the meanings of such equivalence than in the catastrophic mobilities inscribed throughout his most sustained depiction of exploratory travel, *The Narrative of Arthur Gordon Pym*?

Finally published by Harper and Brothers in late July 1838, Poe's only novel had a notoriously difficult passage to market. Likely conceived at first as a quite short serialization for the *Southern Literary Messenger*, where two installments were in fact published in early 1837, the narrative seems to have changed in design once Poe lost his editorial job at that magazine and, having moved to New York to improve his literary fortunes, contracted with Harper and Brothers to produce a novel-length tale. The firm announced *Pym*'s imminent publication in May 1837 and secured copyright to the title the following month, but the concurrent financial panic delayed the book's appearance for more than a year. Although the exact composition history of the text remains uncertain, it nevertheless seems fair to read, in the narrative's unevenness, some material and discursive traces of this difficult moment in Poe's literary career.[13]

In contracting with Harper and Brothers to publish his novel (a decision apparently motivated in part by the firm's earlier rejection of his Folio Club tales on the grounds that they did not comprise an integrated narrative), Poe entered into business with one of the dominant publishing houses of his day—and, more to the point, a key publisher of travel narratives, the genre that, judging from its prominence in the review pages of magazines from the period, was among the most marketable forms of literary discourse in antebellum America.[14] Interestingly, as Joseph Ridgely notes, three of the four main sources for the later sections of *Pym*—Benjamin Morrell's *Narrative of Four Voyages* (1832), J. N. Reynolds's *Address on the Subject of a Surveying and Exploring Expedition to the Pacific Ocean and South Seas* (1836), and John L. Stephens's *Incidents of Travel in Egypt, Arabia Petraea, and the Holy Land* (1837)—were all published by Harper and Brothers, with the first a regular bestseller and the last well puffed by the firm and appearing in the 1837 catalogue even as publication of *Pym* was suspended. Thus worth considering are the ways Poe's narrative may be taken to sublimate its relation to the field of antebellum travelogues and to the literary economy within which they moved, particularly as such relation was structurally established and enforced as a result of the imprint of the house of Harper borne by every copy of his novel. Haunted by the voices of antebellum travelers, in *Pym* Poe narrates not least through ventriloquy.

The novel's first chapter serves to introduce "a longer and more momentous narrative," as Pym himself notes—yet in doing so it supplies a kind of anticipatory precis of the story as a whole.[15] Hence the significance, within the chapter's early emphases, of references to nautical trade and economic speculation: the status of Pym's father as a "trader in sea-stores" refracts as it anticipates the trade in sea stories we subsequently encounter, while the success of Pym's grandfather in stock speculation intimates the necessity, and the risk, of speculative reading to the measure of textual value and interpretive profit (57). If in one sense these details establish the terms of reference for a mundane social reality from which the narrative, in its sensationalism, will quite quickly depart, in another (and, I would argue, more important) sense, they encode the determining coordinates, the omnipresent specters, of textual production and consumption with which the narrative will repeatedly grapple.

The opening gesture toward the public realm of nautical commerce offsets, to suggestive effect, Pym's subsequent account of the particular form of intimacy driving his budding friendship with the young Augustus, son of a whale-ship captain and, even as an adolescent, already a veteran traveler. "I used frequently to go home with him," Pym reports, "and remain all day, and sometimes all night. We occupied the same bed, and he would be sure to keep me awake until almost light, telling me stories of the natives of the Island of Tinian, and other places he had visited in his travels" (57). Undeniable, in this description, is the erotic charge of such narrative transmission. Boys desiring boys, enthralling one another through the phantasmatic displacements allowed by stories of travel: this dynamic suggests that, for someone of Pym's sensibility and social station, even to imagine acts of travel "is to requisition whole societies in the service of fantasy needs . . . [especially, if incoherently] sexual fantasy."[16] And significantly, as stories of travel and intimations of homoeroticism go hand-in-glove in this scene, the relations they establish between author, text, and audience require the mediation that exoticized bodies (the "natives of the Island of Tinian," presumably dark-skinned and "primitive") can provide. To the extent that these bodies orient desire (not to mention labor) in narration, they initiate a telling investment in racialized embodiment that will resound through the ensuing narrative. At least for Pym, the subterranean eroticism charging the exchange of travel stories cannot do without the difference that race makes.[17]

Yet for all the importance of eroticized, racialized mediation to this early instance of the transmission of sea stories, in crucial respects the episode's significance turns on *im*mediacy.[18] The narrative economy and erotics in the scene are resolutely oral: positing a fantasy of the ideal production, circulation, and consumption of narrative, Pym's account makes the creation and reception of travelers' tales individual, intimate, knowledgeable, desiring, face-to-face—an immediate exchange of mediated experience. Such private ritual apparently disentangles the profits of narrative from any conventional measure of economic utility. And as the episode links travel to fantasy *in* narrative, so too it offers a pointed fantasy *about* narrative or, more precisely, about an ideal of narrative circulation (though, since this storytelling ritual serves to inspire the catastrophic, commercially disastrous voyage that ensues, its viability as an ideal remains in doubt). Offering a kind of primal scene for one practice of trading sea stories, the episode acquires its eroticized charge in large part by suspending or mystifying the disciplinary mediation characteristic of the conventions and strictures of the publishing industry.

By the same token, if one implication of this early scene might be that eluding the regulatory norms of commerce yields considerable pleasure in narrative exchange, we should not infer that Poe would want, or could afford, to believe in the ideal he showcased: ironically enough, for authors like him who tried to write for a living, the literary market was anything but predictable in its rules; indeed, it tended to thrive on *unpredictability*. The absence of international copyright haunting Poe in published discourse (such as the *Stylus* prospectus) and private correspondence (such as the Thomas letter) meant that U.S. authors were subject to a volatile industry characterized by rampant republication and plagiarism—precisely, that is, by the unpredictable circulation of literary artifacts, by what most in the period succinctly termed *piracy*. As Meredith McGill observes, decentralization and opportunism were hallmarks of the literary field in this period: the combined effect of "economic depression [triggered by the panic of 1837] and the lack of international copyright brought on an extraordinary demand for cheap publications and fostered the regularization of the system of reprinting. . . . Under this decentralized system of production and reproduction, texts were frequently subject to circulation without editorial or authorial control. Textual integrity and authorial identity were common casualties of the reprint process."[19] Given such a climate, should we wonder at what McGill terms "the pseudonymous strategies deployed by Poe," or for that matter at his ongoing investment in the hoax as a form?[20] Pseudonymity was at best a strategy of indifference, a choice that was no choice—since there was every chance that, in any case, an author's work would not carry his or her name—while the manufacture of hoaxes might at least put to some good use (because potentially profitable) a necessary resignation to the bad faith of publishers and other literary entrepreneurs who maximized profit through swindle. In an industry in which (in a material instantiation of the dynamic later explored in *The Confidence-Man*) the sly trade in false or stolen stories typifies business as usual, how to survive except through mimicry? Publish falsehoods, since the industry will do so in any event.[21]

We should note, at this point, the particular position of *Pym*'s publisher within this literary economy. As Michael Newbury observes, Harper and Brothers, having become "America's largest publisher mostly on the strength of inexpensive reprints of British works," was among the most strenuous opponents of international copyright, precisely because "from very early on . . . [the firm's] business interests [had been] very intimately tied to the laxity of international copyright legislation."[22] By contracting with America's largest publishing house, Poe dealt with the devil, a company whose profits hinged, even before the panic of 1837, on the volatility of the literary marketplace, and whose interests thus undermined in fundamental respects the security and agency of the authors they paid. To an extent unmatched by most publishers in the period, for Harper and Brothers piracy effectively set the terms of commercial policy.[23]

Such details in literary-industrial history will underscore a part of the significance, and much of the irony, of Pym's initial account of his intimate, immediate, resolutely noncommercial consumption of Augustus's sea stories. At the same time, these details will help to put in new light one of the more sensational episodes in *Pym*: the power struggles among the mutineers aboard the *Grampus* that culminate in the gothicized triumph of Pym, Augustus, and Peters over their opponents. This action occurs after an extended reprise by Pym and Augustus of their earlier narrative intimacies, with the former, stowed away for days in the hold of the *Grampus*, learning from the latter the horrific details of the mutiny that has reversed all power on the decks above. In wake of the mutiny, with its scenes of "horrible butchery," we learn through Pym's report of Augustus's narration that two factions have developed among the mutineers—one endorsing "a piratical cruise," the other "bent upon pursuing the course originally laid out for the brig into the South Pacific" (93). At stake, as Pym subsequently clarifies, is a "wavering" distinction drawn "between half-engendered notions of profit and pleasure" (93). And although a majority of the mutineers come to favor piracy as an option, their piratical designs stumble in face of the ingenuity of Pym, Augustus, and the biracial "line manager" Dirk Peters (86): impersonating the dead mutineer Rogers, whose corpse, with its swollen belly, "chalky whiteness," and splotchy complexion, "presented . . . one of the most horrid and loathsome spectacles" conceivable, Pym leads an attack on the rival faction designed to achieve victory through the shocking power of theatrical dissimulation (107). The scheme is a total success: through Pym's performative skills and Peters's aptitude for violence, South Sea adventure, now disentangled from its commercial mandate and anticipated in terms of sensuous "novelty and pleasure," trumps piracy as the chief motive for exploratory travel (93).

The defeat of piracy by exploratory travel, "profit" by "pleasure," is notable for its irony within the plot, since the ensuing events—which include cannibalism, shipwreck, and the wholesale slaughter, on Tsalal, of the rescuing ship's crew—seem anything but pleasurable (though comprehensible *as* an irony in view of what Whalen calls Poe's effort "to evade the curse of utility" that tends to afflict the exploration genre).[24] Still more significant for my purposes, though, is the way profit's defeat by pleasure is subject to a conceptual indifference at the level of narrative production, precisely because the subsequent narration of exploratory travel (the analogue to "pleasure" and the opposite of "piracy" in the binary established by the narrative) relies substantially on *literary* piracy, the unacknowledged borrowing of previously published sources, for effect. Indeed, only paragraphs after we learn that one faction of mutineers desires to pursue a "piratical cruise" and that the two factions waver "between half-engendered notions of profit and pleasure," Poe indulges in the first of many piratical forays with his digression on stowage—a passage that, although as yet unattributed, critics agree has been cribbed (as J. Gerald Kennedy notes) "to pad the narrative."[25] In subsequent sections of the novel, Poe borrows significantly, and without attribution, from Washington Irving's *Astoria* (1836), Alexander Keith's *Evidence of the Truth of the Christian Religion* (1823), Benjamin Morrell's *Narrative of Four Voyages* (1832), J. N. Reynolds's *Address on the Subject of a Surveying and Exploring Expedition to the Pacific Ocean and South Seas* (1836), and John L. Stephens's *Incidents of Travel in Egypt, Arabia Petraea, and the Holy Land* (1837)—the last three being, as I have already indicated, published by Harpers, and Keith's being reprinted by the firm in 1832. Thus in the material dimension of narrative composition, piracy cannot be distinguished from travel's exploratory pleasures: to enjoy the latter we require the former to occur. That Pym's impersonation of the bloated body of the dead Rogers serves to trump piracy for pleasure must be said, in this light, to inscribe a succinct tautology, since as readers we come to profit from the pleasures of exploratory travel through decidedly piratical means. Pym defeats would-be pirates so that Poe the pirate can ply his trade.[26]

As Kennedy notes in the editorial apparatus to the Oxford *Pym*, Poe's digression on methods of stowage in chapter 6 (as already indicated, the first of several instances of unattributed borrowing) can be read as an ironic commentary on the very process of narrative composition, on "his own authorial 'filling up' of the novel."[27] Much of the bite in this irony comes from the scorn Pym expresses for the sloppy manner in which the stowage has been accomplished aboard the Grampus: as its slapdash handling jeopardizes the ship in the event of violent shifts in weather, so Poe's own pell-mell mixture of generic features and rhetorical styles hardly promises narrative stability—a fair warning of the unpredictability, even chaos, of the chapters to follow. As significant, though, to the irony of the digression on stowage is the way it collapses distinctions between well-packaged and ill-packaged, commodity and contraband—distinctions clearly functional in a conceptual sense, but altogether meaningless for the purposes of commercial exchange in a cultural context in which profit could accrue from the indiscriminate and undifferentiated circulation of plagiarized material. Capital thrives on the potential for profit entailed by such collapse, on the differential power of such indifference—as the example of Harper and Brothers, apparently unconcerned by the evidence in the pages of *Pym* of plagiarism from other titles in its catalogue, would itself have taught Poe.[28]

The ironies of indifference I have been exploring here are not restricted to the issues of piracy and exploration, profit and pleasure, raised during the mutiny and materialized through Poe's methods of narrative composition in the second half of *Pym*. They bear as well on the sensational effects that lend affective force to the narrative. Poe's novel is punctuated by a sequence of extreme trials and astonishing occurrences—imprisonment at sea, mutiny and butchery, cannibalism, living burial, paranormal phenomena—all of which, in one sense, seem exceptional or *not* customary, the marks of an absolutely original, unquestionably authentic journey. Yet of course such events are, in another and more important sense, formulaic, the fixtures of an existing and demonstrably marketable genre that Poe, in ironizing, needs also to imitate. And their deployment by Poe in *Pym* tends to evacuate all claim to singularity in sensation, rendering instead extreme trials and inexplicable events sequential and serial so as to make the exceptional predictable, habitual, customary. Recounting, in chapter 1, the instant of crisis when the Penguin overruns the Ariel, Pym asserts that "[n]ever while I live shall I forget the intense agony of terror I experienced at that moment" (60)—a claim contradicted only pages later when, at the beginning of chapter 2, he notes that the passage of a week "proved amply long enough to erase from my memory the shadows and bring out in vivid light all the pleasurably exciting points of color, all the picturesqueness, of the late perilous accident" (65). The disjunction marks a basic failure of narrative memory that, serving to raise questions about Pym's reliability as a narrator, will also enable the serial pattern of sensational episodes to take shape through the incessant invocation of comparably intense agonies of terror punctuating the narrative, whether concerning imprisonment in the ship's hold, or mutiny, or starvation, or cannibalism, or near "inhumation" on Tsalal, or, bathetically enough, "the most excruciating torment" of a diet of filberts (182, 196).

Particularly in light of the bathos of this last example (rendering indigestion on par with cannibalism), the force of sensation becomes oddly deflationary, adding to the sense that Poe aims to undercut the spectacular method he employs. One purpose, we may suspect, has to do with critiquing the tactics, and with them the currency, of popular fiction.[29] Deflating the powers of sensation as a narrative strategy will seem, in this regard, to anticipate the acid summation Poe offers of the English novelist Frederick Marryatt, four years later in the September 1841 issue of *Graham's Magazine:* "He has always been a very popular writer in the most rigorous sense of the word. His books are essentially 'mediocre.' His ideas are the common property of the mob, and have been their common property time out of mind."[30] Serving to damn the popular novelist alongside his anonymous readers, the concept of "common property" names a despicable form of possession, in which shared knowledge is mob knowledge and must, at all costs, be mediocre. Yet in *Pym* the force of the satire entailed by the serialization of sensational effects does not merely encode a relatively secure discrimination in aesthetic judgement; it likewise registers, as an unsettling supplement to such discrimination, the haunting problem of the indifference of aesthetic effects under capitalism, where every sensation is effectively the same, memorable at the moment, forgotten inside the week, because, on the market, any sensation will do.[31]

Against the backdrop of these problems of indiscrimination and indifference, with their resonance for the drama of uncertain circulation within which *Pym* is caught and constituted, I want to examine in greater detail the investments Poe may have had, while writing his novel, in the concept of exploratory travel. A consideration of Poe's own engagement with one of his key source texts, Reynolds's *Address*, and with the issue of Antarctic exploration it promoted, gives a useful focus. The record of this engagement begins with the piece Poe published in *The Southern Literary Messenger* in August 1836 concerning the 31 March "Report of the Committee on Naval Affairs" on the subject of South Sea travel. There, he argues strenuously for the value of the proposed expedition, contending (in an echo of Reynold's own phrasing in an address to the House of Representatives on 3 April 1836) that "[e]nlightened liberality is the truest economy"[32] and then emphasizing, in the heart of the piece, three interrelated justifications for extensive southern exploration: first, "public justice," meaning national support for merchants and fishers; second, national "pride as a vigorous commercial empire"; and last, national "duty . . . to contribute a large share to that aggregate of useful knowledge, *which is the common property of all*"—an argument that, in emphasizing the benefits of useful knowledge, makes "common property" synonymous with democracy and not, as in the Marryatt review five years later, with mob rule.[33] These justifications lead Poe to a stirring exhortation:

> Ought we not, therefore, to be foremost in the race of philanthropic discovery, in every department embraced by this comprehensive term? Our national honor and glory which, be it remembered, are to be "transmitted as well as enjoyed," are involved. In building up the fabric of our commercial prosperity, let us not filch the corner stone. Let it not be said of us, in future ages, that we ingloriously availed ourselves of a stock of scientific knowledge, to which we had not contributed our quota—that we shunned as a people to put our shoulder to the wheel—that we reaped where we had never sown.[34]

The capaciousness of "philanthropic discovery" only intensifies the pull of national duty in this passage. By reminding his readers about the responsibilities of transmitting "national honor and glory," Poe effectively champions, without ever explicating, national expansion over national isolation. What seems striking is the way philanthropic extension and discovery fold so readily into "commercial prosperity," such that the business of profit comes to seem synonymous with the hard work of nationalist endeavor *beyond* the nation's boundaries.

Five months later, in the January 1837 *Southern Literary Messenger,* the issue in which *Pym* debuted, Poe revisits this complex of issues when he reviews Reynolds's *Address*. Given the nation's heavy reliance on whaling and fishing, Poe argues, "[n]o part of the whole commerce of our country is of more importance than that carried on in the regions in question."[35] Yet, he goes on to insist, the preeminent significance of the southern seas for matters of national commerce only underscores, by contrast, the ongoing failure of national commitment to the region's exploration.

> The scene of [the fishery's] operations . . . is less known and more full of peril than any other portion of the globe visited by our ships. It abounds in islands, reefs and shoals unmarked upon any chart—prudence requires that the location of these should be exactly defined. The savages in these regions have frequently evidenced a murderous hostility—they should be conciliated or intimidated. The whale, and more especially all furred animals, are becoming scarce before the perpetual warfare of man—new generations will be found in the south, and the nation first to discover them will reap nearly all the rich benefits of the discovery. Our trade in ivory, in sandal-wood, in biche le-mer, in feathers, in quills, in seal-oil, in porpoise-oil, and in sea-elephant oil, may here be profitably extended. Various other sources of commerce will be met with, and may be almost exclusively appropriated. The crews, or at least some portion of the crews, of many of our vessels known to be wrecked in the vicinity, may be rescued from a life of slavery and despair. Moreover, we are degraded by the continual use of foreign charts. In matters of mere nautical or geographical science, our government has been hitherto supine, and it is due to the national character that in these respects something should be done. We have now a chance of redeeming ourselves in the Southern Sea. Here is a wide field open and nearly untouched—"a theatre peculiarly our own from position and course of human events."[36]

Poe the regionalist and antinationalist is certainly hard to locate in this passage. The persona we encounter is instead zealously patriotic, deploring the cringing cowardice of a "supine" government, sounding the nation's hail in service of global expedition and conquest, and intimating, through the language of redemption and of geographical and historical ownership, something not so far removed from what would soon be called Manifest Destiny, the nascent ideology of American imperialism.[37]

At stake for me is less the issue of genuine belief—was or was not Poe a nationalist and proto-imperialist?—than the question of deployment: how best to comprehend the complex of investments in play that would make, in 1837, expansionist, patriotic ideas profitable ones for the impoverished, professionally desperate writer to endorse in print and so put into circulation. Since several of the topics central to Poe's argument here—the need to chart unknown waters with prudence; the need to extend existing forms of trade; the need to protect sailors; and, most spectacularly, the need to conciliate or intimidate murderous natives—receive extensive treatment, either directly or by intimation through contrast, in the second half of *Pym*, we might suppose that the terms of their articulation in the Reynolds review supply a key to understanding authorial intention and investment in the novel already under way. Alternatively (and somewhat more cynically), we might suppose that the strength of Poe's endorsement of Reynold's proposed expedition serves a legitimating function for the fictional narrative in progress, heightening public awareness of and interest in the currency and significance of South Sea exploration in hopes of helping to determine the conditions of possibility for a trip to the literary marketplace, for bestselling fiction as such (a purpose certainly served by Poe's inclusion, in the excerpt from Reynolds's address that concludes his review, the telling observation that "[i]f we have been a by-word and a reproach among nations for *pitiful remuneration of intellectual labors*, this expedition will afford an excellent opportunity of wiping it away").[38] Nor, I would stress, are the alternatives necessarily exclusive: to imagine only one of a number of possibilities for their interimplication, the pressing material need to write a bestseller may well have produced the felt truth of national and expansionist commitment—what in the August 1836 essay he called "philanthropic discovery" constituting, for him, a project of paramount national and commercial concern because its comprehensiveness could include and legitimate accounts of South Sea exploration (whether factual or fictional) as objects of national and commercial value.[39]

Put another way, the genre of exploratory travel would seem to offer an author such as Poe the long-sought power to determine access to—not to mention the terms of circulation of—socially, politically, culturally, and economically consequential information (power hinging on what Terence Whalen calls "the strange complicity between . . . the exploration narrative and the development of a more or less uniform capitalist economy" characterized by "the rise of information as a form of capital").[40] The generic premise of singularity (with explorer, as author, recording "discoveries" in print) would in this view work to secure the broadest possible socio-cultural significance within the national imaginary. Thus in an important sense *Pym* does take the nation alongside the market as its threshold of legibility—a fact that, as Teresa Goddu maintains, will undermine a critical tradition that inscribes a kind of regional essentialism, equating the novel and its author with "the South" chiefly in order to disarticulate issues of race and racism from the social and cultural politics of the nation. I echo Goddu in her insistence that the point in interrogating this critical tradition is not at all to mystify the racist dynamics in *Pym* but instead to take "issue with how [the novel's] historicization" with respect to issues of race, racism, and slavery as well as ones of region and nation has tended to occur.[41]

For Goddu, the key is to see "that *Pym* records a complex and often contradictory vision of race and sets in motion a national, not just a regional, racial discourse"—an argument that emphasizes the novel's "narrative of racial convertability," its intimation that racial identity "is constructed, and hence vulnerable to change."[42] Although tremendously suggestive, this argument seems least convincing with respect to the episodes on Tsalal, where as Goddu herself notes the racial dynamics are most intensely and rigidly oppositional.[43] Taking seriously such opposition (despite its incompatibility with critical theories of hybridity) I propose that, instead of deconstructing the stark poetics of white and black at text's end, we read them in relation to the problems of indifference haunting *Pym* at the scene and in the materiality of its production. My aim is neither to diminish issues of race and racism in *Pym* nor to downplay their complexity, but rather to emphasize the politics of discrimination necessarily at play in racial representations of the sort we find in the episodes on Tsalal. What if the politics of race offer Poe a context within which questions of difference and discrimination still seem socially relevant, still seem sustainable? The argument has less to do with Poe's commitment to a racist, pro-slavery politics in the first instance, (convinced as I am by Whalen's incisive analysis of Poe's "average racism" and characteristic disinterest in large-scale political causes and debates[44]), than with his capitalization on a deeply inscribed form of social and cultural common sense that would, in spite (or perhaps because) of capitalism's advances, admit discrimination as commercially viable knowledge. At a moment of increasingly indiscriminate commodification in the literary-industrial field, racism *sells*—and, as a viable discursive commodity, its bias *always* discriminates. Thus racism in the episodes on Tsalal can be seen, like nationalism in the Reynolds review, to weld belief to strategy. Poe's is a compound investment: evincing racism by banking on its potential profit, he deploys the politics of black and white to readmit into the marketplace discriminations holding decisive social and material meaning for a majority of antebellum readers, so as to reinvest in authors the agency to *shape* the discriminations people make. In effect, Poe literally mines his national culture's richest vein of discriminatory belief to counter the indifferent political economy that, leveling all differences in the service of capital, haunts him in the literary marketplace—yet he does so, ironically, to *increase* his narrative's commercial viability. To recall and recast an earlier point, the profit and power in trading sea stories will turn on the discriminations that specters of race can afford.

Yet if the dynamics of racism are bankable, in the sense I have just outlined, nevertheless it will be hard to conclude that, by deploying them, Poe offers much in the way of "philanthropic discovery," much less any viable *solution* to the larger problems of indifference that vex him and his narrative. Unlike Whalen, I do not find in *Pym* much effort to chart a middle course between suspiciously foreign sensation and overly mercantilistic utilitarianism; rather, I see a narrative caught in the relentless conversion of these two, haunted by the prospect of their effective indifference in a literary marketplace where, regardless of the integrity of distinctions between commercially useful and commercially useless information, authors had for the most part no agency to make them. Hence the pervasive incoherence of the narrative as an integrated whole, and hence the cryptic opacity of the concluding note, offering as it does the tantalizing hope of an ultimate solution to the narrative's mysteries yet, at the same time, in an incisive inscription of authorial fatalism, foregoing all attribution of responsibility for ideas to which Poe, all too aware of the pervasive threat of unacknowledged reprinting and plagiarism, could not count on laying claim. The prospect of conclusive legibility and interpretability here becomes the office of an anonymous intervention and agency, with the author (as Pym or as Poe) lost in the final bid for meaning. Whose, then, is the voice? Do we read the words of an absolute authority, divinely inspired—or instead some more material, and materialistic, presence, perhaps what Whalen calls "the Capital Reader"? The "field for speculation" is as wide as undecidable (208). Yet by opening it, the final note only closes the narrative's circuit, looping back to the prospect of commercial speculation introduced on the opening page and thereby inscribing the conceptual and material indifference that it cannot, in any event, escape—converting the promise and "throw[ing the] credit" of philanthropic discovery into the fatal traffic that capital requires (207).[45]

Travel's Costs

In 1846, eight years after Poe had failed to capitalize on the popular trade in travel stories, Herman Melville made his name as an author by publishing *Typee*, the first of two narratives about his experiences traveling in the South Seas. Widely praised by critics in England and America for its convincing and realistic depictions of the rigors of exotic travel, the narrative sold very well with the reading public, its compound success ensuring a triumphant first encounter for Melville with the literary marketplace. By the time he published *Omoo*, *Typee*'s companion narrative, in 1847, Melville was already beginning to enjoy the benefits of a budding literary celebrity.

Yet (as Melville scholars will invariably stress) those benefits were, in the long run, effectively crushed by celebrity's attendant costs. In the twentieth-century critical tradition, Melville is celebrated much more widely for his subsequent failures in the literary marketplace, failures typically understood with reference to his reviewers' standard disappointment that his later novels were not more like *Typee* and *Omoo*. Melville's own frustration at such response is already palpable in an 1851 letter to Nathaniel Hawthorne, where he carps at the ignominy of his own reputation—"Think of it! To go down to posterity is bad enough, any way; but to go down as a 'man who lived among the cannibals'!"—and equates *Typee* with the "gingerbread" given to newborns.[46] Ten years later his scorn seems only to have intensified: in a memo to his brother Allan "concerning the publication of my verses," he expostulates "[f]or God's sake don't have *By the author of 'Typee' 'Piddle-dee' &c* on the title-page."[47] The point here is not simply that Melville struggled to get out from under the weight of his own early authorial accomplishment, but more precisely that the name attached to that accomplishment, "Typee," telegraphed a kind of travel and a style of narrative—what together, with respect to *Pym*, I have been calling the trade in sea stories—from which Melville could not escape. As a standard used by reviewers to measure and disparage his subsequent writing, "Typee" (at once material artifact and discursive concept) tended to pressure not just the reception of Melville's works but, I would argue, the conditions of possibility for their circulation in the literary field. Where for Poe the prospect of exploratory travel in the South Seas seems to have represented the promise, however halting, of some authorial agency, for Melville it came increasingly to signify a conceptual imposition or, more strongly still, an uncanny belatedness—the unwonted specter from his own authorial past collapsing *then* with *now*, *there* with *here*, and demanding a (to him repellent) sameness or *indifference* of narrative acts. In *Pym* South Sea travel is haunted; for Melville, it will not stop haunting.[48]

The August 1852 review of *Pierre* in Evert and George Duyckincks's *Literary World* puts the "Typee" effect I have been discussing to use in ways suggestive for an analysis of problems of mobility and uncertain circulation in *The Confidence-Man*. Sharply critical of the "riot" of "remote analogies," the "incoherencies of thought," and the "infelicities of language" in *Pierre*, the reviewer (most likely Evert Duyckinck) makes brutally clear his preference for Melville's earliest works:

> The author of 'Pierre; or, the Ambiguities;' the writer of a mystic romance, in which are conjured up unreal nightmare-conceptions, a confused phantasmagoria of distorted fancies and conceits, ghostly abstractions and fitful shadows, is certainly but a spectre of the substantial author of 'Omoo' and 'Typee,' the jovial and hearty narrator of the traveller's tale of incident and adventure. By what *diablerie*, hocus-pocus, or thimble-rigging, 'now you see him and now you don't' process, the transformation has been effected, we are not skilled in necromancy to detect. . . . We would rejoice to meet Mr. Melville again in the hale company of sturdy sailors, men of flesh and blood, and, strengthened by the wholesome air of the outside world, whether it be land-breeze or sea-breeze, listen to his narrative of a traveller's tale, in which he has few equals in power and felicity.[49]

The acid invocation of necromancy (evidently a skill far beneath this critic's understanding) only underscores, by contrast, the certainty with which "mystic romance" and "traveller's tale" get opposed. For this reviewer, though Melville himself seems to have suffered an unwelcome, even necromantic alteration in authorial ability, it remains unthinkable that such a fate might threaten the integrity of the distinction (ethical as well as aesthetic) between those narrative modes Melville has used during the course of his career.

Such trust, I suggest, is precisely what *The Confidence-Man* erodes. At issue is not so much Melville's conscious authorial intention (though I find persuasive the claim in the Newberry-Northwestern edition that "[t]he Duyckinck blast was an incident that offered [Melville] just the kind of gritty real-life stuff he increasingly seized on, after exhausting his Pacific experiences, to make into fiction").[50] Whether or not by design, Melville's novel of 1857 answers with marvelous irony the call of the *Pierre* review by providing a "traveller's tale of incident and adventure" haunted by "ghostly abstractions and fitful shadows" and filled with "*diablerie*, hocus-pocus, [and] thimble-rigging, 'now you see him and now you don't' process." Incomprehensible except with reference to problems in mobility (to dramas of uncertain circulation), *The Confidence-Man* makes manifest the inextricability of travel's wages from those of necromantic transformation.

When Phillip Fisher observes that "unintelligibility is the first sign of a damaged social space," the insight speaks to the kinds of social and epistemological crisis imagined in so much of Melville's fiction.[51] The question of confidence (the "transparency" of "output," in Fisher's equation) is by no means exclusive to the author's 1857 novel; particularly with respect to interpretation, to the terms by which narrative gets read and understood, crises of confidence (here expressive of what Fisher calls "unintelligibility") erupt throughout Melville's writings.[52] To concentrate on only one instance, the novella "Benito Cereno," serialized in *Putnam's* at the end of 1855, evinces to striking effect the interrelation of "damaged social space" with difficulties of interpretation and readerly trust. Based in part on Amasa Delano's 1817 account of the 1805 slave revolt on the Cuban slaver *Tryal*, and probing a jittery history of slave unrest in the Americas (including the San Domingo revolution of 1791–1805, the *Amistad* revolt of 1841, and the uprisings led by Gabriel Prosser in 1800, Denmark Vesey in 1822, and Nat Turner in 1831), "Benito Cereno" interrogates the racist and paternalistic fictions of slavery's apologists by way of the topos of men at sea central to Poe's *Pym*. Melville's riveting inscription of the monstrosity of chattel slavery depends above all on what Eric Sundquist calls "the extraordinary risk" of "his characterization of Babo and his revolt," a characterization that pushes "to the limit his readers' capacity to discriminate between just political resistance and macabre terror—or rather, to see their necessary fusion."[53] The necessity of this fusion underwrites the shaving scene, where Babo mimes loving service to prevent his captive Benito Cereno from warning the oblivious Amasa Delano about the revolt he has stumbled upon. The razor's blade ironizes intimacy, figuring the ticklish proximity of service to slaughter. As Sundquist argues, "Delano watches Babo's performance without ever seeing it. Although it is Benito Cereno and Babo whose feigned intimacy, undergirded by terror, displays the essential relation of master and slave, it is Delano and Babo who most effectively enact the dynamics of artifice, the construction of the natural, on which both minstrelsy and the defense of slavery are built."[54] Babo's masquerade plays on Delano's obdurate confidence in those naturalizing, racist fictions that always already discount the artifice—and the forms of resistance—they nevertheless help to conjure.[55] Put another way, the overlegibility and illegibility of racialized performance become as inseparable as the two sides of the razor's blade. Granted, Delano's limitations as a reader are evident from the outset, his "singularly undistrustful good nature" implying *less* "than ordinary quickness and accuracy of intellectual perception."[56] Yet, as a result of the narrative's vexed construction (filtered through Delano's perception in the first part, giving over to a legal deposition riddled with ellipses in the second part, and culminating, in the last part, with Babo's haunting silence and deathly gaze, the "shadow" of "[t]he Negro"), Delano's interpretive struggles are not so far removed from our own: any claims we make for the epistemological and political significance of Babo's failed revolt will require us to trust in deeply ambiguous, volatile signs.[57] Delano's failure is precisely that his racist's trust never fails; his confidence is total. Our challenge is to know when to trust and when to doubt the narrative we read. And as the play of the barber insinuates, the cost of misinterpretation can be fatal.

Thus understood, the story of Babo's conspiracy marks the hegemony of confidence *and* its crisis in the United States at midcentury.[58] In 1856, a year after devising such an inscrutable "hive of subtlety," Melville would return in more explicit fashion to the confidence trick, treating it as a capacious symbol of national and, I would argue, transnational tempers.[59] In *The Confidence-Man*, the confidence trick gives the measure not just of an emerging national regime but, more profoundly, of the experience of modernity itself. That Melville would choose to plot his narrative in terms of riverboat travel speaks to the inextricability of problems of confidence and mobility on the cusp of economic panic and civil war.[60]

When Melville finished writing *The Confidence-Man*, sometime around the start of September 1856, the United States economy, built in large part on widespread investment over the preceding three decades in infrastructure and transportation development, still showed all the signs of robust vitality. Yet twelve months later the midcentury boom would crash, a downturn triggered by the failure of the Ohio Life Insurance and Trust Company in August 1857.[61] Thus, while misanthropically out of touch with the confident economic climate of its conception, Melville's last published novel enjoys in retrospect a startling prescience about the mercurial vulnerabilities of confidence under capitalism, dramatizing how (as Marx had observed) the "credit relationship—both on the part of the man who trusts and of the man who needs trust—becomes an object of commerce, an object of mutual deception and misuse," and thus how "*distrust* is the basis of economic trust."[62] Written at a moment of ongoing social upheaval and racial tension, of growing sectional antagonism, of gold fever and westward expansion, and of rail travel's ascendancy at the expense of the riverboat system, *The Confidence-Man* courted readerly censure and, worse, indifference to posit an unsettling interplay among travel, social mobility, and commercial exchange. Its near-unintelligibility an *indictment* as well as a sign of damaged social space, the narrative concentrates on the Mississippi as a prime artery of transport and trade and a great symbol of the frontier so as to show travel as a traffic in hoaxes where mobility can only mean duplicity and social bankruptcy.

At the close of chapter 20, approaching the midpoint of the novel, a transaction occurs that signals the anxious cast given by Melville to problems of trust haunting any exchange. The tubercular miser "grudgingly" concedes to pay full price, two dollars, for the herb doctor's medicine, but the force of his coughs spills the coins from his hand and scatters them across the deck. Charitably helping the invalid with their recovery, the herb doctor makes a damning discovery: "'These are not quarters, these are pistareens,'" he complains, "'and clipped, and sweated, at that.'"[63] Yet, in an apparent display of magnanimity, he accepts the debased payment and gives the miser medicine.

Swindle here comes cheap for the doctor, who seems happy enough to take a reduced rate for what is likely false medicine—mere "'hocus-pocus,'" in the blunt assessment of the Missouri bachelor (106). The obvious point to make (after situating the Missourian within the *Pierre* reviewer's party) is that, so conceived, the confidence trick runs in more than one direction, rendering *confidence*, as such, what Wai-chee Dimock aptly terms "a field of perpetual reversals."[64] Yet as important to the episode is the way the transaction depicted will begin to erode distinctions between well and ill, domestic and foreign: the miser's "pistareens" are twice debased, first because they have left their proper circulation in Spain's economy to infiltrate the U.S. market, and second because, "clipped" and "sweated," they no longer hold the material value that, by face, they promise, and so circulate as tokens of bad faith. Their currency in the United States intimates an imposture and an infiltration foreign in source but catching in kind. Microbe-like, they jeopardize as they capitalize on healthy economic trust, yet they remain no less infectious for their ready detection, since the cure they purchase is by implication a strain of the disease they represent. Binding in this way corporeality to commercial exchange and bodily breakdown to economic betrayal, the transaction between miser and herb doctor intimates the contagions of confidence (with all the semantic resonance this phrase conveys). "The crucial point," as Dimock argues, "is not the confidence man's deviousness, . . . but the apparent syntactical reversibility of the word 'confidence' itself."[65]

Melville's decision to link problems of credit and trust to dubieties of illness and its cure (and not just in this episode, but through the more extended sequence featuring the herb doctor) should not surprise us in view of the widespread antebellum figuration of debt in terms of disease. As Lendol Calder notes in *Financing the American Dream*, Americans in the middle decades of the nineteenth century "subscribed to a loose but identifiable taxonomy of debt that distinguished proper and improper indebtedness, 'getting trusted' from being 'in debt.' The crucial categories were 'productive' and 'consumptive' credit," with the latter strongly associated with tuberculosis—the primary meaning of "consumption" in the period.[66] Productive credit, by contrast, drove "geographical expansion and entrepreneurial business activity," those most prestigious forms of personal and national endeavor, and so was associated with the robust fitness, not the wasting, of social as of human bodies.[67] Thus the force of the *crisis* of confidence in chapter 20 runs to the heart of the economic discourse on trust current as Melville writes his novel. Indicating the distressingly ambidextrous tendency of any scam, the episode exemplifies just how pointedly the narrative as a whole works to trouble the antinomies (well/ill, contagion/cure, production/consumption) on which popular notions of trust relied—so as to undermine confidence in the common sense or hegemony of confidence at midcentury.

As Calder's analysis of the nineteenth-century economic discourse on trust makes clear, Melville's topic in *The Confidence-Man* held an intimate familiarity for the nation's reading (as for its investing) public. By 1857 "[c]redit [had for decades] substituted for money everywhere" in America, "creating what Robert Wiebe has described as a 'giant web' . . . lacing East and West together with paper promises."[68] Regularly baffled, as Calder notes, by "imperialistic" money and the forms of credit that increasingly stood in its place, "people then as never before and never since made . . . great efforts to master" complex monetary meanings.[69] To aid in such efforts, a voluminous "popular literature of financial advice" emerged in the century's middle third, taking "a variety of forms, including sermons, pamphlets, textbooks on political economy, giftbooks for young men and women, didactic short stories, financial advice books, and guides to domestic economy."[70] Such formal variety helped to disseminate a standard lesson: "'character is the poor man's capital.' Character earned the confidence of the community, and confidence established credit. . . . Character was the key, and money the supreme test."[71] The stakes were broadly communal, even national in scope, for if the value of such advice was most immediately individual, its purchase was fully public in extension; as the financial commentator Calvin Colton asserted in 1840, credit gave "the exact measure of the soundness of the social state."[72] The Melville of *The Confidence-Man* would, I suspect, have agreed completely with this estimation, while relishing the volatile cost, for credit as for society, of its slippery imprecision (such that the sound and unsound become completely interchangeable). And I would suggest that, in a sense, the antebellum literature on finance and credit is to *The*

Confidence-Man as exploration literature is to *Pym*, the popular form upon which the novel aimed to capitalize in venturing its trip to market.[73]

I want, in light of this understanding, to focus more particularly on the place of mobility, as concept, as discourse, and as material practice, within the novel's action. Its first insinuation occurs seventeen words in: through the force of analogy that describes the "man in cream colors" arriving as "suddenly as Manco Capac at the lake Titicaca" (1), we experience something of the telescopic dislocations, the compressions in space and time, characteristic of travel writing as a genre. Comprehension depends here on a breadth of readerly knowledge enhanced by the imaginative capacity that travel affords. To envision the man in cream colors, in other words, we need to defeat those temporal and spatial constraints that keep us not just from the long dead Manco Capac but also from the far distant lake Titicaca.[74] The question of mobility becomes still more direct with the introduction of the narrative's setting: "the favorite steamship *Fidèle*" is not just an emblem but a material instance of the increasing economic, social, cultural, and ideological investment, by midcentury, in networks of transport (1). Granting that this ship, as we quickly learn, is overloaded with symbolical significance, nevertheless such ships were familiar, even banal to many Americans in the 1850s—a circumstance unremarkable except as it underscores the full penetration of regulated transit as a routinized aspect of daily life in the period. To favor any ship, after all, will involve a choice of ships and a working knowledge of them. Notable, then, is the way in which the narrative describes the material space on which such familiarity bears and in which such traveling routines unfold:

> Merchants on 'change seem the passengers that buzz on her decks, while, from quarters unseen, comes a murmur as of bees in the comb. Fine promenades, domed saloons, long galleries, sunny balconies, confidential passages, bridal chambers, state-rooms plenty as pigeon-holes, and out-of-the-way retreats like secret drawers in an escritoire, present like facilities for publicity or privacy. Auctioneer or coiner, with equal ease, might somewhere here drive his trade. (8)

The language in this description casts the shipboard environs in terms of ritual and display, as space designed for social performance. Yet, if the effect suggests measured, posing leisure, nevertheless we can, by the presence of the "merchants" at the outset of the passage and the "auctioneer or coiner" at its end, begin to speculate about other uses to which this mobile space will be put. Two rhetorical figures stand out: first, the "murmur [from quarters unseen] as of bees in the comb," suggesting, in close contrast to the buzzing of merchant work, all at once the invisible strains of labor running the ship and the subtler drone of trickery; and second, the "out-of-the-way retreats like secret drawers in an escritoire," associating the social space of transit's retreat with the scene of writing, so that backroom exchange parallels the work of narrative composition. And, in both literal and conceptual senses, between these "quarters unseen" and "out-of-the-way retreats" lie "confidential passages," places where confidence, requiring inconspicuous secrecy, not conspicuous trust, for its operation, apparently has much to hide. The "equal ease" of the auctioneer or coiner, the seller or crook, in making use of this intricate environment will intimate the equivalence of their methods and so, more threateningly, the indifference of their pursuits. In such a context, any meaningful distinction between the "publicity or privacy" of the acts this social space sustains is itself at risk.

The point here, that the space of modern transit gets defined through the forms of transaction and exchange it facilitates, is amplified by the ensuing description of the steamship's progress, from landing to landing, down the Mississippi:

> [T]o right and left, at every landing, the huge Fidèle still receives additional passengers in exchange for those that disembark; so that, though always full of strangers, she continually, in some degree, adds to, or replaces them with strangers still more strange; like the Rio Janeiro fountain, fed from the Corcovado mountains, which is ever overflowing with strange waters, but never with the same strange particles at every part. (13)

So described, the transit system constitutes a mode of exchange, a mobile economy that trades in the relentless supplementation of human strangeness. And the simile comparing this model of transit-as-exchange to a fountain in Rio achieves an effect comparable to that of the novel's first sentence, requiring our imaginative leap from the Mississippi just south of St. Louis to the far reaches of South America. The regional becomes all at once hemispheric: the undeniably familiar becomes always more strange. Such dislocating comparisons, collapsing geographical distance and equating mobility with exchange, all under the sign of ever-increasing strangeness, establish in discourse an analog for the relentless unpredictabilities of the human movements they describe.

These opening passages anticipate the capacity of the narrative to serve as a kind of "transfer book," a ledger where printed marks record material transactions—the signs of physical as well as economic circulation, traffic, exchange (22). And the action therein obviously depends on the acts of travel that finance what I shall call, for want of a better term, the "legitimate" business of the *Fidèle*. Simply by being human, we are told in a celebrated early passage, each passenger on board is a "pilgrim"; more specifically, several of the figures caught up in the plays of confidence are travelers by vocation—the traveling agent of the Widow and Orphan Asylum, the transfer agent for Black Rapids Coal, the herb doctor, Egbert the "thriving young merchant" and "practical poet in the West India trade" (199)—or (as in the case of the cosmopolitan) by avocation. Such narrative emphasis on the place of travel in everyday life, in a book about the trials of confidence, will suggest that the structural interrelation during the antebellum period of expanding transportation and commercial networks—the interrelation, in effect, of physical, economic, and social mobility—was, if necessary, also ripe for exploitation. Hence the irony, in the last chapter, of the "traveller's conveniences" (patent locks, money-belts, and counterfeit detectors) sold by the urchin peddler (244): designed to promote security, they play instead to the anxieties binding suspicion to greed, where only expenditure can secure investment, where only further purchase can protect what is already owned—an irony compounded once we recognize that, as Calder notes, given the "kaleidoscopic variety of monetary forms" circulating in the period, "[c]onfusion and bad money reigned."[75] And hence the irony of the melancholy complaint voiced earlier in the text by the man in gray: "[i]n vain, I wander; no one will have confidence in me" (44). The implication, that just as mobility's project entails the search for confidence so the widespread failure of confidence impels a futile wandering, is one that events in the text will hardly support; they indicate, instead, how ceaseless movement serves the con man as rootedness never could.

So, too, does the traffic in stories. *The Confidence-Man* highlights again and again the significance and power of narrative transmission for the work of manipulating trust (though, since such transmission tends, within the plot, to happen orally rather than through print, it will serve at most as a fractured allegory of literary production). The *Fidèle* in this sense depicts imagined social community as a set of narrative relationships, beguiling because confiding. The stories that get told about abused trust—"Goneril," "Colonel Moredock," "Charlemont," and "China Aster," to mention only the most memorable—manipulate their audiences by playing upon sympathy (a narrative strategy hinting, ironically, at the formula for bestselling fiction during much of Melville's career). The last, "China Aster," is at once the least subtle and most brutally suggestive with respect to the links between the conditions of debt and those of human movement: China takes the loan from Orchis the shoemaker after the latter expresses worry at the sight of the former's son "'paddling about without shoes'" (or, perhaps more accurately, shows an interest in ensnaring by indebting the next generation of customers) (209).[76] Yet if, as this collection of stories will suggest, the narrative habit is a crucial tool in the confidence game, curiously enough in the novel's larger narrative many crucial details of the transactions taking place occur *behind* the scenes. To underscore the supplemental sense of a phrase discussed above, much like the Fidèle on which all action occurs, the narrative itself is filled with confidential passages we are not privileged to read. Our only option is to bring trust or distrust to bear on the ellipses the narrative contains—an option compounding the provocativeness of the digressions on fictional method in chapters 14, 33, and 44, three knowing efforts to set the terms of fiction's circulation that together tempt yet mock readerly trust in narrative art (and so turn what was for Poe a necessary strategy, the art of the hoax, into fiction's irresistible topic and problematic).

One might go so far as to suggest that the webwork of stories here discussed ironizes the emergence of a national literature, and then note the attendant irony of the belatedness, in 1857, of riverboat transport to the dissemination of this literature. Yet I would want to stress that posing the problem of narrative trust in exclusively national terms restricts its full significance. In the first place, these stories are not always clearly "American" in focus. In the second place, and more importantly, the credit economy within which they circulate is globally tentacled. Although subtle, the indications of such extension are decisive. They include the mention, by the man in gray, of travel to the London's World Fair (a story that, by focussing on an "invalid's easy chair," marks a vicious contrast to the tubercular miser's accommodation on the "Procrustean beds" in the emigrant quarters); the World's Charity scheme unfolded immediately thereafter; the French flavor of Charlemont's tale; the debt-ridden move by China Aster into the global market in spermaceti; the participation by Egbert in the West India trade; and, most substantially, the very persona of the cosmopolitan who dominates the novel's second half. As John Bryant makes clear, for midcentury readers this figure would have triggered a whole host of preconceptions about the dangers of too much travel, serving to blur distinctions of home and away, familiar and foreign.[77] Cast, intentionally or not, in the shadow of the early eighteenth-century cosmopolitan financier John Law (Scottish by birth, active in France, touted as the inventor of paper money, credited with the consolidation of New Orleans, and responsible for the original "Mississippi scheme" through which the first millionaires were made),[78] Melville's cosmopolitan enjoys an omnivorous traveling subjectivity; he figures pure social circulation, constantly turning physical mobility into social as well as real capital. His threat, as an incarnation of the con man, involves *saturation*, for cosmopolitanism disdains geopolitical boundaries alongside the membranes of custom. He will obliterate any security to be found in dreams of national integrity. He ensures that, in the narrative's second half, the confidence trick goes global.

Such expansiveness only intensifies the problems at stake, in the novel, concerning the dimensions of publicity and public trust. Sites of normalized, regularized, yet intense public exchange such as the *Fidèle* are particularly vulnerable to the kind of spreading saturation that cosmopolitanism entails. Indeed, reworking an earlier point, we might suspect that the cosmopolitan con man uses the transit system to trade in the relentless supplementation of human estrangement. The veiled transactions in any con job jeopardize public confidence by working themselves out in public life, in forms of common contact. And the crisis they pose only accentuates the absence or evacuation at the heart of the modern public sphere, capitalizing on the fact that, as Michael Warner contends, "[n]o one really inhabits the general public," in order to threaten public life with the prospect of its own bankruptcy.[79]

The larger point at issue here has to do with the social and epistemological significance of the confidence man as a public figure. If no one really inhabits the general public, the confidence man, as empty cipher, is, frighteningly enough, a model citizen. Omnipresent yet always disappearing, he becomes an icon of publicity and, simultaneously, of publicity in crisis. Granted, Melville drew for his inspiration on an historical precedent, as many critics have noted: one William Thompson, whose tour of fraud in 1849 prompted the coinage of the term "confidence man" and the invention, in newspaper accounts, of what Helen Trimpi calls "a new American character type."[80] Thus in one sense the generative capacities of 1850s print culture help to create styles of notoriety and originality on which Melville could capitalize. Yet imagining an "authentic," "original" con man ventures an evident contradiction—and, moreover, risks trust in the prospect of authentic reference. Although much valuable critical work has speculated about historical analogs for figures in the novel, the effect of such speculation is necessarily an investment of critical confidence rendered perilous (yet inescapable) by the narrative we read. Critical interpretation, like other speculative methods, is always already at an impasse, caught and constituted in the double bind of the confidence game.[81]

The lesson underscores the determining illogic—"the dialectic of necessity and contingency, agency and accident"—in credit's materialization.[82] The figure of the con man and the model of the con job offer endless, yet thereby endlessly unpredictable, transformations, so as to measure at once the real profit and the incalculable excess produced by tautology: showcasing to spectacular effect the generative indifference of exchange, they nonetheless make change from no change. In this sense, the problem of confidence raised in *The Confidence-Man* mirrors the dynamic of capital—its near-total power yet also its arbitrariness, accidentalism, vulnerability. And the fact that, as the editors of the Northwestern-Newberry edition observe, relatively little money changes hands though the narrative *intensifies*, rather than diminishes, the social and material emphasis suggested here, precisely by driving home Marx's insight, recorded in his notebook entry on James Mill, that credit resolves the value of money into human flesh.[83] As the cipher of endless credit, the confidence man *stands in* for the money he makes superfluous. The fact that he is at once one and many—that the issue of singularity or multiplicity cannot be determined—thus becomes key to the narrative's significance. Such undecidability underwrites the circulation of capital, and anticipates Marx's argument that the capitalist is capital personified, endowed with consciousness and will. Much like money and the commodity in the general formula for capital outlined in the first volume of *Capital*, the one and many con men "function only as different modes of existence of value itself," with the one, like money, "as its general mode of existence," and the many, like a range of commodities, "as its particular or, so to speak, disguised mode."[84] So conceived, the value at stake in the confidence trick and embodied by the confidence man "is constantly changing from one form into the other, without becoming lost in this movement."[85] "Transformed into an automatic subject," the confidence man embodies the tautological contradictions at work in capital's production.[86] It is as if, in 1857, Melville had read the travel story Marx tells ten years later about capital's mobile tendencies:

> The movement of capital is . . . limitless. . . . As the conscious bearer of this movement, the possessor of money becomes a capitalist. His person, or rather his pocket, is the point from which the money starts, and to which it returns. . . . [I]t is only insofar as the appropriation of ever more wealth in the abstract is the sole driving force behind his operations that he functions

> as a capitalist, i.e. as capital personified and endowed with consciousness and a will. . . . His aim is . . . the unceasing movement of profit-making.[87]

Postscript: Invalidity

"Traveling takes the ink out of one's pen as well as the cash out of one's purse," Melville, writing from Paris, had complained to Evert Duyckinck in early December 1849—a tendency toward expenditure haunting the *The Confidence-Man* yet not at all exorcized by its publication.[88] Seeking some means of earning money in the difficult economic times following the crash of 1857, Melville turned at last to the lyceum circuit, capitulating in full to the mobile information economy—a choice likely preferable, as the Northwestern-Newberry editors suggest, to the grind of magazine publication but nevertheless suspect and troubling to him (as indicated, for instance, by the reference in chapter 9 of *The Confidence-Man* to twenty lyceums as a selling feature of the New Jerusalem scam [63]). A measure of desperation seems to have accompanied his decision to undertake such work, as a letter written to George Duyckink in late December 1858, four stops into a second lecturing season, will indicate: "I should be glad to lecture [in Jersey City]—or anywhere. If they will pay expenses, & give a reasonable fee, I am ready to lecture in Labrador or on the Isle of Desolation off Patagonia."[89] Such readiness on Melville's part to go any distance for profit suggests something of the desolation of financial exigency, not to mention, ironically enough, a commitment to the economics of mobility and the trade in stories worthy of the cosmopolitan himself.

In his first season on the circuit, involving sixteen stops from November 1857 through February 1858, Melville gave a lecture entitled "Statues in Rome." It succeeded neither with his audience nor his critics; the cool reception prompted, in his second season (ten stops from December 1858 to March 1859), a shift to the topic, South Sea travel, that had made his name in the first place. Melville's capitulation to the "Typee" effect, over which he had little control in any event, seems to have worked in securing better reaction, at least with East Coast listeners and the East Coast press. Yet this apparent improvement in lecturing fortune did not prevent him from shifting his topic again for his third season on the circuit (only three stops, from November 1859 to February 1860), this time to more general reflections on the meaning of travel as a practice. Unsurprisingly, the trials of economic expenditure haunt the talk.[90]

"Traveling: Its Pleasures, Pains, and Profits" exists, like the earlier lectures, only in reconstructed form: no manuscripts survive, leaving critics, their trust very much up in the air, to rely on newspaper accounts of Melville's words (a fact helping to dramatize, once again, the uncertainty of circulation at stake in my argument). The reconstruction of the "Traveling" lecture finds Melville dwelling with cautious optimism on the benefits of travel, benefits that his abortive trip from May to November, 1860, between New York and San Francisco by way of Cape Horn evidently failed to realize, and that could not prevent him from abandoning writing as a professional career in search of the more stable type of employment that customs work would eventually provide. Particularly in light of the issues of mobility raised in *The Confidence-Man*, the seeming optimism of Melville the lecturer as reported by the Cambridge *Chronicle* seems perilous at best, as the ambiguities already suggested by his lecture's title, particularly with respect to the concept of travel's "profits," unfold in detail.

According to the reconstructed version, Melville begins by addressing "the kind of experience" in which "the prime pleasure of travel consists": namely, the "delight" of new discovery beyond the landscape of natal environment.[91] He equates natal environment with life in "a deep valley named the Hopper" and new discovery with the eventual ascent of the surrounding "mountains called Greylock"—thereby indicating the confinement (material and spiritual) of untraveled persons, but also, held as if in suspense, the pure possibility of untraveled imagination.[92] On this model, travel differentiates *inside* from *outside*, where the expansive pleasures of the second help to undo the containing tendencies of the first. Entailing movement, travel also involves a potentially transcendent rise in sensibility. Yet to profit from it will require a specific temperament: that of "a good lounger," "young, care-free, and gifted with geniality and imagination."[93] Tacitly linking the ability to profit from travel with a preexisting set of social and cultural privileges, the reconstructed account of Melville's opening remarks recalls Marx's incisive argument about the credit economy, "credit is given only to him who already has," even as it effectively rules out the more complicated circumstances under which Melville himself, careworn and cursed with imagination, traveled to give this lecture.[94]

The "profits" of travel outlined by Melville hold above all to the elimination of prejudice—"a new birth" into "personal humility" that "enlarges the sphere of comprehensive benevolence till it includes the whole human race."[95] The liberalization of attitude and belief here claimed for travel as a practice anticipates the expansion Melville ventures, in concluding his lecture, of the concept of travel itself:

> England, France, the Mediterranean—it is needless to dwell on their attractions. But as travel indicates change and novelty, and change and novelty are often essential to healthy life, let a narrower range not deter us. A trip to Florida will open a large field of pleasant and instructive enjoyment. Go even to Nahant, if you can go no farther—*that* is travel. To an invalid it is travel, that is, change, to go to other rooms in the house.[96]

In the published account, Melville follows this argument with one last statement in summation: "The sight of novel objects, the acquirement of novel ideas, the breaking up of old prejudices, the enlargement of heart and mind,—are the proper fruit of rightly undertaken travel."[97] Reiterating the earlier discussion of travel's profits, such broadly humanistic abstractions cannot dispel the troubling equation of travel with an invalid ("good lounger" in the bitterest sense of that phrase) changing rooms. Liberalized beyond all conventional measure, this expanded concept of travel intimates nothing so much as constriction—the prospect of a claustrophobic confinement undermining the promise of leisured liberation.

Such troubling insinuations only compound the disturbance already set in motion by Melville's earlier claim that "the pleasure of leaving home, care-free, with no concern but to enjoy, has also as a pendant the pleasure of coming back to the old hearthstone, the home to which, however traveled, the heart still fondly turns, ignoring the burden of its anxieties and cares."[98] The statement's irony is hard to ignore: travel, by implication, will turn a carefree heart to worry. Rhetorically and conceptually, the "pendant" weight of homebound pleasure labors to counterbalance the wearying emotional "burden" pressing down on the organ of human feeling. Making travel the cause of anxiety and care, the passage sets up the most intensely unsettling section of the lecture, in which Melville comments darkly on the punitive discipline of the key document of transnational travel in the age of the modern nation-state: the passport. Contending that this item proves "[a] great grievance from first to last," Melville supplies his listeners with a cautionary axiom that, glossing a familiar ritual in travel's routine, underscores lurking corruption in the custom-house: "You soon learn by official demands, what becomes to you an adage,—Open passport, open purse; and its endless crosses at the close of your travels remind you of the crosses it has cost you all the way through."[99] Here the play on "crosses" itself seems "endless": signaling official marks on the passport and the action of bribery, of crossing palms, the term also suggests the material, metaphysical, and geopolitical dimensions of travel (crossing ground, yet also borders) and at the same time the iconic machinery of martyrdom. Thus making the traveler a martyr—forced to bear untold crosses, sacrificed to the ritual deprivations of officially sanctioned scam—the passport records, in the cruel economy of its crosses, the inextricability of travel with economic exploitation. Four years after the appearance of his last published novel, and at the end of a public literary career marked—or, indeed, scarred—by travel's complex crossings, Melville cannot stop dwelling on the alienating power, the excruciating effect, of uncertain circulation. Such, for him, remains the anguish of travel's profit.

3

Secret Circuits, Fugitive Moves

Near the beginning of *The Confidence-Man*, in an episode withheld from discussion in the last chapter, we encounter a character who bears to excess what Michael Warner calls the "humiliating positivity of the particular"—those materialities of embodiment from which citizens under republicanism (white, male, propertied) were privileged to abstract themselves.[1] Black Guinea is "a grotesque negro cripple" who, "owing to something wrong about his legs," is (in a telling echo of Captain Amasa Delano's genial view of "the negro") effectively "cut down to the stature of a Newfoundland dog."[2] Yet subsequently we learn that, improbably enough, Black Guinea's gnarled body is "not the least attractive object" on board the *Fidèle*, presumably because "out of his very deformity, indigence, and houselessness, so cheerily endured," he inspires "mirth in some of that crowd, whose own purses, hearths, hearts, all their possessions, sound limbs included, could not make gay."[3]

Here the antinomies of social life—those forms of possession and dependency structuring capitalist modernity—constitute popular entertainments inseparably fused to the performing body. As we are unsurprised to learn, the violence of commerce lurks in these pastimes: "the cripple's mouth" serves as "at once target and purse" for the coins thrown his way.[4] Those left cold by the possession of wellness find joy, or at least diversion, in the pathetic display of its loss. In effect, the terms of wellness really only come into being in view of Black Guinea's cheerful endurance; the abject is his to perform for the amusement of others. The mirth of the audience depends not least on the cripple's skill in evincing obliviousness to the brutal fact of his anguish. Grotesque not least in the ludicrousness of the trust it evinces, the display drives home some of the social and ideological deformities attending popular spectacle.

But Black Guinea keeps a secret. Or, more accurately, he is *accused* of keeping a secret, which at once draws it into the open and throws it into doubt. As the narrator recounts, even as Black Guinea's "game of charity [is] yet at its height, a limping, gimlet-eyed, sour-faced person—it may be some discharged custom house officer—... who himself on a wooden leg went halt" calls the performance into question by "croak[ing] out something about his deformity being a sham, got up for financial purposes."[5] This charge, we learn, dampens considerably "the frolic benignities of the pitch-penny players"; they become reluctant to reward the cheery endurance of one who may, after all, be only playing at pain.[6]

Given the historical moment, such reluctance should not seem unreasoned: at midcentury the prevailing consolidations of blackness within racist common sense still tended to comprehend suffering as a prime sign of black authenticity. Striving to restore the confidence required by the pitch-penny game, those gathered on the *Fidèle* accordingly call out for some kind of "documentary proof"—an authenticating sheaf of papers, or at least "'some one who can speak a good word'" on Black Guinea's behalf.[7] Not blessed with "'none o'dem waloable papers,'" Black Guinea nevertheless can, and does, supply a list of "'ge'mman'" to testify in his favor—a list that, as several commentators have argued, serves as a fractured catalogue of the incarnations the confidence man will adopt through the novel, and that as such will seem to lend credence to the ex–custom house officer's insistent charge against Black Guinea: "'He's some white operator, betwisted and painted up for a decoy. He and his friends are all humbugs.'"[8]

I should stress here that, in keeping with the analysis of *The Confidence-Man* offered in the previous chapter, my interest in the Black Guinea episode has nothing to do with the determination of authenticity as such—with whether or not Black Guinea is "really" black, "really" crippled—and, by contrast, everything to do with authenticity's problematic, especially as it bears on the broader questions of mobility at stake in this study. The creeping distrust introduced among the crowd by the ex–custom house agent turns on the insinuation of minstrelsy, that theatrical entertainment so popular through the antebellum period. The gimlet-eyed man implies that burnt cork makes for suspect blackness; I would suggest instead that, through the minstrel show, burnt cork rendered its style of blackness hegemonic. As Saidiya Harman contends, "[t]he appropriation of Sambo's affect, the donning of blackface, and the audience's consequent identification with the minstrel mask provided whiteness with a coherence and illusory integrity dependent upon the relations of mastery and servitude, and the possession of a figurative body of blackness."[9] Such is precisely the dynamic on board the *Fidèle*, whether or not Black Guinea is in fact—"in fact"—a minstrel. The traveling collective that participates in his performance achieves a coherence and illusory integrity manifest first in the capacity for genial abuse and next in the capacity for taxing scrutiny. The "game of charity" renders perilous any distinction between being "authentically" black and being a minstrel; the minstrel relation is, on Melville's ship as throughout the antebellum period, always already constitutive of the dynamic linking black performer to white audience.[10] Hence the particular complexity, and pointed irony, of Black Guinea's immobility: crippled, he embodies the ceaseless circulation and circulability of a fixed yet fungible cultural type.[11]

In her analysis of the subjections bound up in slave performance, Hartman rightly insists that "[t]he culture of cross-racial identification facilitated in minstrelsy cannot be extricated from the relations of chattel slavery."[12] At the outset, Black Guinea indicates ruefully that he is "der dog widout massa," yet he remains bound to the system of testimonial and patronage (valuable papers, gentlemen to speak on his behalf) that in the period served to calibrate freedom as a social and political resource by regulating and legitimating the public movements of *both* the enslaved and the escaped. This cripple cripples the antithesis between freedom and enslavement: his performance renders the two states perilously intimate precisely by dramatizing how, in Hartman's phrase, "the simulation of good times ... [could serve] to incite the flow of capital."[13] On board the *Fidèle*, much as on the plantation or at the auction block, "gaiety articulates the brutal calculations of the trade."[14] At stake (only months before the *Dred Scott* decision denying any possibility of black citizenship) is a striking instance of what Hartman calls the "economy of enjoyment" in which black subjectivity entails black subjection—in which any black is "'[b]ound' to be a darky, whether slave, contraband, or free."[15]

Understood in these terms the Black Guinea episode highlights the continued profitability of the cultural and social circulation of hegemonic ideas of blackness on the eve of civil war while, at the same time, intimating some of the anxieties such circulation could inspire. Although Black Guinea can go nowhere, nevertheless in some sense his subjectivity, evading full disclosure, acquires a kind of fugitive energy. Thus his leglessness marks as it ironizes an ongoing problem of black mobility, one addressed yet extended in the Fugitive Slave Law—a piece of legislation that, in serving to secure the proper relations and movements of persons within the nation by making disclosure about fugitives the duty and the business of citizens, worked not least to marshal the common knowledge it compelled against secrets troublesome to social and national hegemony. Particularly when read in such light, the Black Guinea episode will anticipate many of the key questions addressed in this chapter. At one level, I am concerned with the interimplication of mobility and secrecy at midcentury, through which crises of motion becomes crises of knowledge. Such interimplication informs what can be discovered, comprehended, revealed, and circulated by persons in transit. At another level, I am concerned with the ways instabilities of bodily knowledge sometimes compromise, sometimes assist those persons who must move to survive. The texts focal to this compound inquiry—Henry Bibb's 1849 *Narrative of the Life and Adventures of Henry Bibb, an American Slave*, Sarah Edmonds's 1865 *Nurse and Spy in the Union Army*, and Harriet Tubman's 1869 and 1886 memoirs (both transcribed by Sarah Bradford)—emerge from modes of social being and practices of cultural production distinct from and yet enmeshed in the dramas of uncertain circulation explored in the previous chapter. Contesting what Shirley Samuels calls the habitual "imagination of national embodiment" that "repeatedly excluded the racial and gendered body," these texts show the significance of struggles over knowledge for the politics of mobility in the United States at midcentury.[16]

Materializing Fugitivity

In distinct yet provocatively complementary ways, the texts I address in this chapter work to trace the interrelation of national belonging with risky, contested forms of movement, circulation, and travel. As such, they all register the viability, the *circulability*, within the literary field of a problematic intensely absorbing across the social sphere. The Fugitive Slave Law bears out, to graphic effect, the fully national significance of such absorption. The force of its legislation, commanding "all good citizens . . . to aid and assist in the prompt and efficient execution of this law," delineates the state's attempt to secure social relations within the nation's imagined community by requiring its subjects to aid in policing illicit mobility.[17] And access to knowledge is key: targeting both fugitives and those who would "knowingly" obstruct their recapture, the law insists on the juridical and political necessity of common knowledge and full disclosure over against the social threat of fugitivity's open secret.[18] Thus the problem of mobility as a social resource becomes not just geopolitical (about managing bodies in space), but also informational (about controlling the circulation of discourse).

Passed as one of five enactments in the 1850 Compromise, the Fugitive Slave Law undertook to regulate the situation as well as movement not only of slaves but of *all* inhabitants of the United States.[19] The stakes were evidently economic as well as ideological: as Eber Pettit notes in his 1879 *Sketches in the History of the Underground Railroad*, "[t]he facilities offered by the fugitive slave law for capturing runaway slaves had made it a profitable business."[20] That the law did so not least by rewarding acts of *disclosure* underscores by contrast the compound anxiety provoked by the intrication of secrecy and mobility in the United States at midcentury. Yet if the law's passage sought to turn the unknown (methods enabling the escape of the enslaved) into the known (information enabling their recapture), by contrast fugitives and their abolitionist allies proved resilient in turning the known into the unknown: in using mobility's secrets to make bodies disappear. In effect, then, in the very effort to legislate a politics of movement for the enforcement of which each citizen was responsible, the Fugitive Slave Law threw into high relief the unpredictable, even volatile, conditions of movement in the antebellum United States.[21]

The anxiety inscribed in this law over the capacious dynamics of unpredictable, unchecked mobility will not simply reflect, but instance, what James Beniger terms "the crisis of control" beginning to take shape in the United States at midcentury, when "[f]or the first time in history... the social processing of material flows threatened to exceed in both volume and speed the system's capacity to contain them."[22] Although such an association may at first seem tenuous, its purpose is not at all to discount the specific significance, within the larger contest over slavery, of the 1850 legislation, but instead and additionally to emphasize the position of this law within a constellation of projects aimed at counteracting often volatile unpredictabilities of movement, in the transport of human bodies as in the circulation of commodities, by regulating them within networked information systems. In other words, although the Fugitive Slave Law registers most immediately within a temporally attenuated, conceptually particular genealogy of slave-holding control, in complementary ways its significance derives from a more historically specific, conceptually diverse complex of developments occurring in the years around 1850: the start of what Beniger calls "the control revolution" characterizing the consolidation of industrial capitalism. When read this way, the law, codifying deeply felt investments in the regulatory force of systematic, systematically produced knowledge, comes to seem a key apparatus within a spreading material and information economy, its status as an instrument of state repression more clearly interleaved with its contribution to the disciplinary manufacture of useful knowledge. Here we can begin to address Lawrence Buell's recent critique—that all too often in current American literary and cultural studies "the American 1850 is [taken to be] a more important litmus test of the social themes of mid-nineteenth-century American literature than, say, the growth of the international market economy, the impact of European socialist thinking, or the European revolutions of 1848"—by arguing for its *inextricability from* a constellation of events within the articulation of modernity.[23] And here we can also begin to trace the intimacy and interimplication of enslavement with "free" labor under capitalism, an intimacy and an interimplication that, as Saidiya Hartman and Samira Kawash among others have recently insisted, a liberal juxtaposition of freedom to slavery and a liberal ethic of self-possession only serve to mystify.[24]

For fugitives from slavery, as for black and white abolitionists, one response to the type of regulation endeavored by the Fugitive Slave Law was an increasing commitment to those modes of clandestine movement and surreptitious assistance we have come to associate with the underground railroad. This loose assemblage of escape routes seems, at least in hindsight, to have enabled resistance to this law (as, more broadly, to the violently proprietary worldview it sanctioned) through the material facilitation of acts of secret travel. The secret character of such acts is likewise key to the discursive production of the underground railroad (a largely retrospective venture that, as I will discuss below, tends in the view of contemporary historians to involve a strategic romanticization)—so much so, in fact, that in narrative reports of activity on the road, the *opening up* of secrecy comes to seem the crucial dynamic within its operation. Anthologies and reminiscences published in the postbellum era repeatedly insist that the underground railroad, despite the open secrecy of its workings, managed to make fugitivity nearly systematic in the decades before the Civil War—such that slaveholders could only rage against a system they knew to exist but could not find to stop. These narratives solicit the perception of such open secrecy about the systematicity of fugitive escape, not just with the kinds of stories they tell but also with the serial quality of their telling—deploying reiterative force to drive home the failure of slavery's agents to master the secrets of the underground railroad. The sheer volume of disclosure makes manifest the scope of such open secrecy.[25]

According to Levi Coffin, Eber Pettit, and William Still, among others, the secrets of "the mysterious road" held most immediately to the practices enabling escape: forgery, concealment, dissimulation, disguise.[26] In the preface to his record, the black abolitionist William Still outlines such secretive methods at some length: "Occasionally fugitives came in boxes and chests, and not infrequently some were secreted in steamers and vessels, and in some instances journeyed hundreds of miles in skiffs. Men disguised in female attire and women dressed in the garb of men have under very trying circumstances triumphed in thus making their way to freedom."[27] Still goes on to indicate, however, that concealment and disguise were not the only means of escape. Physical signs of miscegenation and airs of social privilege could likewise aid in fugitive dissimulation:

> And here and there when all other modes of escape seemed cut off, some, whose fair complexions have rendered them indistinguishable from their Anglo-Saxon brethren, feeling that they could endure the yoke no longer, with assumed airs of importance, such as they had been accustomed to see their masters show when traveling, have taken the usual modes of conveyance and have even braved the most scrutinizing inspection of slave-holders, slave-catchers and car conductors, who were ever on the alert to catch those who were considered base and white enough to practice such deception.[28]

The passage suggests acutely the incoherencies of racial categorization—yet also, for African Americans, its punitive double-binds: in the eyes of slavery's agents, the ability and willingness of some slaves to pass as white only affirms the baseness intrinsic to their underlying blackness. As importantly, the passage underscores the educative powers of travel by indicating that, although slaves who travel with their masters enjoy movement without freedom, they can use the experience tactically to gain knowledge invaluable for the purpose of escape. Unexpectedly enough, travel's habitus (the material and conceptual inclusions and exclusions normalized through traveling practice, such that "airs of importance" will always already signal freedom) here enables fugitivity to occur.

Comparable "airs of importance" could surround discursive artifacts, the forged documents employed by fugitive slaves: as Still notes, "[p]asses have been written and used by fugitives, with their masters' and mistresses' names boldly attached thereto, and have answered admirably as a protection, when passing through ignorant country districts of slave regions, where but a few, either white or colored, knew how to read or write correctly."[29] Punning on the interrelation of forgery, movement, and masquerade—those discursive and material means to slave escape—this sentence only intensifies the clench of ignorance with knowledge that drives both the moves and the discourse of fugitivity. Dissimulation here draws its force from the uneven configuration of literacy's power against racial and social privilege.[30]

As Still's volume will suggest, in postbellum accounts of the underground railroad dissimulation through disguise tends to enjoy special prominence, presumably for commercial as well as documentary reasons: the strategy makes for thrilling narrative. Regularly, the methods of disguise reported in these accounts exploit an instability of bodily markers—in effect, the vulnerable relation between body and social identity as performative categories—in service of outlawed movement. By manipulating the public visibility of a body, of the social signs making it remarkable while distinguishing it from others, dissimulation through disguise can also be taken to stand in intimate contrast to, and so in surreptitious ways to answer, the rituals of public exposure and display central to slavery's specular apparatus.[31] To take only one example, in his *Sketches*, Eber Pettit tells of Cassey's escape from enslavement in Baltimore to freedom in Philadelphia: "She disguised herself in sailor's clothes and walked boldly to the Philadelphia boat. There she walked up and down the deck smoking a cigar, occasionally passing and re-passing the constables who had been sent to take her. The constables left the boat after waiting till it was about to start; they were watching for a colored woman to come on board answering to her description."[32] Cassey's strategy trades on social signs of white manhood to dupe the agents of slavery's racial order. Key for my purposes is the punning insistence on "passing and repassing" that, recalling with a twist the "passes/passing" play in Still's account, serves to secure the link between dissimulation and movement: conceptually as semantically, the body's disguise and its motion become as if one act. Here the very possibility of fugitive mobility becomes indivisible from—indeed, synonymous with—secrecy. And fugitivity's power seems liminal, working the interstices of bondage and freedom: Cassey uses the power of physical proximity to confound a regimen deeply invested in the absolute difference of the enslaved and their masters. Her closeness to the constables charged with her recapture flouts the authority (and mocks the effectiveness) of a system obsessively reliant on the power of discriminatory surveillance. The disjunction between what seems to us her striking visibility and what seems to the constables "his" unremarkable invisibility confirms a blind spot in slavery's vision—in its scopic tendencies but also its worldview—concerning the transparency of the relation between exterior and interior states. Cassey's masquerade calls into question the essentializing expression of nature (as slave or chattel) through skin, and thereby turns the trick on slavery's monstrous skin show.[33]

Significantly, the prospect of intimate difference raised by the story of Cassey's dissimulation tends not just to characterize particular accounts of fugitivity recorded in these narratives but also to inflect the overarching sense they impart of the underground railroad as an enterprise. Often its postbellum historians will mimic the rhetoric of corporate culture, depicting the road as a corporation in which shareholders invest so as to have an interest—what in his *Reminiscences* Levi Coffin terms "assessments on Underground Railroad stock."[34] The force of such mimicry would seem to situate the underground railroad within the arc of northern corporate influence. As Pettit argues in his *Sketches*,

> It should not be supposed that the few humble individuals actually engaged in the active operations of this institution, were the only persons interested in it. Some of the best men in the nation were stockholders; men of wealth and influence, men in office, State and national,—men, women and children identified themselves with its affairs. It had the aid and approval of the most distinguished philanthropists of the age, and many far-seeing politicians, descrying the conflict between slave and free labor, took sides with the latter.[35]

Suffusing the project to assist fugitive slaves with a desire to mobilize bodies in service of the ideological cause of free labor, Pettit's final claim here intimates some of the complexity of the investment of America's corporate classes in the contest over slavery. Finessing the vexed question of the freedom of "free labor" under capital, the passage concentrates instead on persuading its reader of the fully national scope of the underground railroad as an institution. Compelling across all regions and to children and philanthropists alike, this secretive institution would seem, judging from Pettit's description, to have marshaled a fundamentally democratic polity against slavery. The glory of the underground system, we might well conclude, inhered in its congruence with the nation's imagined community, epitomizing and impelling an epochal shift from slavery's tyranny to capitalism's liberty.

As more recent commentators emphasize, such an understanding is typical of what Larry Gara terms the "romance" of the underground railroad. In actuality, it was never as organized or systematic as popular accounts maintain.[36] As the editors of *The Black Abolitionist Papers* point out, "[a]bolitionist and southern propaganda frequently mythologized [the railroad's] networks as highly complex secret organizations, but they were often haphazard, localized, and semipublic in nature."[37] Thus the underground railroad's systematicity and the openness of its secrecy are at best retrospective, historicizing fictions—key elements in the production of northern freedom's ideal against southern slavery's evil.[38]

One of the more troubling aspects involved in the production of this myth is the way it tends to displace African Americans as agents within the fugitive dynamic. As Gara maintains, the romance of the underground railroad has tended to overstate the contributions of white abolitionists, positing a phantasmatic network of white organizers at the expense of those fugitives and black abolitionists most immediately and committedly involved in assisting the enslaved to escape. What, we may ask, underlies the effort to produce and to circulate such romance in retrospect? Does it speak, perhaps, to a lingering anxiety about the widespread failure of whites before the Civil War to do much at all to assist in the material emancipation of the enslaved? Does it indicate a determined effort to occlude the intimacy of capitalist freedom with plantation bondage? Does it demonstrate the ongoing marketability of scenes of black suffering and white benevolence in the Jim Crow era, and a subtle reinscription of racial hierarchy into the history of the fight against slavery? Such possibilities are evidently disturbing ones; together they speak, by contrast, to the ongoing problem—the crises of legibility—posed by fugitivity for hegemonic conceptions of liberty in the nineteenth-century United States.

Fugitive Habits

In the "Narrative of the Life and Escape of William Wells Brown" with which *Clotel* begins, Brown reflects on the testing challenge that knowledge entails for the ends of mobility and subjectivity. He describes (as if at second hand) the effect of the realization of free status as it strikes his fugitive "character," William. The runaway has just received shelter and comfort and, most consequentially, is on the verge of receiving a surname from a white Quaker, Wells Brown.

> "I have frequently been asked," says William, "how I felt upon finding myself regarded as a man by a white family; especially having just run away from one. I cannot say that I have ever answered the question yet. The fact that I was, in all probability, a freeman, sounded in my ears like a charm. I am satisfied that none but a slave could place such an appreciation upon liberty

> as I did at that time. I wanted to see my mother and sister, that I might tell them that 'I was free!' I wanted to see my fellow-slaves in St. Louis, and let them know that the chains were no longer upon my limbs. I wanted to see Captain Price, and let him learn from my own lips that I was no more a chattel, but a MAN. I was anxious, too, thus to inform Mrs. Price that she must get another coachman, and I wanted to see Eliza more than I did Mr. Price or Mrs. Price. The fact that I was a freeman—could walk, talk, eat, and sleep as a man, and no one to stand over me with the blood-clotted cow-hide—all this made me feel that I was not myself."[39]

So described, the charming sound of freedom's "probability" resonates with an unsettling, uncanny force. It entails at once a desire for performative testimonial (where William might enact, not least in jeopardizing, his freedom by traveling to proclaim it at scenes of his enslavement) and a deep sense of defamiliarization neatly limned by Brown choosing to ventriloquize his "own" imagined speech as if at second hand, as if the speech of another. "'[A]ll this made me feel that I was not myself'": what typically we will understand as subjectivity, Brown's free *I*, comes into being at the instant of its fracture ("not myself"); the bodily habits indicative at most of liberty's routine materialization (walking, talking, eating, sleeping) produce a knowledge of conflicted selfhood. The fact that Brown loses the feeling of self (or perhaps more accurately feels selfhood's negation?) at the instant of freedom's recognition indicates the impossibility of an unproblematic association of liberty with self-possession for the fugitive (even as it intimates, more polemically, the sense of self proper to the slave despite slavery's ideology). Liberty literally materializes in the *dis*identification it entails. Thus, although adamant about the joy of escape and the value of freedom, Brown calls the naturalness of liberal subjectivity into some doubt, intimating instead that for the ex-slave in a systematically racist society such subjectivity threatens—as Saidiya Hartman has argued so convincingly—to become another form of subjection, through which any white, empowered with access to benevolent as to vicious discrimination, can deign (or fail) to regard any black "as a man."

Central to the introduction to Brown's 1853 novel, then, is the lesson that fugitive practice makes self-possession—the state foundational to modern bourgeois identity—troublesome business for escaped slaves. In the *Narrative of the Life and Adventures of Henry Bibb, An American Slave, Written by Himself*, Henry Bibb is tenacious in describing the costs of this lesson.[40] Published by Bibb himself in 1849, three years before *Clotel*, the account is notable, as Charles Heglar observes in his introduction to the Wisconsin edition, for its "recursive pattern of escape and return, which is a significant variation from the conventional linear pattern of escape and transformation into a freeman" exemplified, most famously, in the 1845 narrative of Frederick Douglass.[41] Significant in view of this recursive pattern is the way Bibb's narrative foregrounds links connecting rival yet intimate forms of motion: the circulatory economy of slavery and the fugitive practice of escaped slaves. In so doing, it shows how the outlawed movements of the enslaved make the question of mobility a contest for knowledge. At stake are not least the materialities of social circulation.

The *Narrative of the Life and Adventures of Henry Bibb, An American Slave* is the most well-known of a constellation of contributions by its author to the abolitionist cause. Enslaved from birth, starting in 1837 Bibb ventured several attempts at escape before finally succeeding in 1841; that year, he began a very successful career condemning slavery on the abolitionist lecture circuit. The passage of the Fugitive Slave Law in 1850 helped to inspire Bibb's move, with his second wife, Mary Miles, to Chatham, Canada West, where the two founded and ran *The Voice of the Fugitive*, an abolitionist newspaper dedicated to emigration. Although cut short in its run by Bibb's untimely death in 1854, *The Voice of the Fugitive* offered, under his editorship, relentless critiques of slavery in the South and racism in the North and in Canada—critiques grounded in the conviction that, as Bibb maintained in an address delivered (along with John Fisher and James Tinsley) to the North American Convention of abolitionists in September 1851 and published one month later in *The Voice of the Fugitive*, "there can be no real freedom in the land while the great body of our people are held in slavery."[42] A comparably incisive understanding of the intimate interrelation of freedom and bondage characterizes Bibb's 1849 narrative.

Bibb begins the account of his harrowing escape from slavery with a bleak joke about upbringing. Observing first that "I was brought up in the Counties of Shelby, Henry, Oldham, and Trimble" (64), Bibb quickly revises himself in the interests of precision: "Or, more correctly speaking, in the above counties, I may safely say, I was *flogged up*; for where I should have received moral, mental, and religious instruction, I received stripes without number, the object of which was to degrade and keep me in subordination" (64). The ironizing substitution, through which flogging takes the place of upbringing, marks the violent methods proper to the Peculiar Institution, methods that, through their subordinating lessons, render growing up a process of being beaten down. The effect is among other things to ironize the educative relation, indicating that the key lessons in slavery's pedagogy reinscribe—

literally into enslaved flesh, by means of "stripes without number"—a dehumanizing brutality. And Bibb's insistence in this context on the four counties in which he was relentlessly "flogged up" makes it hard to disassociate geographical locale from the threat of violence. The emphasis is counterintuitive, and effectively geopolitical: the mode of regional affiliation that, in the context of freedom, typically signifies "home" becomes, under slavery, inextricable from alienation and affliction. The flogging into being of the slave renders the material space of origin foreign, even contrary, to any sense of self. Against such brutal pedagogy, fugitive practice—a means of escape from the double-bind of flogging-as-upbringing and a mode of material existence emphasizing what Paul Gilroy calls "routes" over "roots"—becomes by contrast enlivening and life-sustaining.[43]

As his narrative makes clear, Bibb embraces illicit mobility as a kind of routine. Throughout, he positions such practice in opposition to the degrading lessons of the lash. For, although "[s]laves were not allowed books, pen, ink, nor paper, to improve their minds" (65), nevertheless Bibb gains an education through routinized escape:

> But it seems to me now, that I was particularly observing, and apt to retain what came under my observation. But more especially, all that I heard about liberty and freedom to the slaves, I never forgot. *Among other good trades I learned the art of running away to perfection.* I made a regular business of it, and never gave it up, until I had broken the bands of slavery, and landed myself safely in Canada, where I was regarded as a man, and not as a thing. (65; emphasis added)

This passage counters, to pointed effect, the pedagogy of the lash used to flog Bibb up. Here (in ways resonant with those outlined by Eber Pettit in the passage discussed above) illicit mobility holds a kind of tutelary power. In Bibb's case, practice makes perfect the fugitive moves that finally permit him to elude slavery's carceral mastery. The full status of personhood (a shift from thing-ness to man-ness contingent, ironically enough, on the regard of others) requires for its success the "regular business" of running away. And the representation of fugitivity as a business will underscore the ways its practice works to counter the slave mode of production: tirelessly rehearsing "the art of running away," the fugitive adopts what he calls a trade—what amounts, polemically, to a form of labor—through which to break the bands and, with them, the labor relations central to his enslavement.[44]

The power of Bibb's illicit movement is at once intimate with and antithetical to the forms of transformation proper, under capitalist modernity, to travel's hegemony. As I argued in chapter 1, the common sense of travel involves a change in consciousness, intellect, being, and affect through the defamiliarizing knowledge that traveling ostensibly produces. Yet, at the same time, any assumption of such change typically takes for granted an enduring stability of social subjectivity—that is, the identificatory attributes proper to liberalism. The revelatory logic of transformation under such a traveling practice thus holds in suspense the precepts of selfhood that ensure the underlying unchangeability of the traveling subject. In effect, the material forms of mobility at stake presume, as they require, social stasis for their operation. The sorts of transformation available to members of the traveling class will tend to require the fixity and security of the social system, and the habitus, legitimating their travels. Violently abjected by such a system while enslaved, when in flight Bibb confounds its power, not least by troubling the social stasis it requires. As Bibb the fugitive will not sit still, so his fugitivity, a decisively transformative practice in its own right, undermines the naturalized bond between the social privilege of movement and the material ability to move.

Rhetorically, at key points Bibb's narrative trades, in knowing, ironic ways, on the privilege at issue here. The moments I have in mind are apostrophic ones that, in recording existential longing or lament, limn to dissonant effect the kind of epiphany standard in travel writing from the period. The point, as we see in the two passages below, is not only to deploy the strategic power of desire and regret in the discursive contest against slavery, but also to intimate the ideological bonds on their circulation. In Bibb's treatment, the isolating yet universalizing veneration of nature, familiar from the Romantic tradition, shifts decisively in implication and impact:

> Sometimes standing on the Ohio River bluff, looking over on a free State, and as far north as my eyes could see, I have eagerly gazed upon the blue sky of the free North, which at times constrained me to cry out from the depths of my soul, Oh! Canada, sweet land of rest—Oh! when shall I get there? Oh, that I had the wings of a dove, that I might soar away to where there is no slavery; no clanking of chains, no captives, no lacerating of backs, no parting of husbands and wives; and where man ceases to be the property of his fellow man. These thoughts have revolved in my mind a thousand times. I have stood upon the lofty banks of the river Ohio, gazing upon the splendid steamboats, wafted with all their magnificence up and down the river, and I thought of the fishes of the water, the fowls of the air, the wild beasts of the forest, all appeared to be free, to go just where they pleased, and I was an unhappy slave! (72)

In her analysis of imperial travelogues on Africa, Mary Louise Pratt argues that, in a telling expression of what I have been calling travel's hegemony, "the 'face of the country' is presented chiefly in sweeping prospects that open before or, more often, beneath the traveler's eye. Such panoramic views are an important commonplace of European aesthetics, of course, and that undoubtedly accounts for much of their appeal."[45] Here, Bibb exports the panoramic view for critical ends. The difference between steamboats, fishes, fowl, and beasts, on the one hand, and slaves on the other—that boats move magnificently and beasts roam freely while slaves can do neither—underscores the extent of the degradations entailed by the Peculiar Institution, situating as it does slaves beneath machine and beast, and tacitly damns the logic of chattel slavery as at once mechanistic and truly beastly. In an incisive, ironic pun, the thoughts that revolve a thousand times in Bibb's mind—of a place without slavery's torments, "where man ceases to be the property of his fellow man"—are historically and philosophically revolutionary, proper to the revolutionary generation that, founding the American republic in protest against bondage to the Crown, demonstrated the bankruptcy of its own ideals by naturalizing slavery as a part of the republican landscape.

Subsequently Bibb expresses such irony in terms of vision, where the sense of sight (permission to gaze) triggers an exercise of insight that the slave as chattel is deemed too base to enjoy:

> while I was permitted to gaze on the beauties of nature, on free soil, as I passed down the river, things looked to me uncommonly pleasant: The green tress and wild flowers of the forest; the ripening harvest fields waving with the gentle breezes of Heaven; and the honest farmers tilling their soil and living by their own toil. These things seemed to light upon my vision with a peculiar charm. I was conscious of what must be my fate; a wretched victim of Slavery without limit; to be sold like an ox, into hopeless bondage, and to be worked under the flesh-devouring lash during life, without wages. (93)

Aesthetic appreciation is in this instance less disinterested than defamiliarizing; it acts as a kind of spur to existential consciousness and political critique, capacities held, under slavery, to be far beyond the reach of any slave. Here, as in the earlier passage, Bibb moves from panoramic contemplation to institutional analysis, this time so as to indicate the ideological underpinnings of the pastoral mode, to find the politics within the panorama (a strategy evident in the equivalence drawn between "the beauties of nature" and "free soil"—the name of the abolitionist political party in which Bibb participated from its founding a year before the publication of his narrative). Pastoral glory supplies the very terms by which to comprehend, by contrast, slavery's horror; the aesthetics familiar from and proper to the travelogue mark, here, the consciousness of bondage. Again the bestial allusion serves to intimate the bankruptcy of the slaveholding tendency to identify slaves as mere beasts; by expropriating the posture and viewpoint proper to socially and culturally sanctioned travelers, Bibb makes ludicrous the bestialization that, bound by chattel slavery, he cannot escape. Subject yet object, person yet chattel, traveler yet slave, Bibb scripts the circumstances of what W. E. B. Du Bois would later call "double-consciousness": his conscious *I* emerges at the instant of its fracture—an existential condition reflected and engaged, materially and spatially, through the practice of fugitivity or illicit travel.[46]

The two passages at issue bear out W. T. J. Mitchell's contention that "landscape is what Marx called a 'social hieroglyph,' an emblem of the social relations it conceals."[47] Revealingly, the second of the vistas charming Bibb's vision will fail and, by failing, *fulfill* Emerson's test of landscape, as outlined in "Nature": "the landscape has no owner," and so one "cannot *freely* admire a noble landscape, if laborers are digging in the field hard by."[48] The crucial difference, of course, comes with the problem slavery poses: in Bibb's account the prospect of honest, self-sustaining toil throws into brutal relief the obliteration of self by forced labor. Bibb's experience bears out the literal sense, and with it the unintended truth, of Emerson's dictum, precisely because the slave's witness of free labor constitutes the material condition of unfreedom, the paradox of enslaved admiration. If in Bibb's account the relation between the enslaved and the honest farmer is ostensibly one of contrast, it still turns on a supplementarity in which the reminder (or remainder?) of slavery literally underwrites the material practices proper to the condition of liberty. Thus deployed, the panoramic view makes graphic the emergence of slave subjectivity in an ongoing subjection.[49]

Bibb meets this double bind, in which slavery is not so much opposed as requisite to the liberal ideal of freedom, through the fugitive practice delineated at the start of his narrative and documented at length in its pages. What he terms the "regular business" of illicit travel becomes, by means of relentless repetition, effectively habitual, redressing the felt need for escape—yet what can a traveling *habit* mean for automatic presuppositions of self-possession, agency, and free will? Dedicated to the pursuit of material freedom, and answering routinized abjection with routinized unpredictability, the habitual fugitive confounds the stark juxtaposition of slavery to liberty, exploiting instead the incoherences entailed in their interimplication. In effect, the depiction of fugitivity as a habit works to puncture slavery's discourse: by habitualizing illicit movement, a fugitive practice incomprehensible simply in terms of choice and agency, Bibb resists the pathology that would come to be inscribed as *drapetomania*, while refusing the false promise that free will, as a liberal ideal, holds out for the enslaved.[50]

By using mobility against slavery's interdictions to fashion a kind of contradictory subjectivity, Bibb the fugitive jams the circuit linking personality and property that marks the condition—indeed, the open secret—of self-possession within bourgeois modernity. Bibb uses his habit, fugitivity, to affirm an ideological and metaphysical attribute, free will, that is, under slavery's rule, off limits to the slave. Such use underscores an inescapable entanglement of habit with volition, and contests the culturally normative opposition between habit-forming and freely chosen practices, thereby showing the very concept of free will to be a tool of ideological power, delimitation, and control, rather than an abstract, absolute, and transcendent value.[51] Effectively, the secretive moves of fugitivity confound the plantation system while also troubling liberal ideals of freedom that, supposedly antithetical to slavery, require its existence for their meaning and materialization.

Not surprisingly, Bibb's traveling habit can exact from his owners resolutely material costs. As a habitual runaway, he threatens not just to disrupt with his potential escape the smooth working of a local economy, but to provide a contagious example—a source of knowledge—for slaves on neighboring plantations. And because he represents such a risk to potential buyers, as a commodity Bibb is difficult to keep in circulation: suspecting his fugitive tendencies, no slaveholder wants to chance his purchase. The challenge, then, for any owner wishing to sell Bibb is to hide the fact of habitual fugitivity requiring his sale in the first place—to bank, that is, on the commercially uncertain security of secrecy against the commercially volatile prospect of notoriety.[52]

Judging from Bibb's narrative, the success of such strategy is doubtful at best. As Kawash notes, "his notoriety as an incurable runaway serves him well" since, time and again, his owners struggle to sell him, a struggle having to do with the openness, the insufficient secrecy, of this tendency.[53] In hopes of correcting his fugitive habit, each time Bibb is recaptured his captors (sanctioned, as Bibb notes, by the law declaring that "'[a]ny slave, for rambling in the night, or riding horseback without leave, or running away, may be punished by whipping, cropping, and branding in the cheek, or otherwise, not rendering him unfit for labor'" [76]) bind him with chains and submit him to the lash. But, in its commercial effect, such discipline proves disastrous, since the material signs of chains and scars, composing the stark text of his habitually fugitive history, discourage potential owners from his purchase. Here what Hortense Spillers calls the "undecipherable markings on the captive body"—"lacerations, woundings, fissures, tears, scars, openings, ruptures, lesions, rendings, punctures of the flesh"—prove altogether too legible for slaveholding taste.[54] The disciplinary methods aimed at discouraging outlawed movement and so securing slaves as property work instead to vex the trade in flesh that American slavery, as a racist mode of socioeconomic circulation, requires.

As Bibb tells it, the slavecatchers who recapture him following his second attempt at escape try to circumvent this conundrum through a grotesque malformation of the "gentleman's agreement." Aiming to discourage Bibb from disclosing "that [he] had been a runaway," so as not to "lessen [his] value . . . in market," they present him with what amounts to a parody of verbal contract hinged on the paradox of object (chattel) made subject (trustworthy partner) (95). Free from chains, he is to be bound by his word: "the understanding between us was, I was not to be tied, chained, nor flogged; for if they should take me into the city handcuffed and guarded by five men the question might be asked what crime I had committed? And if it should be known that I had been a runaway to Canada, it would lessen the value of me at least one hundred dollars" (96). This sort of understanding will indicate the potential in slavery for a nearly capitalistic mercantilism. Such self-possession holds punitive significance: the show of docility or self-discipline, designed to induce purchase, to perpetuate enslavement, bears a perversely contractual obligation. Caught between the suspicion of criminality (when bound) and a specious freedom (when unbound), Bibb indicates in this passage the violence of subjection that, as Hartman argues, will attend the perilous humanization by whites of the enslaved. At stake in such an agreement, though, is a haunting recognition on the part of slavery's agents: the physically damaging methods of preventing Bibb's escape will impede his continued circulation as a commodity on the market. For if the habit of running away makes the fugitive conspicuous and notorious in absentia, from view as from labor, nevertheless the more conventional disciplinary tools of slavery (whips and chains) broadcast the fugitive tendencies they work to prevent. The dilemma for Bibb's captors is precisely that the need to restrict movement will advertise habitual fugitivity—and thereby impede commercial exchange. Again, we see an instance in which anxiety surrounding the proper terms and contents of public knowledge, and more specifically of the constitution of a public in witness to the signs of a slave's fugitive tendencies, troubles slavery's ideology and material procedure.

In Bibb's account, corporeality and intellection can likewise intimate fugitivity's open secret. Within slavery's economy, bodies are legible, disclosing through the signs of their suffering, their endurance, their strength, their racial constitution what amounts to their marketability.[55] Before one of his masters, the ironically named William Garrison, can sell Bibb at the New Orleans slave market, he must submit him for inspection "by a city officer, whose business it [is] to inspect slave property that was brought to that market for sale" (114). This official looks for whip-scars, examines the muscles, and checks teeth and skin for signs of age; yet, according to Bibb:

> the most rigorous examinations of the slaves by those slave inspectors, is on the mental capacity. If they are found to be very intelligent, this is pronounced the most objectionable of all other qualities connected with the life of a slave. In fact, it undermines the whole fabric of his chattelhood; it prepares for what slaveholders are pleased to pronounce the unpardonable sin when committed by a slave. It lays the foundation for running away, and going to Canada. They also see in it a love for freedom, patriotism, insurrection, bloodshed, and exterminating war against American slavery. (114)

What Bibb calls "the mental capacity," linking intellect to the fugitive habit, is one of the open secrets that as readers we already know intimately. The slave inspectors predict the difficulty of Bibb's sale: "After conversing with me, they have sworn by their Maker, that they would not have me among their negroes; and that they saw the devil in my eye; I would run away, &c" (114). Here conversation uncovers intelligence, which marks a devilish possession—rhetorical and ideological code for habitual fugitivity in the enslaved.

As the recurrence of such "discovery" renders Bibb's secret increasingly notorious at the scene of auction, Garrison has no choice but to send Bibb out to sell himself, a decision that, in its resolutely alienating attribution of self-possession to the slave, will again indicate the intimacy of slavery with capitalist practice. Made responsible for his own marketability, for his successful circulation as a commodity, Bibb labors under an obligation that will throw the status of mobility as a form of social contest into high relief. Daily over an unspecified number of weeks he tours New Orleans, during which time he hears the same complaints over and over again; "I was too white; . . . [potential owners] were afraid that I could read and write; and would never serve as a slave, but run away" (117). In the eyes of the slaveholding classes, a problem of pigment ("I was too white") marks the alarming prospect of that ontological conundrum, *intelligent property*, and, with it, systemically debilitating habits of fugitivity. Underscoring the mutability of racialized embodiment, here the legible signs of miscegenated physiognomy, of a body made in the crucible of slavery's American reproduction, disclose to the slaveholding eye a secret about the habitual propensity of that body to move, to fly, to transgress the material and ideological boundaries erected to prevent its travel.[56]

As the foregoing analysis will indicate, with respect to the question of fugitivity in Bibb's narrative I share the view advanced by Kawash in *Dislocating the Color Line:* "Bibb's narrative . . . is less about the ultimate condition of freedom with which it concludes than it is about the intermediate condition of escape."[57] Yet we need to attend with care to the material circumstances pressuring fugitivity as an intermediary practice, especially as these circumstances have in Bibb's case significantly to do with familial obligation and desire: what (as I have already noted) Helgar calls the "recursive pattern of escape and return" structuring the narrative corresponds pointedly to the fact that, although unwilling simply to abandon his enslaved wife and daughter, Bibb can never successfully manage to enable their escape alongside his. Thus, although evocative, Kawash's contention that for Bibb "the action of escape is driven by its own internal logic, . . . as an end in and of itself" would seem to overlook the material social relations complicating his fugitivity.[58] If, as I noted above in echo of Gilroy's pun, Bibb's illicit travel favors "routes" over "roots," still, judging from his account, the space of separation between these two is perilous at best. For Bibb, familial roots are indeed the ties that bind.

The implications are troubling, emerging from a tendency, within the narrative, to associate marriage and family with bondage. Conceivably this association may be historically and biographically particular, resulting from the distinct conditions governing the enslavement of Bibb, on the one hand, and of his wife Malinda, on the other, that prevent their mutual escape. Still, from early on in his narrative, Bibb pointedly contrasts escape and liberty with romance and bondage—the habit of "waiting on the girls" at once "perfectly congenial to [his] nature" and a distraction from the countervailing habit of "running away" (30). Hence his ongoing indignation at "[t]he circumstances of [his] courtship and marriage" (33):

> To think that after I had determined to carry out the great idea which is so universally and practically acknowledged among all the civilized nations of the earth, that I would be free or die, I suffered myself to be turned aside by the fascinating charms of a female, who gradually won my attention from an object so high as that of liberty; and an object which I held paramount to all others. (33)

Retrospective disbelief registers as much in the sentence's grammatical instability as in the infinitive with which it begins. Unsettlingly enough, Bibb relies here on the charge of seductiveness ("fascinating charms") prime among the mystifications employed by slave holders to veil their sexual abuse of female slaves.[59] Where for Frederick Douglass, as Kawash argues so incisively, marriage, in keeping with the liberal social contract, "marks the self-possession of the man through and in terms of the possession of a wife," for Bibb nearly the obverse seems true—yet nevertheless, and ironically, his association of marriage with an intensified bondage for the male slave turns on a set of gendered oppositions close to the heart of modern liberal theory.[60] The dynamics are complex: as Russ Castronovo observes, "[w]hen Bibb represents 'the society of young women' as a threat to freedom, he objects to society first and foremost; he resorts to misogyny only because woman—much more so than man—has a social body, which he conflates with the constraint of the South's domestic institution."[61] At stake is an understanding that, in Lora Romero's words, "divides the world into (on the one hand) a public and masculine sphere of abstract rights and (on the other hand) a private and feminine sphere of affective bonds," and that typically associates masculinity with motion and femininity with stasis, such that the freedoms entailed through fugitive practice are not only unavailable to but actively hindered by women.[62] We find, in this dimension of Bibb's text, a gap in its challenge to the antinomies structuring liberal versions of possession and self-possession, bondage and freedom, along with a reminder that, as Romero argues, "the color line is really a double line (the double line of color and gender)."[63]

Thus compromised by specific blindspots and contradictions within Bibb's narrative, any estimation of the contestatory significance of his fugitive practice tends as well to falter, at the level of textual production and circulation, before the generic and commercial strictures imposed by the slave narrative as an institutionalized form. For if, in Bibb's case, illicit travel and habitual escape disrupt not just slavery's routine but also its knowledge economy (those informational flows assisting in the maintenance of the plantation system), nevertheless the highly codified production and circulation of fugitivity as a narrative commodity in the literary marketplace will begin to intimate subtle constraints on its practice.[64]

For Kawash, the critical tendency (exemplified by James Olney and Robert Stepto, among others) to question the authenticity of Bibb's narrative is specious at best, illuminating much less about the text than about critical investment in "the priority of the autonomous, authentic subject, implicitly the classical subject of autobiography."[65] In the view of such critics, generic regularity confirms authorial veracity: since freedom from slavery will necessarily realize liberal self-possession, any account that ignores or refuses such transformation cannot be an authentic product of slave experience. In answer, Kawash works to "reinterpret Bibb's seeming authorial failure as a successful and strategic *refusal* of the centrality of the self-contained, authentic subject," contending that his "narrative challenges the priority or necessity of such a subject, and of the political and economic relations it presupposes, by refusing to equate freedom with becoming a subject."[66] The argument is a compelling one, yet notwithstanding its incisiveness it does not distinguish between Bibb's refusal of authentic subjectivity *within* his narrative and the imposition of authentic subjectivity *by* the genre as a marketable literary commodity. Precisely because, as Carla Kaplan reminds us, "literary conventions index social ideologies," the force of such generic imposition proves normative and disciplinary, bearing heavily on the terms of slave narrative circulation—on the politics of discursive alongside material mobility.[67]

What Kawash calls "the political and economic relations" presupposed by the liberal discourse of authentic subjectivity—relations reinscribed, I am suggesting, by the slave narrative as a commercial genre—underwrite the prefatory apparatus with which Bibb's account, like so many other slave narratives, begins, and also the critical evaluations from the periodical press with which it concludes. In the introduction, the New York minister Lucius Matlack marshals an array of testimonial writings to affirm the trustworthiness of Bibb's account and, accordingly, Bibb's entitlement "to public confidence and high esteem" (3). By excerpting, from the Detroit Liberty Society's report on its investigation of Bibb's veracity, letters from his former masters Silas Gatewood, W. H. Gatewood, and Daniel Lane alongside ones from the abolitionists Hiram Wilson, William Birney, W. Porter, and Ross Porter, Matlack employs a two-pronged strategy in which the affirming endorsements of prominent abolitionists and the specious charges of slaveholders together legitimate the narrative we have yet to read. Clearly such strategy aims to preempt critiques of the narrative, as of the larger abolitionist project it assisted, by inscribing the views of a credentialing authority while undermining representative spokesmen for slavery. As Heglar notes in the appendix to the Wisconsin edition of Bibb's narrative, Bibb "faced challenges to his credibility as a writer" since "his very eloquence undermined the notion that he had ever been a slave" (thus in a sense the signs of intelligence compromising his value at the auction block again cause trouble, even as they enhance the value of his autobiography as a commodity in the literary marketplace) (215). Yet if this problem suggests a pointed political necessity to the inclusion of the prefatory documents, nevertheless in reading them we struggle to separate political from commercial strategy—so much so that when, near the outset of his introduction, Matlack insists that "the narrative of the life of Henry Bibb . . . is equally distinguished as a revolting portrait of the hideous slave system, a thrilling narrative of individual suffering, and a triumphant vindication of the slave's manhood and mental dignity," the purpose of narrative composition and circulation seems less about the projects of political intervention than about the affects associated with readerly gratification.[68] To the extent that it can produce such affects, Bibb's eloquence proves key to the commercial viability and circulability of his narrative, linking the distinction of his account to the vindication of his manhood and mental dignity—to the authenticity, that is, of his subjectivity.

The issues at stake become still more problematic when we note that, in all likelihood, Bibb himself bore primary responsibility for soliciting and assembling testimonials to his veracity, a responsibility suggested by his February 1845 letter to the former slaveholder turned abolitionist James Birney, but effectively occluded through the authenticating signature of Lucius Matlack attached to the prefatory material in the 1849 *Narrative*. In the Birney letter, Bibb indicates his desire "to colect some facts to prove the reality of my Narative," a desire motivated in part by his previous encounter with Birney in which the latter "suposed that I was an imposter & was kind a neugh to tell me for my own good."[69] Whatever intentions motivated Bibb in writing this letter, its posture indicates the social constraints placed upon the escaped slave—bound by the benevolence of white discrimination, obliged "for [his] own good" to submit to the kindness (!) of white distrust to legitimate the terms of personal experience and thus any claim to personhood. Graphically demonstrating the forms of social abjection awaiting fugitives in the free North, the Birney letter exemplifies Hartman's analysis of the particular ways in which, for African Americans, subjectivity could reinforce subjection.

The "facts" collected by Bibb served to satisfy the Detroit Liberty Society of the truth of his oral account and, subsequently, to entice prospective readers of his written narrative. Thus, in a sense the prefatory apparatus published under the guiding hand of Lucius Matlack in 1849 only continues the process of abasement in service of liberty so evident in the Birney letter of 1845. The excerpt from the Liberty Society report included under Matlack's guidance describes how, in facing the committee, Bibb "was subjected to a rigorous examination" (3), a fact not just literally true but ideologically decisive, and a process in no way concluded but carried forward again and again through readerly consumption of the commodity *Life and Adventures of Henry Bibb, an American Slave*. By the very terms of the apparatus framing and legitimating his narrative, Bibb is constantly subject to the rigors of an examination determining the conditions under which his experience will circulate. So conceived, the procedures of narrative evaluation in the free literary marketplace begin to indicate their intimacy with the perils of the auction block, an intimacy chillingly suggested in the "wish," expressed in the excerpt from the *Liberator* review included at the end of Bibb's narrative, "that as many copies of [the book] might be sold during the present year, as there are slaves in the United States" (206). Risking what Joseph Roach calls "surrogation, the tendency to substitute one commodity for another by symbolic transfer," such desire will indicate the capacity, in even the most fervent opponents of slavery, to tighten the fetters of *racial* subordination.[70]

Travel's Wardrobe

Eleven years after Bibb's untimely death in Canada West, another author with cross-border allegiances produced a memoir comparably absorbed with the power of mobility for the investment—and the interrogation—of human subjectivity. Published in concert by W. S. Williams and Co. of Hartford, Jones Bros. and Co. of Philadelphia and Cincinnati, and J. A. Stoddard and Co. of Chicago in 1865, Sarah Edmonds's widely popular *Nurse and Spy in the Union Army* ("an instant best seller" eventually selling over 175,000 copies) recounts the compound service given by its author to the Union cause in the fight against southern secession.[71] In so doing it details the mobilities and dissimulations of an agent whose subjectivity depended in deeply complex ways on the links connecting the management of secret knowledge with the practice of covert travel. As such, it shares with Bibb's narrative a concern for the power of mobility as a social resource and for the significance of knowledge to mobility's material operation. Making inextricable surveillance from secret travel, spying is to Edmonds much as fugitivity is to Bibb: an art and a calling, but also (although to a lesser extent) habitual and habit-forming. And, as with fugitivity for Bibb, for Edmonds spying cannot occur without dissimulation.

Such similarities, however, do not constitute the only source of resonance between the two texts. Although Edmonds does not say so explicitly, her account likewise issues from and writes against an association of family ties with bondage. As Elizabeth Young indicates, Edmonds tended in interviews following the success of her book to refer to her early childhood as a period of enslavement to a tyrannical father, and to describe her discovery of cross-dressing (through reading *Fanny Campbell, the Female Pirate Captain*, an 1844 novel about a cross-dressing heroine in the revolutionary war) as the means to her emancipation.[72] Thus where Bibb explicitly counterposes freedom to family in his narrative, Edmonds reveals only in retrospect the comparable dynamics that invest her account, dynamics in which dissimulation enables escape from familial bondage.

If the constraints of family constitute a latent secret in *Nurse and Spy*, nevertheless we must recognize the openness of that secret's larger social significance. The equation by a white woman of the patriarchal family with a form of enslavement was, of course, a well-publicized practice by 1865, contentious common knowledge for any audience reading Edmonds's memoir. For many feminist abolitionists in the antebellum era, the family constituted its own "peculiar institution," the critique of which held to an analogy drawn between women's subjection in family life and the subjection of the enslaved on the plantation. As Karen Sánchez-Eppler takes care to emphasize, however, "[a]lthough the identifications of woman and slave, marriage and slavery, . . . may occasionally prove mutually empowering, such pairings generally tend toward asymmetry and exploitation. . . . The bound and silent figure of the slave represents the woman's oppression and so grants the white woman access to political discourse denied the slave, exemplifying the way in which slave labor produces—both literally and metaphorically—even the most basic of freedom's privileges."[73]

I take this vexing problematic to underpin Edmonds's autobiographical anecdote about familial enslavement and, particularly in view of her repeated disguise as a contraband slave, to haunt the memoir she writes about cross-dressed espionage in the Civil War. The prospect of such haunting will enrich yet complicate our understanding of another secret withheld by the text: namely, that, as Young points out, Edmonds can enter the Union army only by masquerading as a white man, one "Franklin Thompson."[74] Although periodic hints in *Nurse and Spy* at Edmonds's military costume leave this secret less secret than Young suggests, nevertheless her conclusion, that the "memoir as it stands is thus a form of textual counterfeit, as much a disguise for its protagonist as the inks, wigs, and accents Edmonds adopts within her story," is richly provocative.[75] Even so, I would want to shift the weight of argumentative emphasis: the full significance of such counterfeiting really only registers when read against the ongoing social currency, after midcentury, of the fraught discourse ("the inks, wigs, and accents") linking white woman with slave, an association predicated on both the regulatory recognition and the liberatory potential that impersonation affords. If, as Young contends, "[c]ross-dressing is at once theme and technique in *Nurse and Spy*," such compound valence will mark, in turn, drag's status as an ideological relation rooted in the convolutions of race and gender.[76]

Nurse and Spy is what William Stowe, following Bakhtin, calls a heteroglossic narrative, one that serves as a "meeting place for various voices, literary styles, levels of speech, and kinds of subject."[77] For Edmonds, the force of narrative has less to do with the authority or singularity of its account than with the malleability of its utterance and address; polyvocality thus underscores and extends the manipulation of racial, national, and engendered subjectivity continually emphasized within the action of her book. Its tremendous success in the literary marketplace certainly suggests that, for postbellum readers, the promise of titillating secrets—of illicit knowledge—more than repaid their material cost, a lesson confirmed again and again by events in the memoir itself.

Advertising masquerade as a source of interest yet also of anxiety, the "publishers' notice" launching Edmonds's narrative makes the malleability of gender an issue of substantial commercial concern. After first dismissing the need to apologize "for adding one more to the numerous 'War Books' which already fill a large space in American Literature," on the grounds that such accounts respond to a nearly insatiable interest in "the general reader," and then briefly outlining Edmonds's exploits as nurse and spy, the publishers hasten to quell in advance any readerly discomfort at the prospect of cross-dressing: "Should any of her readers object to some of her disguises, it may be sufficient to remind them it was from the purest motives and most praiseworthy patriotism, that she laid aside, for a time, her own costume, and assumed that of the opposite sex, enduring hardships, suffering untold privations, and hazarding her life for her adopted country, in its trying hour of need."[78] This reminder works to constitute Edmonds's public, her readership, affectively—on the patriotic ground of national identification over any anxiety provoked by cross-dressing. Dubious sartorial practice here confirms not indecency but instead patriotic devotion. Where by implication proper "costume" expresses true gender, the sacrifice of such truth through drag's dissimulations will serve the larger interests of the nation-state.[79] "Patriotism" (national affection) can glorify gender betrayal. All the more ironic, then, that, in passing for "Franklin Thompson" at the time of her enlistment, Edmonds is already a *national* impostor, an expatriate Canadian enamored with the Federalist cause of her "adopted country." Young contends, in fact, that Edmonds's fuller biography will suggest that patriotism serves at best as a cover for her investment in adventure and social transgression.[80] The lineaments of drag thus complicate even as they consolidate the affect proper to the national subject.

As it continues, the "publishers' notice" endeavors to capitalize on the understanding that women nurse by nature—a view that, serving on the battlefield to facilitate the secret practice of women spying, helps in the literary marketplace to manage the scandal of drag:

> In the opinion of many, it is the privilege of woman to minister to the sick and soothe the sorrowing—and in the present crisis of our country's history, to aid our brothers to the extent of her capacity—and whether duty leads her to the couch of luxury, the abode of poverty, the crowded hospital, or the terrible battle field—it makes but little difference what costume she assumes while in the discharge of her duties.—Perhaps she should have the privilege of choosing for herself whatever may be the surest protection from insult and inconvenience in her blessed, self-sacrificing work. (6)

The double emphasis on "privilege" (by nature to nurse, by culture to cross-dress) binds gender to labor so as, I would argue, at once to diminish and to increase the scandalousness of the prior hints at drag. Thus the claim that "it makes but little difference what costume she assumes while in the discharge of her duties" is flatly disingenuous, since of course such details make all the difference in a text designed to sell on the basis of its titillating, sensational disclosures. Accordingly, the suggestion guiding the last sentence, "[p]erhaps she should have the privilege of choosing for herself," serves less to defend a principle of female autonomy than to circulate (within the constraints of blessed self-sacrifice) the largely specious yet commercially enticing "privilege" of female fashion choice. Viewed in this way, the "publishers' notice" serves as a discursive dissimulation, miming sober vindication in the interests of the open secret of market sales.

As significant to the textual precis offered by the "publishers's notice," particularly in light of the narrative we come to read, is what in Edmonds's dissimulative practice is *not* cause for concern. Anticipating, and aiming to forestall, readerly objection to male impersonation, the publishers stay silent about racial masquerade. All risks of outrage evidently fall elsewhere: blacking up is, by implication, among the most unremarkably natural practices in the world. The omission may well lead us to conclude that, for Edmonds's publishers as for her readership, the trappings of blackness effectively constitute a part of the proper costume still available to a white woman in the 1860s; they remain, that is, "her own." Here the open secret of racialized crossing and the common knowledge of minstrel practice collude, their interimplication widely available (and deeply enticing) for purposes of commercial circulation.

Absent from the "publishers' notice," racialized masquerade looms large in the memoir itself. And its indispensability to Edmonds the spy will begin to indicate the fraught significance, for national security, of a strategic elasticity in social being. At issue is the meaning of miscegenation, in the broadest sense of the term.[81] On her first three missions, Edmonds assumes some of the most overdetermined signs of abjected identity in midcentury America—male contraband, Irish peddler woman, female contraband—to capitalize on the neglected anonymity attending social debasement. Precisely because such figures lack any social power, they enable the spy's easy insinuation into the circuits of informational secrecy.

Yet as Edmonds's first mission, in particular, will indicate, determinations of the skin can threaten as well as assist the manipulation of social being. Disguised as a male contraband, she proves unrecognizable in the union camp—but, across enemy lines, to pass as a slave she must toil with the slaves, with the result that her hands blister "from wrists to finger ends" (113). Literally materializing patriotic sacrifice, the peeling away of skin from flesh puts patriotic service in jeopardy (since the test of enslavement and, with it, the success of this espionage remain functionally manual). The impermanence of pigment only compounds the problem: where, during her mission, her whiteness threatens to show through a rapidly fading blackface, upon her return she cannot remove the dye entirely and, with her complexion "a nice maroon color," is not recognized by the general to whom she reports, so must chalk her face in order successfully to convey the information she has retrieved.[82] In a sense, the act of chalking gives a way to understand as untrustworthy not just the markers of disguise but the signs of race, whether white or black: whiteness seems less a stable ground than a tenuous, enacted application, a performative standard against which a culture can measure its racialized fears and desires. Seen in this way, the instability entailed by racial dissimulation complicates those modes of knowing through which the social order comes to imagine itself and its others. Yet I would stress that the larger significance is not obviously liberatory: despite its ironies the episode serves to affirm that the worth of knowledge always depends on the whiteness of skin.

Positioned in the narrative's action between Edmonds's two contraband disguises, her impersonation of an Irish peddler woman holds a more convoluted but no less telling significance for the enacted analogy between white woman and slave. Although necessarily informed by the common nineteenth-century understanding of the Irish as black—such that, as Young observes, "Irishness functions as a form of costume congruent with blackness"—the significance in question has more particularly to do with conditions of material practice: Edmonds's Irish peddler gets "blackened" by what she *does*.[83] Having "abandon[ed] the African relation" for "that of the Hibernian"—an abandonment that, to reiterate, is for midcentury common sense no departure at all—Edmonds finds herself caught at the outset of her mission without knowledge of the roads or the distance to the enemy lines, and so required to "spend the first night in the swamp, as the only safe retreat" (148). Here the concealment endured to ensure the safety of the spy cannot but recall the overdetermined scene of slave escape. Foregoing, this time, the actual trappings of the contraband, as a result of her movements Edmonds the peddler finds herself effectively contraband once more. The "'dismal swamp'" (149) brings on fever, but also feverish contemplation:

> I took great interest in carefully tracing each link in the chain of circumstances which had brought me to the spot wheron I now lay, deserted and alone, in that notorious Chickahominy swamp. And ere I was aware of it, I was sighing over a few episodes in my past history—and mentally saying, well, only for this intense love of adventure, such and such things "might have been," and I should now be rejoicing in the honorable title of ———, instead of "wasting my sweetness on the desert air," in the wilderness of the Peninsula. (150)

The passage is perhaps the closest Edmonds comes to addressing the autobiographical trace of familial enslavement that, as I have suggested, haunts her memoir; what she calls "love of adventure" works, in preventing her exchange in marriage, to prompt her flight from the familial institution, and, through "the chain of circumstances," leads to her hiding, fugitive-like, in the dismal swamp—a situation, at least as represented, fraught with tension, ambivalence, and longing.

All the same, for Edmonds the results and rewards of espionage more than offset its material and emotional demands. As she observes after blistering her hands on the first mission, "[n]otwithstanding the hardships of the day I had had my eyes and ears open, and had gained more than would counterbalance the day's work" (113). This claim literalizes the information economy, making knowledge labor's recompense. At stake is not just the strategic value of specific information but the power of information control: where the nurse enjoys the privilege to attend the wounded, the spy enjoys the privilege to modulate inside information with common knowledge.

Hence Edmonds's pointed concern with the "numberless papers and hundreds of correspondents in the loyal [Union] army": "Freedom of opinion and the press is certainly a precious boon, but when it endangers the lives of our soldiers and frustrates the plans of our Government, surely it is time to adopt measures to control it, just as much as it is necessary to arrest the spies who come within our lines" (333, 334). At issue in this caution is precisely the way the wide circulation of knowledge jeopardizes, by broadcasting, the movements of military men. Edmonds's investments may well be genuinely patriotic, but they remain acutely self-interested: what Young rightly calls "the extraordinary mobility possible for white women within the context of wartime espionage" clearly requires for its continuance the careful regulation of information's currency and flow.[84] Promiscuous transmission threatens the knowledge economy enabling Edmond's traveling practice.

This contention brings me back to consider the conditions under which Edmonds's espionage can take place, and the kinds of knowledge, both common and secret, those conditions make possible. The "extraordinary mobility" espionage affords is, in a sense, nothing less than the mobility it requires. In the early missions these requirements concern labor (so that, for instance, the itinerancy of the peddler serves as necessary cover for the worker in the information economy), but by the end the terms have shifted from labor to leisure: dressed in "citizen's clothes" so as to impersonate a foreigner, on her last spy mission Edmonds makes touristic travel—the search for manners and customs of the wartime South—her cover for espionage. Particularly as this final mission finds her spying, "inside of [Union] lines," on pro-rebel agents in Kentucky, it only underscores the extent to which espionage, as a practice linking surreptitious movement with the regulation of knowledge, elicits (and, moreover, demands) the convolution of foreignness and familiarity.

Although strategic, such convolution involves real risks—since its example is socially volatile, and since, once ventured, it becomes so hard to check.[85] Hence the significance of moments in the text that emphasize more measured differences in social being. Such moments, I would argue, are strategic in their way: delimiting access to social mobility, they serve to regulate its distribution and so protect its distinction, in much the way that spying works to manage the flow and value of knowledge.

Significantly, the work of such differentiation becomes most efficient and effective when Edmonds takes a break from spying to go on leave. Traveling to Washington under cover of a tourist's anonymity, she suspends the search for secrets and commits instead to the broadcast of common knowledge about the terms of social difference in midcentury America. The sense of diversion and posture of detachment characterizing her reflections will help to measure the forms of social power at stake. The disinterested discriminations hegemonically proper to the leisured traveler constitute, as they occlude, discriminatory interest. This narrative dynamic emerges most decisively in Edmonds's account of her vacationing visit to a contraband camp in the national capital. Her time there, she remarks, is "amusing and instructive" (240), a characterization that will render education and entertainment co-constitutive:

> Here were specimens of all grades of the negro character, from the genuine pious, cheerful trusting christian, to the saucy, lazy, degraded creature, which generations of slavery has made almost on a level with the beasts of the field. But all of them kind-hearted, merry-tempered, and quick to feel and accept the least token of kindness. Their cheerfulness is proverbial; old women, with wool white with age, bent over the wash-tub, grinned and gossiped in the most cheerful manner—girls romped with their dusky sweethearts, and mothers tossed their babies with that tender pride and mother-love which beautifies the blackest and homeliest face. All were happy, because they were free—and there seemed to be no room for anything like gloom or despondency in their hearts. Men, women, and children sang, whistled and laughed together—and whether their songs were of heaven, or of hoe-cakes, they were equally inspiring. (240–41)

Recalling Edmonds's observation earlier in the same chapter that, in Washington, "everything is regulated according to caste" (238), the categorizing imperative in this passage indicates the quite fine differentiations enabled by gross bias. Here taxonomy presumes the familiarity, as it perpetuates the circulation, of racist stereotypes; rhetorically, the force of "proverbial" knowledge allows white readers the curious privilege of learning from lessons that, by dint of acculturation, they always already know (a logic that can help to explain why Edmonds herself enjoys instruction in the racialized types she has already proved so adept at impersonating). Not surprisingly, given the sustaining cultural force of sentimental discourse at midcentury, Edmonds endeavors to elicit white sympathy by emphasizing the black capacity to feel (whether kindness, merriment, gratitude, cheer, desire, or mother-love). These affects are "universal," such that the common sense of racial difference takes shape in the intimate familiarities white folks deign to grant their others. Graphically demonstrating the perilous bonds of liberty confronting freed slaves—what Hartman calls "the forms of violence and domination enabled by the recognition of humanity, licensed by the invocation of rights, and justified on the grounds of liberty and freedom"—the process makes the foreign familiar in order to *fix* differences in social being along with their attendant asymmetries of power.[86]

If this episode purports to edify Edmonds and, through her, her readers, an earlier account of contraband life, reproduced by Edmonds from her journal, emphasizes instead the potential for contraband instruction. According to Edmonds, the contrabands "'are exceedingly ignorant, yet there is one subject upon which they can converse freely and intelligibly, and that is—Christ—the way of salvation. Almost all with whom I conversed to-day were praying men and women. Oh, how I should like to teach these people! They seem so anxious for instruction, I know they would learn quickly'" (73).[87] The pedagogic relation that serves here to structure authorial fantasy underscores, once more, the link between knowledge and social mobility: quick learning will clear the fast track to subjection in liberty. And Edmonds's apostrophic exclamation only underscores the will to *conversion* suffusing every dimension of the narrative as a whole. An ideological project serving religious and nationalistic ends, conversion provides the educative analogue to the convertability of social self that espionage, with its use of masquerade, deploys in the struggle to command enemy secrets. Both make the acquisition and deployment of inside information the means to power.

Surfacing repeatedly as the purpose guiding all action in *Nurse and Spy*, the drama of conversion is perhaps most striking in a set piece near the narrative's close. The passage recounts Edmonds's electrifying encounter with "a poor old, blind, palsied slave" on board a Mississippi steamer (339). The episode epitomizes conversion's dynamic:

> Reader, has your heart ever been taken by storm, in consequence of the mere intonations of a voice—ere you beheld the individual who gave them utterance? On this occasion, I turned and saw "one of God's images cut in ebony." Time had wrinkled his face, and the frosts of four-score winters had whitened his woolly locks, palsied his limbs, and dimmed his vision. He had been a slave all his life, and now, at the eleventh hour... he was liberated from bondage, and was rejoicing in freedom from slavery, and in that freedom wherewith Christ makes His children free.
>
> By some invisible attraction, a large crowd gathered around this old, decrepit slave, and every eye was upon his sable withered face, as he gave a brief and touching history of his slave life.
>
> When he had finished, the soldiers eagerly began to ask questions—but suddenly the old colored man turned querist, and raising himself up, and leaning forward toward the crowd, he asked, in a voice strangely thrilling and solemn, "Are any of you soldiers of the Lord Jesus Christ?" (338)

I understand this scene to depend for its force on a kind of Uncle Tom effect, the touching spectacle of a slave abject in body yet transcendent in spirit. At the same time, and even more disturbingly, it recalls the Black Guinea episode in *The Confidence-Man*, in which the attraction of a suffering yet serene blackness brings an audience, a public, to life. Given such complex resonance, any meaning we extract will depend for its force on the prior success of mass mediation; the captivating authenticity of the old slave signifies nothing less than the pervasive circulation and continued circulability—the full saturation in public discourse—of the type he so evidently represents. The "invisible attraction" of his type, in other words, bespeaks its ubiquity in traveling the networks of culture. At stake is the value of stasis to mobility's political control: the fixed familiarity of discriminatory typology enables its ready and extended circulation.[88]

For Edmonds, I would argue, the advantages of deploying such stasis are decisive: the traffic in racialized types brings capital rewards while, at the same time, helping to consolidate a quite privileged access to real and social mobility. In the broadest sense, her narrative's open secret is that so much of its inside information trades in commodified forms of common knowledge drawn straight from the repertoires of a racist culture. The problems and possibilities of movement key to *Nurse and Spy* and bound up with its knowledge economy require both literal and more broadly conceptual impersonations of the enslaved—impersonations legible, I would stress, to the extent that their objects of imitation remain discursively and socially fixed, immobile. Thus the text is not just a discursive counterfeit; it marks as well a grim contraband, thieving mobility at the expense of those it would claim to help set free.

Fugitive Careers, Fugitive Commodities

On the same Washington trip in which Edmonds finds amusement and instruction in the contraband camp, she has another encounter—this one occurring at the ubiquitous scene of touristic enjoyment, the museum—that shows, less predictably, the potential of the flesh for treachery. "Wrapped in reverence," she contemplates a painting of George Washington, when a friend draws her attention "to two paintings which I had not noticed before . . . represent[ing] the surrender of Lord Cornwallis and General Burgoyne" during the Revolutionary War (239). The effect is electric: "I felt a warm current of blood rush to my face, as I contemplated the humiliating scene—the spirit of Johnny Bull triumphed over my Yankee predilections—

and I left the building with feelings of humiliation and disgust" (239). Edmonds's blush marks bodily betrayal by native essence. Involuntary and automatic, the rush of blood to cheek limns the heat of paradox no less than the shame of national pride. Otherwise so adept at impersonation, suddenly Edmonds, born in British New Brunswick, can no longer pass for an American, as the red glow of natal bloodline shows through the cover of political commitment. Where the spy uses surreptitious travel to gain precious intelligence, the tourist through her rambling gives intimate secrets away.

In part, perhaps, to redress her shame, upon returning from vacation Edmonds resumes her masquerades and, on the eve of Antietam, secures important information while disguised as a female contraband. She is far from the only one in the Union Army invested, at this moment, in complexities of wardrobe; some ten months later, one of her compatriots writes from Beaufort, South Carolina, to friends in Boston, outlining a concern over clothes. "Last fall," notes Harriet Tubman in a letter dated 30 June 1863,

> when the people here became very much alarmed for fear of an invasion from the rebels, all my clothes were packed and sent with others to Hilton Head, and lost; and I have never been able to get any trace of them since. I was sick at the time, and unable to look after them myself. I want, among the rest, a *bloomer* dress, made of some coarse, strong material, to wear on *expeditions*. In our late expedition up the Combahee river, in coming on board the boat, I was carrying *two pigs* for a sick woman, who had a child to carry, and the order "double quick" was given, and I started to run, stepped on my dress, it being rather long, and fell and tore it almost off, so that when I got on board the boat there was hardly anything left of it but shreds. I made up my mind then, I would never wear a long dress on another expedition of the kind, but would have a *bloomer* as soon as I could get it. So please make this known to the ladies, if you will, for I expect to have use for it soon, probably before they can get it to me.[89]

This passage makes graphic not just the value of dress for military expedition but more pointedly the utter insufficiency of women's "proper" clothes to its conduct. The anecdote intimates the exigencies attending a much more mundane kind of exposure—and, in so doing, anticipates to resonant effect Tubman's subsequent characterization of the contrabands for whom she cares at the Beaufort hospital: "Most of them coming from the mainland are very destitute, almost naked" (perhaps—to risk a grim joke—because the spies have claimed their clothes).[90] By emphasizing the loss of clothing and intimating the price of nakedness, Tubman's letter necessarily puts the material cost of impersonation in new light. And her insistence on "bloomers" only compounds this effect: subject, as the editors of *The Black Abolitionist Papers* note, to "widespread criticism and ridicule," such costume served in the period "as a badge of [feminist] radicalism."[91] Turning on this open secret, Tubman's request to her Boston friends links the promise of improved mobility—as, more obliquely, of social power—not to sartorial dissimulation, but instead to sartorial display.

As a figure, Tubman, with Sojourner Truth "one of the two most famous nineteenth-century black women," according to Nell Irvin Painter, brings into sharp focus the complex of issues at stake in this chapter.[92] After escaping from bondage in 1848, Tubman committed herself tirelessly to the fight against slavery, and to the achievement of racial and sexual equality in America—first, and most famously, as a conductor on the underground railroad, then as a nurse and spy in the Union army. The power of mobility as a resource in the material contest over knowledge was thus crucial to her activist practice in ways that complement the case of Henry Bibb and complicate the case of Sarah Edmonds. Yet, in the years following her wartime service, Tubman was constantly threatened with material want, so much so that twice she collaborated in the production of an account of her life in order to raise money for personal and communal sustenance. Both written by Sarah Bradford, a white teacher of devout religious conviction and evident antislavery dedication, these two narratives—*Scenes in the Life of Harriet Tubman*, published in 1869, and *Harriet Tubman, the Moses of Her People*, published in 1886—indicate the force of Tubman's political commitment to the elimination of slavery, and underscore the importance of secret travel to the practice of such work. Yet both are fraught with difficulties, precisely because, as Jean Humez observes, such "highly mediated text[s]" raise "daunting suspicion and resistance, especially for modern readers sensitive to racial power dynamics."[93] In detailing the often thrilling details of Tubman's life in regularly censorious and racist language for the purpose of commercial purchase, the two accounts raise exactly the problems I have emphasized in my analyses of Bibb and Edmonds: commodifying the details of African American suffering and perseverance for purposes of circulation in the literary marketplace, the narratives reckon the material price of Tubman's freedom through a continuing commercial subjection. The latter account makes the problem acute; concluding its appendix of testimonials to the authenticity of its subject with a collation of the passes she procured to facilitate her movements during the war, it deploys a record of the state sanction of black mobility to induce credence in the truth, and the commercial desirability, of its narrative. The archive of passes effectively determines the terms of subsequent motion—such that the capacity to move in the postbellum social moment requires that Tubman stay fixed in the past. Read this way the narrative of 1886 will only underscore, nine years into the viciously racist sociality of a post-Reconstruction America, the curious commercial viability and, with it, the conflicted, volatile significance that fugitive stories could sustain.[94]

4
Mobility's Disciplines

> Certainly we are moving faster than before. Or, more correctly, we are being moved faster.
>
> —*Henry Ford,* Today and Tomorrow

In 1905, a cinematic attraction called Hale's Tours debuted to great acclaim at K. C.'s Electric Park in Kansas City; during the next half decade, it took the U.S. amusement industry by storm.[1] "Designed like a railroad car, complete with conductor and simulated sways and jolts, clickety-clack and brake sounds, this theater projected scenic views taken from a moving train."[2] Marshaling the hypnotic bond between travel and cinema,[3] Hale's Tours traded in redundancy by making rail, the principal motor of system and industry since the middle of the nineteenth century, what it already was: a method of commodification realized between motion and stasis, mediation and immediacy. Celluloid mimicked the materialities of modern travel so as to supplement while capitalizing on its practice. Such is one way for capitalism to keep its subjects in their proper place: spending money to remain stock still, transfixed by recorded movement. In the case of Hale's Tours kinesthesis was key, holding viewers in thrall not only with a simulation of travel, an illusion of motion through space, but indeed with the very fact of motion from reel to reel.[4]

Such enthralled fascination helps to suspend and at the same time to make profitable the manifest unpredictabilities that, at the turn of the nineteenth century, attend travel's prevailing modes, methods, and effects. In so doing, it exemplifies the operation of a concept I want to call "disciplinary pace." As evident in the ensuing discussions, to the extent that this concept serves to explicate regimental, mechanistic forms of subjectivity circa 1900, it will complement Mark Seltzer's influential account of "disciplinary individualism," a key object and outcome of what he terms the body/machine complex.[5] But where Seltzer attends to the work of individuation, my emphasis falls instead on mediatory movements—on the material and ideological relations at issue in struggles over physical and social mobility at the turn of the nineteenth century. In its characteristic deployments, disciplinary pace marshals the technologics of motion control to achieve a productive *regulation* of velocity that, in anticipating (or, indeed, in establishing the conditions of possibility for) the Fordist spectacle of "faster and faster," a spectacle reliant upon the strategic potential of *inertia* at the core of modern speed, aims to make bodies in motion the objects, not agents, of their velocity. We can imagine the work of such regulation with reference to the customers who, in taking Hale's Tour, enjoyed the paradoxical thrill of sitting still at locomotive speed. Thus the commodified spectacle of high velocity institutes a political economy of stasis; instantaneity, the thrilling prospect of "faster and faster," enjoys only halting distinction from immobility. At stake, I contend, is a desire to manage unpredictable, even insurgent, bodies. Held to the *standard* of speed, they can only race in place.[6]

Evidently the widespread institution of forms of technology rich with disciplinary potential in the last decades of the nineteenth century supplied the means through which to materialize disciplinary pace and figure its effects—in response, precisely, to problems occasioned in large part by these same technological forms. Thus the regulation of velocity, social as well as physical, constitutes a particularized solution to an historically concentrated problem: in helping to manage the volatile, promiscuous intimacies (among social classes as among races, genders, and ethnicities) necessarily entailed by everyday exchange in a fully technologized, newly mass-mediated society, what I call disciplinary pace promised to restore some measure of cultural propriety and social control by recalibrating social relations among persons through their movements. In this quite specific sense, the instantiation of disciplinary pace worked, at the century's turn, to rearticulate the material and social conditions of mobility by suspending or transforming unpredictable and threatening kinds of movement.

I would stress, though, that instantiations of disciplinary pace signal not simply an increase, around 1900, in regulatory social and cultural practices but also (and perhaps more importantly) the unsettling power of movement in this period. The new terms of mobility, evinced most strikingly in the transnational extension and growing ubiquity of train travel, offered unprecedented opportunity to unprecedented numbers to unpredictable effect. As Lynne Kirby observes with respect to rail, "[t]he instability of the railroad... lies [not least] in bringing together for a brief period individuals from all walks of life, while dynamizing and hence destabilizing relations among them."[7] And if, as Catherine Cocks demonstrates, postbellum changes in the railway system (especially the introduction of extra-fare service) served to reinforce material barriers against such instability, nevertheless we must recognize, in the very fact of such innovations, the working out of pervasive, intractable anxieties.[8] Thus, social potential constitutes social threat: the triumph of rail, relentlessly putting persons and things into motion, signals its own greatest danger. The very terms of network power—to annihilate time and space in achieving ceaseless social and material circulation—figure forth the signs of systemic vulnerability.

The great strikes of the last decades of the nineteenth century can begin to make manifest the constitutive contradiction here. Occurring when the "control revolution" seemed fully hegemonic in modern industrial life, these upheavals indicated the alarming possibility of another kind of revolution exploding from within the networked industrial system. That striking workers in the postbellum period typically began by targeting the railway network points at once to the concentration of labor in this industry, to the brutality of its increasing monopolization, and to the widespread recognition of its value—and its vulnerability. Viewed in retrospect, the strikes of 1877, of 1886, and of 1894 all dramatize the enormous significance, as precarious as decisive, of motion for nation in the U.S. context, such that the disruption of transport could bring national business, at least for a time, to a halt. Hence the significance of disciplinary pace: where the great strikes mobilized immobility (the unexpected *seizure* of system) as a method of political resistance, attractions such as Hale's Tours managed, in an attenuated compensation, to commodify frozen motion, rendering it fully profitable. Yet if, in one sense, disciplinary pace must thus be understood as a strategy deployed from within the cultural field to manage social crisis by converting it to capital, in another sense, as I will argue, disciplinary pace demonstrates its inadequacy to that project, unable, even when making regulatory seizure constitutive of system itself, to avoid putting into circulation traces of the sort of crisis it would contain.[9]

I shall locate the signs of disciplinary pace across a range of quite disparate materials—etiquette manuals from the last decades of the nineteenth century and the first decade of the twentieth, Stephen Crane's 1895 Mexican travel dispatches, Jack London's tramp writings around 1900 and his 1909 autobiographical novel, *Martin Eden*. The differences in genre, composition, and discursive address belie a shared investment in the articulation and dissemination of manners and customs, and a shared concern over problems in social and cultural pedagogy. In distinct ways, but to provocatively comparable ends, these materials take up entanglements of touristic travel, colonialism, and social mobility—precisely to worry over the contingency and accidentalism of human movement under capitalism at the turn of the nineteenth century.

Conduct, Custom, and the Stasis Effect

As I argued in the introduction, the 1893 World's Columbian Exposition, a touristic destination of global significance at the end of the nineteenth century, undertook to commemorate the anniversary of American "discovery" not least by celebrating the power and potential of mobility in the present. Hence its emphasis, in elaborating a nationalist and imperialist pedagogy, more particularly on educing properly mobile subjects—on instituting, in service of cultural propriety and social control, new terms for the proper relations of bodies to one another through their movements in an era of persistently unpredictable physical and social mobility. Yet, I would suggest, the evident urgency of such lessons within the fair's pedagogical project indicates how problems of conduct could supplement the coming ubiquity and widespread extension of human traffic and transit. Not surprisingly, such problems in the conduct of new forms of mobility at the turn of the nineteenth century supplied a key focus not just for the grand spectacles of public culture but also for more routinized, everyday pedagogies found, among other places, in the discourse on manners and etiquette ("maddeningly porous rules of behavior anxiously followed by 'good society' when coerced into contact with indecorous natures," in Martha Banta's wonderful phrasing).[10] What *is* surprising is the extent to which this discourse took up interrelated issues of conduct and mobility in language rich with traces of disciplinary pace.

Aiming to bring behavior up to speed with newfound material wealth and social status yet at the same time to regulate with care movements along the social circuit, the discourse on manners tends to deploy stasis effects of its own. Handbooks on proper behavior produced at the end of the nineteenth century typically seek to indoctrinate readers through tabulations of mannerly behavior, an effort displayed most spectacularly in Florence Howe Hall's 1902 *The Correct Thing in Good Society*, where the book's very organization, with left pages headed "It is the correct thing" and right pages headed "It is not the correct thing," suggests itself as a digital system, the "1 or 0" of manners.[11] Through such tabulations, the authors of these books and the industry that produces them undertake to render orthodox manners—specific, particular custom envisioned as general, universal custom—not just natural but, in keeping with the function of disciplinary pace, more nearly automatic.

Instancing the decisively technologizing dimensions of social unpredictability in the late-nineteenth century moment, the discourse on manners often intimates an uneasy sense of the mechanistic constitution of U.S. social life. "Society is like a great machine," writes Julia Dewey in 1899, a machine "that will not work smoothly until every wheel and cog is fitted to its place. Therefore it is best that there should be a code of social laws well understood and rather carefully adhered to."[12] The trope here typifies the period's concern with the intrication of bodies and machines, just as, more particularly, it indicates an anxiety about the proper relations between the constituent parts of this "great machine," relations best calibrated through "social laws" isomorphic to the physical ones that explain the workings of a real machine. By emphasizing the fittedness (and arguably the fitness) of individual placement within this social mechanism, Dewey's comparison works not so much to naturalize as to technologize the common sense of social stratification. In so doing, it directs our attention more particularly to mobility as an issue, rendering *social position*, the place of "every wheel and cog," inextricable from *social motion*, the smooth working of all parts within the social whole.[13]

By implication, of course, such smoothness is precisely what turn-of-the-century America fails consistently to provide; otherwise, the discourse on manners would be superfluous. In promising to teach "a code of social laws" that will help social subjects work smoothly by learning their proper places alongside their compatriots' (and, for that matter, their *others'*), Dewey tacitly imagines the society she inhabits grinding its gears to unsettling effect. So conceived, this "great machine" remains in development, its parts or population still indeterminate in character and unpredictable in action. At issue are not least the felt disruptions to American society from increased industrialization, immigration, urbanization, and massification in the closing decades of the nineteenth century. Such processes determine, yet are likewise determined by, the new social subjectivities they help to produce—a dynamic that, although necessary to the operation of real factory machines as to the consolidation of material and ideological power through their ownership, still manages to generate the sort of anxiety so palpable within Dewey's interest in "social laws." (And, of course, the anxiety latent in Dewey's handbook is the anxiety on which, socially and commercially, it capitalizes.)

In articulating the terms of a code through which to regulate the workings of the American social machine, the discourse on manners can be said to function as the everyday counterpart to travel writing and ethnography, complementing the emphasis in those genres on what Mary Louise Pratt calls "manners-and-customs description" of foreign cultures by rehearsing for Americans what are claimed to be their *own* manners and customs, so as to prevent any dilution or contamination of them—a project that, in standardizing etiquette, obviously aims to make hegemonic the behaviors of a specific class fraction.[14] The terms of such enterprise begin to come clear in the argument made by Margaret Sangster at the start of her 1904 handbook, *Good Manners for All Occasions*: "The immense ingress upon our shores of foreign peoples with ideals different from ours has somewhat modified our universal gallantry, yet we are glad to observe that in the assimilating processes of the republic the most ignorant peasantry acquire our ideas, while there is no excuse whatever for our absorbing theirs."[15] Like a kind of double filter, state bureaucracy and national character work together, in this pronouncement, to supply the necessary prophylaxis against foreign contaminations. Fifteen years earlier, in a volume entitled *Manners and Social Usages*, Mrs. John Sherwood outlines a comparable project for the cultivation and maintenance of native etiquette in considerably greater detail. After listing the "national faults" and "inelegancies" charged to Americans by "foreigners" visiting the United States ("our bumptiousness, our spread-eagleism, . . . our too great familiarity and lack of dignity," and, perhaps most tellingly, "the greater freedom allowed in the manners of our young women—a freedom which, as our New World fills up with people of foreign birth, cannot but lead to social disturbances"), she recommends patience, not rage, to her readers:

> Instead of growing angry over these criticisms, . . . We can . . . decide for ourselves on certain points of etiquette which we borrow from nobody; they are a part of our great nation, of our republican institutions, and of that

> continental hospitality which gives a home to the Russ, the German, the Frenchman, the Irishman, and the "heathen Chinee." A somewhat wide and elastic code, as boundless as the prairies, can alone meet the needs of these different citizens. The old traditions of stately manners, so common to the Washington and Jefferson days, have almost died out here, as similar manners have died out all over the world. The war of 1861 swept away what little was left of that once important American fact—a grandfather. We began all over again.[16]

Sherwood's concern involves social rupture, expressed in terms of loss—the violent demise through civil war of the institution of the "grandfather"—but also in terms of addition—the immigrant arrival (of "the Russ, the German, the Frenchman, the Irishman, and the 'heathen Chinee'") "fill[ing] up" America "with people of foreign birth" and so transforming the social landscape in the late nineteenth century. Her project involves bringing manners into line and up to speed with the new conditions of mobility at century's end. The solution she proposes, constructing etiquette as native essence, borrows wholesale from a well-worn mythology of new birth in the new world: nothing less than an exceptionalism and manifest destiny of manners derived from the very landscape—a "wide and elastic code, as boundless as the prairies."

The need for such a boundless code responds to the "flood of questions" caused by this "newer world" of social rupture:

> How shall we manage all this? How shall we use a fork? When wear a dress-coat? How and when and on whom shall we leave our cards? How long and for whom shall we wear mourning? What is the etiquette of a wedding? How shall we give a dinner-party? The young house-keeper in Kansas writes as to the manners she shall teach to her children; the miner's wife, having become rich, asks how she shall arrange her house, call on her neighbors, write her letters? Many an anxious girl writes as to the propriety of 'driving out with a gentleman,' etc. In fact there is one great universal question, what is the etiquette of good society?[17]

This catalogue of questions will help us to comprehend more precisely still the terms of social rupture at issue here and, in so doing, to envision something of the readership Sherwood, like other contributors to the discourse on manners, anticipates. Those who, in 1889, would rely on a book like *Manners and Social Usages* are themselves new arrivals of a sort; "having [recently] become rich," they hold substantial social power and must assume the responsibility, and the privilege, of managing "all this," the "newer world" without stately traditions or grandfathers and overrun "with people of foreign birth." The demands of such management, entailing the regulation by this newly empowered class of itself alongside (and over against) its others, will correspond to intimate yet competing forms of mobility—social rise from within the nation, spatial ingress from without. Reflecting on the significance of the questions she has catalogued, Sherwood makes plain this dynamic: "[m]any people have found themselves suddenly conquerors of material wealth, the most successful colonists in the world, the heirs of a great inheritance, the builders of a new empire. There is a true refinement manifested in their questions. Such minds are the best conservators of law and order."[18] In a move that recalls even in recasting for a new social moment the midcentury discourse termed by Amy Kaplan "Manifest Domesticity," Sherwood counters the unpredictability of foreign arrival by envisioning imperial extension—a mode of territorial and commercial dominance in the international arena that, linking the command of space and wealth to the exercise of an expansive mobility, empowers its agents on the national (as on the global) stage to conserve "law and order" not least by regulating unruly movements *within* American society.[19] And, tellingly, the new wielders of such power demonstrate their fitness for its use through the "true refinement" their questions (in effect, their ignorance) reveal. Here what Bourdieu calls "[t]he ideology of natural taste . . . , converting differences in the mode of acquisition of culture into differences of nature," serves to bind together resources of sensibility with ones of capital in a fully imperial frame so as to normalize yet mystify the violence Sherwood directs toward her putative inferiors.[20] In effect, Sherwood's questions veil the inquiry they advance: what is the etiquette of control and coercion? Working to calibrate developing itineraries of colonization through rituals of social propriety, the mannerly American becomes a secret agent of empire for whom manifest destiny is customary, a habit of mind. That the management of this ruptured world appears almost exclusively to concern the etiquette surrounding conspicuous consumption begins to intimate something of the dynamic that, a decade later, Thorstein Veblen would analyze so trenchantly in his *Theory of the Leisure Class*.

Given that the code elaborated in the discourse on manners for the governance of the "great machine" of U.S. society responds, as anxiously as attentively, to forms of movement and circulation at the core of emergent social and geopolitical relationships, we should not be surprised to find that, almost as a rule, the etiquette books here described showcase proper manners for traveling. Travel in these books is ubiquitous. As Sangster observes, echoing and reinscribing the well-worn common sense about American restlessness, "[m]ore or less as a matter of course, we travel."[21] Moreover, travel's practice will, ideally, improve the culture, providing contact between those with taste and those in need of it. Sherwood glosses the potential for such enriching improvement:

> The travelling world, living far from great centres, goes to Newport, Saratoga, New York, Washington, Philadelphia, Boston, and gazes on what is called the latest American fashion. This, though exploited by what we may call for the sake of distinction the "newer set," is influenced and shaped in some degree by people of native refinement and taste, and that wide experience which is gained by travel and association with broad and cultivated minds. They counteract the tendency to vulgarity, which is the great danger of a newly launched society, so that our social condition improves, rather than retrogrades, with every passing decade.[22]

In strong contrast to the Emersonian argument, in which "[t]ravelling is a fool's paradise" and "immitation [is] but travelling of the mind," by Sherwood's definition travel fosters forms of social emulation necessary for social progress.[23] The cultivation that travel supplies comes in two stages, first to those persons of "native refinement and taste" who live in "great centres," and only then to those in the larger "travelling world" who venture from the social and cultural periphery to gaze on fashion's spectacle. In the social machine of the postbellum nation, citizens do the work of what Emerson earlier in the century called the "true *member*" not by detaching themselves from social contact, but by aping their supposed betters—a ritual and a practice to which travel proves indispensable.[24] And by linking "the tendency to vulgarity" with the prospect of social retrogression, Sherwood tacitly pits emulation as fostered by travel against the threat of degeneracy that, for many commentators, haunted the fin-de-siècle moment.

Yet, if social improvement through individual emulation constitutes travel's ideal effect, in practice the results tend to be much less predictable—and accordingly much more volatile, especially in an era when, as Florence Hartley worries in her 1882 etiquette manual, "the mania for traveling extends through all classes."[25] The physical sensations of modern movement, epitomized by train travel with what Sangster calls its "jerking and swinging motion that wears terribly on the nerves," jeopardize the composure of the traveling subject with the threat of neurasthenia, a physiological loss of self-control compounding travel's potential for *social* pathology.[26] Emulation, after all, requires social intimacy, and social intimacy carries real risk. Hence the standard concern, in the discourse on manners, with contamination by bad behavior, a danger only increased by the loss of nervous control, and hence the vigilant commitment to etiquette as a prophylactic. As Hartley avers, "[t]here is no situation in which a lady is more exposed than when she travels, and there is no position where a dignified, lady-like deportment is more indispensable and more certain to command respect."[27] The danger of exposure is at once external (through the negative example of others) and internal (through unintentional disclosures of self), as Dewey, in her *Lessons on Manners*, makes clear:

> It is often remarked that there is no better opportunity for studying human nature than that afforded by traveling. In the hurry and rush, on crowded cars and boats, and in the midst of strangers, people are off guard, and unconsciously exhibit their actual traits of character. We need not take a long journey to witness selfishness that few would indulge in, if they thought themselves observed. The true lady or gentleman is never betrayed into a display of ill-manners.[28]

Alarmingly, in this passage etiquette starts to sound like a social veneer, rendering the "true lady or gentleman" a kind of con artist adept at disguise and dissemblance, at suppressing "actual traits of character." Yet at the same time, the absence of agency in the concluding sentence makes travel itself the cause of etiquette's betrayal. For Dewey, it seems, even the shortest trip offers opportunities for emulation to disastrous effect. Surrounded by unconscious exhibitionists, the traveler encounters precisely what, according to Sherwood, travel should ideally counteract: "the tendency to vulgarity, . . . the great danger of a newly launched society." Particularly when read in light of Dewey's own sense of society as a "great machine," the behavior of the unconscious exhibitionist proves treacherous for everyone, since the failure of one cog jeopardizes every cog, threatening to cause a full-scale breakdown in the proper behaviors and movements of the constituent parts of the U.S. community. Thus can crises of motion turn into crises of nation.

At stake are what I would call contingencies of contact in the practice of modern mobility, contingencies that likewise haunt an otherwise very different instance of manners-and-customs instruction, the Mexican travel dispatches of Stephen Crane. Although generically these journalistic sketches stand at a considerable remove from the etiquette manuals I have been discussing, they too demonstrate a concern for problems in traveling conduct and an anxious fascination with contamination and accident—the arbitrary, even volatile character of social contact—unavoidable in the practice of modern mobility. And they elaborate, to striking effect, the ways in which crises of motion exceed the national frame in the U.S. 1890s, drawing specters of empire into view.

The Worth of Worthless Literature

In late August 1896, Crane received a brief letter from Teddy Roosevelt. After thanking Crane for an autographed copy of *George's Mother* and expressing a desire one day to see his copy of *The Red Badge of Courage* likewise signed, Roosevelt offers a sidelong critique of Crane's recently published "A Man and Some Others": "Some day I want you to write another story of the frontiersman and the Mexican Greaser in which the frontiersman shall come out on top; it is more normal that way!"[29] Emphasizing (through the word "normal") an animadversion to signs of deviance from the doctrines of American exceptionalism, Roosevelt's cheery suggestion marks one index of federal and national opinion against which Crane's ambivalence as traveler and writer had, by 1896, already measured itself. More than a year earlier, recourse to the representational moves of disciplinary pace offered him one way to contend and cope with a sense of the normalizing force of U.S. imperial relations with Mexico.[30]

In the nearly four months between the end of January and the middle of May 1895, Crane undertook a frantic tour of the southwestern United States and Mexico, a tour financed by the Bacheller, Johnson, and Bacheller syndicate, among the most prominent and influential news corporations in the period. Over the course of his travels, during which, repeatedly broke, he had on several occasions to wire his syndicate sponsors for additional funds, Crane wrote fourteen travel dispatches, all but three published by papers in the Bacheller chain. Typically short, these sketches are consistently marked by irony and cynicism. In the Mexican dispatches (my chief focus here) emphasis falls heavily on the traffic in custom as it shapes social space, and by extension on the troublesome tracing of cultural semblance within cultural difference. As a result of such emphasis, the signs of stasis-in-motion I attribute to the pressures of disciplinary pace emerge in these sketches as at once topic, problematic, and effect. At issue is the evident power and latent crisis of American colonialism at the end of the nineteenth century.

As Bill Brown observes, the Mexico Crane visited in 1895 had, over the course of the previous decade, "appeared as the leisure space in which Americans could fully inhabit alternatives to modern life."[31] Such newfound attraction to Mexican culture grew out of "two economic relations—travel and trade" that, in turn, "depended on the Mexican Central Railway... connect[ing, since 1884,] Mexico City in a continuous standard-gauge line to the United States."[32] The Bacheller decision to send Crane to Mexico underscores the entanglement of travel with trade: indicating a desire, as Brown notes, "to share in the 'Mexican' profits," the syndicate's venture banked at once on the commodification of Mexico through travel and the commodification of Mexican travel itself—on the ready commercial mobility of travel accounts focused to the south.[33]

If indeed the discourse on manners current at the turn of the nineteenth century supplies a counterpart to travel writing and ethnography by mapping the empire of etiquette, in his Mexican dispatches Crane underscores the extent to which American custom has helped in colonizing Mexico. Homegrown habits offer a necessary supplement to the more foreign pleasures found south of the border, rendering Mexico's difference liminal, not absolute. Thus, in "The City of Mexico," one of the three unpublished sketches, Crane indicates, without comment, that the institutions of emergent mass tourism have come to occupy the architecture of an older empire: "The old palace of the Emperor Iturbide is now a hotel over-run with American tourists. The Mexican National Railroad has its general offices in a building that was the palace of a bygone governor of the city and the American Club has the finest of club-houses because it gained control of a handsome old palace."[34] Renovating and revitalizing the abandoned spaces of imperial contest and early nationalism, the exploding tourist industry in Mexico constitutes a new mode of colonial control, yet enjoys, as Brown observes, a success "to which Mexico as such is all but superfluous."[35] Not surprisingly, then,

> [t]here is a certain American aspect to the main business part of the town. Men with undeniable New England faces confront one constantly. The business signs are often American and there is a little group of cafes where everything from the aprons of the waiters to the liquids dispensed are American. One hears in this neighborhood more English than Spanish. Even the native business purpose changes under this influence and they bid for the American coin. 'American Barber-shop,' 'The American Tailor,' 'American Restaurant' are signs which flatter the tourist's eye. (431)

Attributed by Crane to the universality of "the reputation of Americans for ability to spend money" (431), these signs of "American aspect" will also indicate an ability in Americans to *make* money, to consolidate capital by disseminating U.S. culture through travel and trade. The effect is precisely supplemental, as the spreading hegemony and creeping globalism of U.S.

custom compound by displacing the exoticism of the foreign locale, establishing for the purposes of economic domination the commodified interplay of difference with sameness.

The clearest indication of such interplay occurs when Crane reflects on the dynamics of currency conversion in "Free Silver Down in Mexico," a sketch published in several Bacheller papers in the last week of June 1895. "The rate of exchange," Crane notes, "is always about two for one. For fifty American dollars [travelers] receive one hundred of the dollars of Mexico. It is a great thing to double money in this fashion. The American tourist is likely to keep his hand in his pocket and jingle his hoard" (444). Yet since pricing is likewise "always about two for one," this same tourist typically "exclaims that he can as yet see no benefit in this money exchange" (444). Here the formal differentiation instituted through currency conversion, registering most visibly in the aesthetic excess of Mexico's "gaudy script," bespeaks an underlying process of economic standardization and, with it, the apparent failure of the tourist's economic advantage (444). Mexico's distinction, its difference, is, in this understanding, indifferent after all.[36] The irony, of course, is that the coordination of Mexican with American economics, seeming to undercut what for the tourist is the "benefit in this money exchange," requires exploitation on a systematic scale, the commercial colonization of Mexico by American "travel and trade." Not surprisingly, though tourists cannot immediately see the advantage they gain from changing money, Mexicans comprehend all too well the full force of the losses they bear. The political economy underpinning tourism in Mexico correlates differences and extracts value at the expense of Mexicans. The point is perhaps most telling with respect to the question of rail travel, that material network enabling the tourist industry to thrive. "Railroad fares in Mexico are usually quoted at double the mileage in the United States," Crane notes (445). "That is to say, reduced to a common basis, they are equivalent. This doubling of the rates, then, does not affect the tourist from the United States, because he thinks in American coin, but it plays havoc with the Mexican citizen, who earns his money in the coin of Mexico" (445). What to tourists seems the indifference of economic difference works, for natives, to distribute—or indeed to withhold altogether—mobility as a material practice and social resource, so as to map to negative effect Mexico's space for its citizenry. The exacting measures and real costs of material difference, in other words, occur beneath the commodified circuitry of touristic exchange.

When, in "Free Silver Down in Mexico," Crane contends that "[t]he author of this article . . . merely recites facts" (446), he claims for his reportorial voice a disinterestedness in perspective that, amounting to a kind of stylistic signature, remains disingenuous in view of the incisive ironies registered throughout his Mexican sketches. Although the posture seems nearly photographic, claiming only to record the impress of surface details on consciousness, its very detachment bears the trace of devastating social critique.[37] We encounter to telling effect this capacity for ironizing attack cast as detachment in the second of two sketches published under the title "Stephen Crane in Mexico." In this dispatch, appearing in a number of Bacheller newspapers in the third week of July 1895, Crane recounts the experience of taking the train from San Antonio into Mexico City, as illuminated by the responses of two American travelers, a "capitalist from Chicago" and an "archaeologist from Boston" (446). Rendered generically, in outline only, these travelers typify pure occupation: two means to the extraction of value from Mexican land, one emphasizing materiality in the present, the other emphasizing materials from the past. Exploitation is, tacitly, their common endeavor, and plunder their common object. Thus the trip they undertake is characterized as an "invasion" facilitated by the "conquer[ing]" power of the train they ride (447, 452). Like the anonymous tourists in "Free Silver Down in Mexico," these two delight in the "beautiful game" of money exchange, the two-for-one conversion that, substituting American currency with the aesthetically excessive Mexican scrip, entails (as we know from the earlier dispatch) for tourists but not for locals an indifferent difference (449). Against, however, the expectations primed by monetary delight (if in keeping with the contradictions of financial exchange), the initial encounter of the two travelers with the Mexican landscape entails a bewildering disappointment: "[t]he train again invaded a wilderness of mesquite. It was amazing. The travellers had somehow expected a radical change the moment they were well across the Rio Grande. On the contrary, southern Texas was being repeated" (450). The emphasis here on geographical repetition works to counter the exoticizing desire for stark difference that helps to produce "Mexico" as a commodity within travel's political economy, at the same time intimating the blindness of these travelers to the geoeconomic exploitation they help to perpetuate—the effects of travel and trade, capitalism and archaeology, that render Mexico's *social* landscape importantly dissimilar from Texas's. Crane's ironizing insistence on frustrated touristic expectation and the absence of "radical change," rendered all the more cutting through detached, disembodied narration, thus attacks the processes of exoticizing differentiation and market exploitation through which the tourist industry works to establish and regulate Mexico's commercial appeal. At stake is not least Crane's effort to exempt himself from the fascinated desire for difference, to distinguish his own reporting practice, as a mere recitation of facts, from the invasive conquest that archaeological and capitalist excavations entail.

One consequence of the effort at such exemption will be to undermine the standard enterprise of the genre, travel writing, to which Crane's Bacheller dispatches rather uneasily belong. The tensions at issue emerge most explicitly in the last of his 1895 reports, a piece entitled "Galveston, Texas, in 1895" that, detailing for purposes of commercial circulation the particularities of the coastal city, frames its account by calling into question the value of the emphasis on difference typically privileged by travelogues. "It is the fortune of travellers," Crane wryly begins,

> to take note of differences and publish them to their friends. It is the differences that are supposed to be valuable. The travellers seek them bravely, and cudgel their wits to find means to unearth them. But in this search they are confronted continually by the resemblances[,] and the intrusion of commonplace and most obvious similarity into a field that is being ploughed in the romantic fashion is what causes an occasional resort to the imagination. . . . And travellers tumbling over each other in their haste to trumpet the radical differences between Eastern and Western life have created a generally wrong opinion. . . . In a word, it is the passion for differences which has prevented a general knowledge of the resemblances. (474–75)

The implications are clear: confronted by an economy in which "[t]he declaration [of resemblance] has no commercial value," travelers wishing to profit from the publication of their experiences must manufacture the striking differences they claim only to report (474). Such is precisely the imperative that Crane the mere reciter of facts undertakes to evade.

Thus when, in the unpublished "Mexican Lower Classes," he legitimates his commitment to the certitude of "two things, form and color" by arguing that "[i]t perhaps might be said—if anyone dared—that the most worthless literature of the world has been that which has been written by the men of one nation concerning the men of another" (436), the axiom (daring not least because it threatens to cancel the worth of the discourse that Crane writes and that we are in the process of reading) might lead us to expect another critique of the "passion for differences" driving the market in travel literature. Ironically enough, however, the ensuing sketch exemplifies its lesson in the bankruptcy of cross-national literature with reference to the figure of "the Indian," measuring the worthlessness at issue against the irreducibility, not the immateriality, of indigenous difference. Whereas, in Crane's view, "[t]he people of the slums of our own cities . . . are becoming more and more capable of defining their condition," he "cannot ascertain" in "the lower classes of [Mexico's] Indians" any signs of their "feel[ing] at all the modern desperate rage at the accident of birth" (436–37). Instead, they evince in "their faces . . . a certain smoothness, a certain lack of pain, a serene faith . . . [a] superiority of contentment" (438). Crane here estimates a compound difference, one that interweaves serenity with inscrutability against rage and legibility. Yet the impossibility claimed by Crane of reading "the Indian," such that he cannot determine the nature of the difference he knows to be present by nature, will establish the ready familiarity of these aboriginals, their affiliation with the stereotyped propensity of their race toward an inscrutable fatalism, resigned as serenely as incomprehensibly to the inevitability of immiserated disappearance. Undercutting his own axiom, Crane's reflection on impoverished indigeneity in Mexico cannot fairly be termed "worthless," since the ideological value (not to mention commercial appeal) of its discursive lineage is at the close of the North American nineteenth century as well established as substantial.

Significantly enough, the well-worn figure of the illegible Indian, triggering in "The Mexican Lower Classes" a near-crisis in interpretation, serves Crane elsewhere as a more reliable, less disruptive marker of difference in Mexico—as the necessary counterpoint to the semblances he encounters. Thus although, as Crane asserts in "Hats, Shirts, and Spurs in Mexico" (a sketch appearing in print over a year after his tour, on 18 October 1896), "above all the reader must remember that the great mass of humanity upon the principal business street of Mexico City dress about the same as they do in other places," nevertheless the figure of "the Indian"—"utterly distinct"—gives the exception to this mandatory reminder (467):

> The Indian remains the one great artistic figure. . . . Whether his blanket is purple or not or of some dull hue, he fits into the green grass, the low white walls, the blue sky as if his object was not so much to get possession of some centavos as to compose the picture.
>
> At night when he crouches in a doorway with his sombrero pulled still further over his eyes, and his mouth covered by a fold of his serape, you can imagine anything at all about him, for his true character is impenetrable. He is a mystic and silent figure of the darkness. (467–68)

Elsewhere committed to a nearly photographic detachment, here the reportorial voice foregoes mere fact for pure imagination, claiming, on the grounds of "Indian" impenetrability, license to posit an indigenous cipher, a blank screen for racialized projection. The ironies at issue are as obvious as decisive: the reportorial identification of absolute difference entails a discursive performance and an ideological dissemination of intimate familiarity. For readers used to invocations of "Indian" mystery, the "picture" composed by Crane's "mystic and silent figure of the darkness" could not be any closer to home. It trades in "form and color" about which white Americans, in 1895, had been "certain" for generations.

The presence of "the Indian" as the exception (yet also the supplement) to Mexican semblance within Crane's Bacheller sketches certainly complicates his wish to differentiate his discourse (mere fact) from the colonizing moves of trade and tourism. When Crane's capitalist and archaeologist see from the train's window a sombreroed silhouette sleeping in a doorway, "[t]he figure justified to them all their preconceptions": "proving . . . certain romances, songs, narratives . . . [h]e renewed their faith" (450). Although Crane evidently aims to puncture these preconceptions and critique the forms of imperial excavation they help to legitimate, by trading in typologies of indigenous impenetrability he risks making his own difference from the material and ideological forces of trade and tourism indifferent after all. The enduring romance of backwardness, the timeless inertia of the serene indigene, here sets the conditions of possibility for the inclusion of Mexico within the high-speed circuitry of modern mass mediation. Fixed through the difference that "the Indian" makes, static Mexico must be moved faster and faster—a process to which Crane, despite (or perhaps through) his ironized detachment, certainly contributes.[38]

Vagabond Wages

In *The Material Unconscious*, Brown rightly notes another dimension of Crane's concern in "The Mexican Lower Classes": what Crane terms "the first thunder of rebellion" (436), glossed by Brown as "the facts of American labor."[39] Crane's "first thunder," Brown observes, "had already been heard during the Great Strike of 1877, the Haymarket Riot of 1886, the Pullman Strike of 1894."[40] Such crisis likewise haunts the description, in Crane's dispatch about the capitalist and the archaeologist, of the image on the Mexican silver dollar—"the face of it intended to represent a cap of liberty with rays of glory shooting from it, but it looked to be on the contrary a picture of an exploding bomb" (449). This coin bears the trace of Haymarket, and so limns, in the imperial context, the latent threat and excess of capital, the supplement of its commerce, the violent opposition it can breed.

The labor unrest glossed by Crane as "the first thunder of rebellion" managed, among its many effects in the last decades of the nineteenth century, to provoke in anxious response the invention of a new kind of mobile, nomadic subjectivity: the tramp, that figure who served to concentrate and concretize a whole host of inchoate social fears about the volatility of mobility in the United States. As Michael Denning notes, "[t]he 'tramp' is no myth or symbol in the 'American mind,' no eternal archetype of 'America.' It was a category constructed in the wake of the 1893 depression and the 1877 railroad strikes to designate migratory and unemployed workers; indeed it was ideological naming of the new phenomenon of unemployment."[41] Such ideological naming, I would stress, serves to mystify the crimes of capital by pathologizing not just job loss as a condition but also the socially unsettling forms of movement it inspires. The figure of the tramp, in other words, circulates discursively so as to veil the contingency, the violence, the *illogic* of capitalism—occluding yet confirming how, in Brown's formulation, "accidents within the market might significantly change one's understanding or material experience of the market."[42]

Eugene Debs's 1894 meditation, one month into the Pullman strike, on the Commonweal armies then heading to Washington will help to clarify, in answering, the process of ideological naming that brought "the tramp" into social being:

> Out of work, out of money and without food, ragged, friendless and homeless, these Commonwealers began their march to the capital city of the nation while Congress is in session. . . . Faster and still faster they rallied as the bugle call echoed through the land. They walk, they ride, they float; the storms beat upon them, their tent their skins; their couch the mother earth, their pillows stones. Some fall by the way and are buried by their comrades, unknelled and unsung, to sleep their last sleep in unknown and forgotten graves. But the survivors press forward to Washington, and as they march, recruits start up from almost every center of population in all of the land, from mountain and valley, from hill and dale, from abandoned mine and silent factory, shop and forge—they come and tramp to the muffled drum—funeral march of their throbbing hearts. The cry is, "on to Washington," where, on the marble steps of the nation's capitol, in their rags, and barefooted, they would petition Congress to enact laws whereby they might perpetuate their wretched existence by toil—laws that would rekindle the last remaining spark of hope, that their future would be relieved of some of the horrors of hunger and nakedness.[43]

"They walk, they ride, they float": so described, tramps take up collective mobility in hopes of redressing alienated misery, welding pilgrimage to protest at the nation's legislative center and symbolic heart. Resisting the political and ideological inertia of industrialized speed, Debs's tramps counter their superfluity and abjection under capital precisely by reclaiming, for the purposes of protest, the power to move "faster and still faster."

Jack London is among the most celebrated participants in the tramping marches that occurred during 1894, having spent a part of his cross-continental tramping expedition that year as a member of Charles Kelly's Industrial Army, the western wing of Coxey's Army of tramps and migrants. Although when he joined Kelly's Army, London had intimate experience with the miseries of impoverishment and was fully committed to the struggle against capitalist exploitation, the tramp writings he published over the ensuing two decades evince a striking ambivalence of perspective, combining clear signs of experience—what Jonathan Auerbach terms "an intimate investment"—with the detachments of taxonomy, the knowledge of the native informant with the posture of the ethnographer.[44] The resulting authorial persona, evidently devised to document yet also capitalize on the crisis in labor relations to which the tramp, as a social presence, necessarily corresponded, instances not just London's ongoing attempt, in Auerbach's phrase, "to make himself somebody in print as well as by that very print," but also the significance, and the entanglement, of physical movement, social mobility, and discursive circulation within this endeavor.[45]

As London indicates in the 1897 essay "The Road," the problem posed by the tramp in America is not least one of ignorance: "We have met [the tramp] everywhere, even desecrating the sanctity of our back stoop, . . . [yet] his land is an unknown region, and we are less conversant with his habits and thoughts than with those of the inhabitants of the Cannibal Islands."[46] The ubiquity, even inescapability, of tramps, as intimate as unsettling, constitutes (ironically enough) their social insignificance. Beneath contempt for the desecrations they commit, they are also beyond consideration. Converting ignorance into knowledge thus becomes the mandate of these writings: London offers what Auerbach calls "a typology of tramps . . . much as a field anthropologist might do" so as to show how, "[s]trange as it may seem, in this outcast world the sharp lines of caste are as rigorously drawn as in the world from which it has evolved."[47] Yet the effort to illuminate the tramp's "unknown region" alongside "his habits and thoughts" (the manners, customs, and attitudes proper to tramp life) will evidently situate this discourse in jarring proximity not just to ethnography but also to travel writing—enlivening, for the reader, ethnological reportage and sociological analysis with a kind of vicarious tourism. Hence (in ways comparable to Crane's Mexican sketches), London's tramp writings venture to give, even as they grimly mimic, what Richard Brodhead terms "the reading of regions" characteristic of literary regionalism, a mode that, contradictorily enough, "purports to value a culture for being intactly other at the very time that it is offering outsiders the chance to inhabit it and enjoy its special 'life.'"[48]

The tensions at issue in the attempt to render vicarious tourism through the methods of ethnographic reportage emerge to striking effect in "Rods and Gunnels," an essay rejected by four magazines, including *Harper's* and the *Saturday Evening Post*, before being accepted for publication by *The Bookman* in 1902. Written, as London notes, "to correct some of [the] misinformation" circulating about tramps and their traveling practices, "Rods and Gunnels" locates the source of such misinformation not just with outsiders reporting on tramp life but also with newcomers to that life: "*when the lesser local tramps are themselves ignorant of much of the real 'road,' the stray and passing sociologists, dealing only with the lesser local tramps, must stand in corresponding ignorance*."[49] Thus the essay's pedagogical project, in correcting misinformation, is compound: to underscore the importance of instruction in the manners and customs of tramping for tramps themselves as well as for their observers. The "single instance" London uses to illustrate his project is, on the face of it, merely semantic: the distinction between rods and gunnels.[50] The latter serve as trusses connecting train cars, while the former constitute part of the wheel trucks on passenger coaches. Thus "riding the rods" names "not various kinds of acts, but one particular act," an act that—unlike riding the gunnels, which, involving "no special trick or nerve," "[a]nybody with arms and legs can [do]"—"requires nerve, and skill, and daring."[51] To render this distinction more vivid, while legitimating his own authority in making it, London shifts from the taxonomic to the experiential mode so as "to explain how such a rod is ridden."[52] Using "for clearness . . . the first person" and for immediacy the present tense, he takes us underneath the carriage of the passenger coach:

> The train is pulling out and going as fast as a man can run, or even faster. Time, night or day; to one who is familiar it does not matter. I stand alongside the track. The train is approaching. With a quick eye I select the coach and truck . . . [and] begin to run gently in the direction the train is going. As "my" truck comes closer I hit up my pace, and just before it reaches me I make one swift spurt, so that when it is abreast of me the respective velocities of the train and myself are nearly equalised. At this moment (and it

> must be the moment of moments and neither the moment before nor the moment after)... I [use one of the gunnels to]... swing my body under the car and bring my feet to rest on the brake-beam.... Between the top of the truck and the bottom of the car is a narrow space, barely sufficient to admit a man's body. Through this I squeeze, in such a manner that my feet still remain *outside* the truck on the brake beam, my stomach is pressed against the *top* of the truck, and my head and shoulders unsupported, are *inside* the truck, I say "unsupported," and I mean it, for beneath my chest is the rapidly revolving axle. This I dare not touch, but must thrust my head and trunk, snake fashion, over and past it and down till I can lay my hands on either the brake-rod or the cross-rod. This done,... I must draw my hips, legs and feet over and down across that moving axle without touching. Squirming and twisting, this is accomplished, and I sit down on the cross-rod, back resting against the side of the truck, one shoulder against the cross-partition, the other shoulder within a couple of inches of the whirling wheel.... Six or eight inches beneath me are the ties, bounding along at thirty, forty, or fifty miles an hour, and all in the world between is a slender swaying rod as thick as a man's first finger. Dirt and gravel are flying, the car is bounding overhead, the earth flashing away beneath, here is clank and clash, and rumble and roar, and... this is "riding the rods."[53]

Accustomed (and thus indifferent) to the tramp on "our back stoop," here we find ourselves imaginatively wrenched from the contemplative comforts of home into the perilous, cramped space of nomadic transit, in all its sensory excess. The passage makes nearly incomprehensible the convolutions of the tramp body that enable this means of transport to occur. We experience the pure presence of an endeavor that remains powerfully foreign, even inconceivable. The effect, I would stress, is the aim, not failure, of this discourse. Dramatizing the literal insinuation of the outsider's body into the mechanics of industrial culture, London's account of riding the rods drives home to us the fact, and the fascination, of intimate distance (measured explicitly in the closeness of the ties below) and intimate difference (measured tacitly in the closeness of the sanctioned travelers above).[54] By riding the rods, the tramp becomes a parasitic passenger, exploiting the networked system from within, extracting use value from the mass transit he cannot otherwise afford. And by sharing his experiential knowledge of such extraction with readers who are much more likely to pay for train travel, London the native informant serves as both our antithesis and our prosthesis—our means to possess, through print circulation, illicit forms of modern mobility we cannot really comprehend.

At the end of "Rods and Gunnels," London articulates the more general form of the epistemological quandary of tramp knowledge in striking terms.

The problem, in his formulation, has everything to do with the "sharp lines of caste" in trampland:

> The 'profesh' [or veteran tramps] are the aristocracy of their Underworld. They are the lords and masters, the aggressive men, the primordial noble men, the *blond beasts* of Neitzsche [sic], lustfully roving and conquering through sheer superiority and strength. Unwritten is the law they impose. They are the Law, the Law incarnate. And the Underworld looks up to them and obeys. They are not easy of access. They are conscious of their own nobility and treat only with equals. Unless the investigator qualify... he will never know them. And unless he be able to qualify and know them, he will be no fit exponent of the Underworld to the Upperworld.[55]

To the extent that knowing tramp life and explaining it to others require what London calls qualification, the interrelated projects of comprehension and communication entail the conversion of outside to inside, of epistemology ("the tramp" as analytic category) to ontology ("the tramp" as experiential identity). Accordingly, the attempt to know trampland becomes tremendously difficult, its endeavor resonating with the problem of worthlessness held by Crane to afflict literature seeking to span different nations or, in this case, different class formations, different worlds. Yet where Crane rejects the value of such literature, London *rarifies* it, precisely by indicating the exclusiveness of the qualification that permits passage between "Underworld" and "Upperworld." The challenge of such literature, to avoid "misinformation" while producing "fit" accounts of trampland, will mark the preciousness, not the worthlessness, of the discourse we read—and of the "exponent" who has written it. Here London effectively turns the debased habits of abjected outcasts into the prized knowledge he has gleaned, for us, from an elect.

As the invocation of Nietzschean "blond beasts" begins to make clear, this elect is in London's formulation not just culturally exclusive and protective; it is racially distinct. This emphasis will in turn help to shed light on London's decision, in the already discussed 1897 essay "The Road," to counterpose tramps with "the inhabitants of the Cannibal islands." His effort in this essay at educating readers to consume the homely, "back stoop" exoticism of the tramp turns, much as in "Rods and Gunnels," on the difference that race makes—a difference *implicit* in the insinuation that any attention paid to foreign "primitives" occurs, like a kind of investigative cannibalism, at the tramp's expense, and *explicit* in the ensuing query, inspired by racial politics closer to home: "is not the increasing, shifting, tramp population, not passive like the Negro but full of the indomitability of the

Teuton, equally worthy of consideration, and by the whole race?"[56] So conceived, the effort to understand tramps—social outcasts who, according to London, "adventur[e] in *blond beastly* fashion"—takes nativism and white supremacy as its latent principles.[57] Where Crane in Mexico tries to supplement the indifference of cultural differences with indigeneity, London in trampland retools social division through the discriminating power of white supremacy.[58]

London's investment in the supremacism of some tramps, as articulated in "The Road" and "Rods and Gunnels," becomes all the more unwieldy when read in light of the systemic critique he advances in the 1901 essay "The Tramp," where, converting supremacy back into abjection, he argues that tramps represent the "waste" of the industrial system, nothing more than "perambulating carcasses."[59] Offering a devastating account of the necessary relation between capitalist production and a surplus labor force, the essay locates tramps as "the by-product of . . . [the] economic necessity" of such surplus.[60] "The tramp is one of two kinds of men: . . . either a discouraged worker or a discouraged criminal," a distinction that is, for London, functionally meaningless, since the first produces the second.[61] "But," he emphasizes, "the tramp does not usually come from the slums. His place of birth is ordinarily a bit above, and sometimes a very great bit above. A confessed failure, he yet refuses to accept the punishment and swerves aside from the slum to vagabondage."[62] Hence the particular significance of tramp mobility:

> The "road" is one of the safety valves through which the waste of the social organism is given off. And *being given off* constitutes the negative function of the tramp. Society, as at present organized, makes much waste of human life. This waste must be eliminated. Chloroform or electrocution would be a simple, merciful solution of this problem of elimination; but the ruling ethics, while permitting the human waste, will not permit a humane elimination of that waste.
>
> And so the tramp becomes self-eliminating. And not only self! Since he is manifestly unfit for things as they are, and since kind is prone to beget kind, it is necessary that his kind cease with him, that his progeny shall not be. . . . Sterility is his portion.[63]

The vision of tramping supplied by this passage seems impossible to reconcile with the celebration of "primordial noble men" and the insistence on qualification and fitness with which "Rods and Gunnels" concludes, until we recognize in the apparent contradiction the signs of what Auerbach takes to be London's "unusual motto—master *and* be mastered (or, be mastered *to* master)."[64] The significance of such similitude, capturing and constituting the tramp between abjection and supremacism, registers to powerful effect in London's invocation of "vagabondage," an overloaded term that, bringing bondage to the vagabond, effectively ties the tramp to nomadism. That is, consigned to "vagabondage," to master and be mastered, the tramp has no choice but to pursue self-elimination in Fordist terms and be moved so as to be removed, faster and faster.

The point here is precisely to locate in London's tramp writing powerful traces of disciplinary pace. We can see such traces to vivid effect when we turn to "The Apostate," a tramping fiction London wrote in 1906 and placed with the *Woman's Home Companion* the same year. In this story, London recounts the transformation of an impoverished slum child, Johnny, from factory worker to invalid to human calculator and finally to tramp. This compound shift confirms the relentless, pulverizing display of the systematics of mobility within naturalist discourse, such that work fuses with vagrancy and incarceration with escape. These fusions mark a crisis of differentiation, which from the outset plays itself out temporally, against the calendar: "All days were alike. Yesterday or last year were the same as a thousand years—or a minute. Nothing ever happened. There were no events to mark the march of time. Time did not march. It stood always still. It was only the whirling machines that moved, and they moved nowhere—in spite of the fact that they moved faster."[65]

Here, the passage that narrates such crisis of differentiation concludes with a perfect figure for disciplinary pace: the machine that races in place, that has no start or stop, no departure or return; the time-piece that tells no time; the regimental round that, going nowhere, levels all rituals with its ritual, all anomalies with its anomaly. So understood, the regimen I call disciplinary pace calibrates not just a similitude but an exchange between static and frantic motion, thereby working at once to expose and to preclude unpredictabilities of movement. At the same time, by flattening hours, eliminating the event, and so seeming to stop time, it strives (though, I would stress, never really manages) to occlude the *historicity* of industrial and economic determinations under capitalism. Thus in "The Apostate" disciplinary pace corrects in advance the apostate's "wayward" turn to tramp life, a turn indicating a shift in the terms but not the ends of social agency. As Mark Seltzer argues, in this story "the apostate to the work ethic reinvents, in inverted form, the principle of movement without volition, which is here the very principle of machine-work, as the pathologized and moveless state of his resistance."[66]

Now, if "movement without volition" entails the premise of "machine-work" and at the same time, through inversion, the premise of its "resistance" ("be mastered *to* master," in Auerbach's formulation), very quickly the clear separation of a host of ideas clustered around work and leisure (including stasis/motion, animism/automatism, domesticity/migrancy, property/vagrancy, and rest/travel) becomes obsolete. The effect is not so much one of confusion as of coordination or coupling, through which ordinarily distinct concepts such as work and leisure, rest and movement, become intimate, inextricable, bound together as if on a circuit.[67] In the story, such coupling means not least that London's apostate continually endures the punitive genetics (and also erotics) entailed by a prosthetic or automatic subjectivity: "There had never been a time when he had not been in intimate relationship with machines. Machinery had almost been bred into him, and at any rate he had been brought up on it."[68] Here, the terms bring into line, grooved together, pressures of biology and industry, such that *motorism* constitutes the gene pool. Given that Johnny's sole "impression of his father," "that he had savage and pitiless feet," marks the "dim and faded" memory of his mother and father in bed, copulating, the double, brutal duty of the foot as oedipal part and traveling part, fetish and motor, in signifying the absent, abandoning father will give a means by which to gauge Johnny's transformation from worker-machine to tramp-machine.[69] As if inevitably, such transformation only confirms familial coherence and continuity in the image of familial fracture: this family consists in its tendency to fall apart. Johnny leaves just as his daddy has left; waywardness constitutes his patrimony.

Yet, as the story shows, the apostate's capacity to *escape* by leaving is undecidable at best. Since "[f]rom the perfect worker he had evolved into the perfect machine," since "he had attained machine-like perfection," and since "[a]ll waste movements were eliminated," his "move" to tramp life further refines his body as motionless machine, coupled to the boxcar it rides and, "in spite of the fact that [it] move[s] faster," nevertheless moving nowhere.[70] If in one respect this paradox suggests death (with the boxcar as coffin and the tramp's motionless motion as a corpse's rotting), in another it helps to measure the body's radical and automatic redaction under disciplinary pace, where (against its conventional meaning as leisured liberation) mobility can only signify the *labor* of leisure in the image of the body/machine at rest or, indeed, entranced.[71] Thus indicating how tramps get caught and constituted within the dynamics of moveless movement, "The

Apostate" calibrates, to dramatic effect, motion with stasis: the condition of "vagabondage" determinant for the tramp and intimate, at least in London's account of the "Underworld," with the operations of disciplinary pace.[72]

In London's treatment, the industrial grind that drives the apostate to vagabondage, to the "self-elimination" constituting the tramp's "negative function" under capitalism, thus serves to gloss (though not really to historicize) the determinate relationship between industrialized motion and social expulsion. Yet if, for the apostate, "the whirling machines . . . moved nowhere—in spite of the fact that they moved faster," for London himself the concept and the figure at issue in such machines prove as moveable as malleable, linking the punitive dynamic of mass manufacture to the less rationalized or rationalizable regimen of literary production. This linkage appears most strikingly in a celebrated passage from London's essay "Getting into Print," published in *The Editor* of March 1903, where he describes his formative decision to go "up against the magazines":

> I had no one to give me tips, no one's experience to profit by. So I sat down and wrote in order to get an experience of my own. I wrote everything—short stories, articles, anecdotes, jokes, essays, sonnets, ballads, vilanelles, triolets, songs, light plays in iambic tetrameter, and heavy tragedies in blank verse. These various creations I stuck into envelopes, enclosed return postage, and dropped into the mail. Oh, I was prolific. Day by day my manuscripts mounted up, till the problem of finding stamps for them became as great as that of making life livable for my widow landlady.
>
> All my manuscripts came back. They continued to come back. The process seemed like the working of a soulless machine. I dropped the manuscript into the mail box. After the lapse of a certain approximate length of time, the manuscript was brought back to me by the postman. Accompanying it was a stereotyped rejection slip. A part of the machine, some cunning arrangement of cogs and cranks at the other end (it could not have been a living, breathing man with blood in his veins), had transferred the manuscript to another envelope, taken the stamps from the inside and pasted them outside, and added the rejection slip.[73]

So understood the process of literary refusal constitutes an industrialized grind from which all evaluative nuance has been removed. Supplementing the fiction factory, here rejection itself—"stereotyped" for maximum efficiency—gets mass-produced. Although Auerbach correctly notes that this "key passage . . . pits the 'soulless machine' of publishing, imagined as an impersonal system of mail, against the personal integrity of the struggling author, embodied (by implied contrast) as 'a living breathing man with blood in his veins,'" we should also recognize that, alongside and against such differentiation, the anecdote outlines a telling complementarity of indifference—the novice author indiscriminate in writing "everything," the magazine industry indiscriminate in rejecting it all.[74] The effect of such complementarity (not strictly symmetrical, since the losses register much more heavily with London than with the "soulless machine") is, I would argue, to emphasize the ceaseless circulation of this mechanical process, the relentlessness of the traffic entailed by this failure to traffic in literature. Judging from the retrospect supplied by "Getting Into Print," at the start of London's authorial career his writing must have seemed doomed to a kind of vagabondage, going nowhere faster and faster.

Ironically enough, even as London published "Getting into Print" to educate novice authors with the tips, the experience, from which they might profit so as to evade the circuit of relentless rejection, he remained caught in a drawn-out struggle to publish "The Tramp," a process starting in 1901 with its submission to *McClure's*, entailing its refusal by "twenty well-known national magazines," and finally ending in 1904 with its acceptance by *Wilshire's Magazine*.[75] Written (as already outlined) to account for the social circulation of what London understood as human waste, the essay threatened to fall victim to a comparable process, to meet the self-eliminating fate of discouraged discourse and so, in a sense, to become what it named. That eventually it avoided such an end offers a basic lesson in historical contingency, an accidentalism that, in his encounters with the literary field, London knew intimately, yet that, in his accounts of social and human circulation, he remained surprisingly reluctant to credit. All the more ironic, given this reluctunce, that, against the developmental fantasy in "Getting Into Print," where the titular accomplishment pulls a writer beyond relentless rejection, in London's case the "soulless machine" tended, more messily, to haunt his authorial practice even after his inaugural printedness had been achieved.

We should not be too surprised to find London transposing and expanding this scene of self-tutelage and industrial discipline in his 1909 novel *Martin Eden*. When the novel's protagonist (a semiautobiographical surrogate for London himself) decides to begin writing, not just to secure his livelihood but also to improve his social identity—to gain cultural alongside real capital—he chooses for his first topic what, as a sailor, he knows: travel, and more specifically "the voyage of the treasurehunters" (a topic that doubles as an ironical précis of *Martin Eden* itself).[76] Thus, in ways not specified in "Getting Into Print," in the 1909 novel the experience of mobility afforded by travel establishes the conditions of imaginative possibility for authorship as a material practice.[77]

Much like the young London, Eden composes prolifically, driven by "creative fever" to blaze through his first piece, and then many more, "at white heat" (116). Yet such compositional speed leads not to quick publication but, instead, to a kind of stasis-in-motion that, depriving Eden of any control over the effect of his authorial velocity, sees the concept of travel, in reconfigured form, writing back to establish for the novice author a more disciplined pace. "[D]estined to receive many stamps and to be started on many travels" (257), Eden's manuscripts, regardless of subject matter, literally become a travel literature—traveling endlessly, failing to find placement in magazines, circulating in a "perpetual motion" that takes them nowhere, so as to discipline the ambitions of the neophyte.[78] And, because Eden's poverty regularly prevents him from purchasing "stamps with which to continue [his manuscripts] on their travels," they spend much of their time "piling up" (174), by-products of surplus in the literary field that instance its investment in stasis.

Highlighting issues of idealistic authorial trust ("[h]e poured his soul into stories, articles, and poems, and entrusted them to the machine") and of discursive travel ("[manuscripts] traveled across the continent"), the passage in *Martin Eden* that reproduces, in expanded form, the account of rejection initially provided by "Getting into Print" pointedly amplifies the meaning and impact of mechanized rejection:

> It was the rejection slips that completed the horrible machine-likeness of the process. These slips were printed in stereotyped forms and he had received hundreds of them—as many as a dozen or more on each of his earlier manuscripts. If he had received one line, one personal line, along with one rejection of all his rejections, he would have been cheered. But not one editor had given that proof of existence. And he could conclude only that there were no warm human men at the other end, only mere cogs, well oiled and running beautifully in the machine. (161)

Aestheticizing the efficiency of anonymous brutality, beauty here is viciously ironic. The literary traffic in which Eden becomes caught evacuates all trace of authenticity ("one personal line") from its workings. Piling up by the "hundreds," the stereotyped rejections supplement the literary waste given off by the system, yet in so doing only perpetuate its ceaseless circulation. Eden's rejection slips constitute the souvenirs of a punitive traveling regimen.

Appropriately, when "the smooth-running editorial machine [finally breaks] down" (262) and *The Transcontinental Monthly* agrees to publish "one of his horror stories" for a paltry five dollars (263), Eden lapses into a delirium that, punctuated by visions of burning sums "in fiery figures" (265), only affirms the grind of the literary machine. Upon pulling an imaginary "lever . . . [that makes] his mind revolve about him, a monstrous wheel of fortune, a merry-go-round of memory, a revolving sphere of wisdom," he finds himself transported back to the laundry where, at an earlier moment of impoverishment, he had gone to make money through unending toil (267). In his feverish fantasy about this past experience, laundry work becomes inextricable from literary industry—he "before the mangle," receiving blank checks (not cuffs) fed by "an editor of a magazine" "for a million years or so," seeing his coworker Joe "starching manuscripts," then finding himself "back in the ironing room in the midst of a snow-storm . . . [of] checks of large denomination, the smallest not less than a thousand dollars" (268). Notwithstanding its surrealism, the fantasy holds an exactingly predictive power: subject for years to discipline by the literary industry, first through outright rejection and subsequently through miserable recompense coupled with the regular deferral of payment, Eden suddenly finds his writing in demand and himself a celebrity who can command for his labor "checks of large denomination." "At first, so great was his disgust with the magazines and all bourgeois society, Martin fought against publicity; but in the end, because it was easier than not to, he surrendered. . . . Money poured in on him, fame poured in on him; he flashed, comet-like, through the world of literature" (435–37). The result is to transform yet reinforce Eden's fraught relation to the mangling mechanics of literary traffic: although fame and fortune replace nonentity and poverty as the effects of ceaseless circulation within the literary machine, that change—monumental, in material terms—only exacerbates his alienation.

At issue is the arbitrary nature of the process, the illogic driving bourgeois discriminations in the capitalist marketplace:

> It was the bourgeoisie that bought his books and poured its gold into his money-sack, and from what little he knew of the bourgeoisie it was not clear to him how it could possibly appreciate or comprehend what he had written. His intrinsic beauty and power meant nothing to the thousands who were acclaiming him and buying his books. He was the fad of the hour, the adventurer who had stormed Parnassus while the gods nodded. The hundreds of thousands read him and acclaimed him with the same brute non-understanding with which they had flung themselves on [his friend and mentor] Brissenden's [long poem] "Ephemera" and torn it to pieces—a wolf-rabble that fawned on him instead of fanging him. Fawn or fang, it was all a matter of chance. (441–42)

Figuring the senselessness of middle-class taste, here the call of the wild articulates pure accident (by way, I would note, of a concept, "wolf-rabble," that bleakly finds the wolf-man London confronting himself in his imagined audience). The "intrinsic beauty and power" necessary to the ideology of literary genius hold an at best irrational relation to purchase and acclaim, the interimplicated means to real and cultural capital. As Loren Glass rightly argues:

> [t]he problem of Martin's fame is a problem of value, specifically [what Eden himself sees as] the "purely fictitious value" of literary work. This value is a problem—is fictitious—because it seems to have nothing to do with its author and everything to do with its public circulation. This circulation—through a sort of fantastic retroactivity—creates an authorial source—the famous writer—who occupies the helpless body of the original author.[79]

And the arbitrariness of such public circulation is acute: the pieces that, compounding Eden's sudden celebrity in wake of the success of his essay "The Shame of the Sun" and his novel *Overdue*, ensure the continuous and far-flung circulation of his name, are without exception works previously subject to relentless rejection by the literary machine. Baffled by the mercurial change in fortune of what remains no more or less than "work performed"(437), the celebrated author has neither will nor desire to write; much like the tramp typologized by London in the essay of the same name, he finds that "[s]terility is [now] his portion."[80] Appropriately enough, given the arbitrariness of the publishing industry, in a perfect gesture of archival elimination Eden the author simply mails his way to fame.

For Martin Eden, the alternative to the bad faith of a literary industry that turns to profit the bankruptcy of its judgments and to the crushing predicament of a celebrity that evacuates identity through an irrational transformation lies in a recurring fantasy of exoticized South Sea travel. This fantasy first strikes him just before he is struck by fame, when he realizes that Brissenden's "Ephemera," the masterpiece Eden misguidedly negotiated into print, has been butchered by the magazine in which it appears:

> How long he sat there he did not know, until, suddenly, across his sightless vision he saw form a long horizontal line of white. It was curious. But as he watched it grow in definiteness he saw that it was a coral reef smoking in the white Pacific surges.... he made out a small canoe... [in which] he saw a young bronze god.... He was Moti, the youngest son of Tati, the chief, and this was Tahiti.... It was the end of the day, and Moti was coming home from the fishing.... Next, [Eden] was no longer an onlooker but was himself in the canoe, Moti was crying out, they were both thrusting hard with their paddles, racing on the steep face of the flying turquoise. (410–11)[81]

The force of such fantasy depends on the way it counters the sterile circuitry of literary labor with the restorative, erotic work of strenuous physical exertion conveyed by the hard "thrusting" in the vision.[82] The piston-like quality of such labor recasts the motor principle of industrial automation in service of purposeful movement not pointless circulation. Thus the scene posits an outside to the entrapment entailed by literary labor, one that becomes more and more detailed in its elaboration as Eden becomes more celebrated—and more wealthy. Concretized against the arbitrary rewards of fame, Eden's tropical dream transforms into a material project:

> He knew a valley and a bay in the Marquesas that he could buy for a thousand Chili dollars. . . . He would buy a schooner—one of those yacht-like, coppered crafts that sailed like witches—and go trading copra and pearling among the islands. He would make the valley and the bay his headquarters. He would build a patriarchal grass house like Tati's, and have it and the valley and the schooner filled with dark-skinned servitors. He would entertain there the factor of Taiohae, captains of wandering traders, and all the best of the South Pacific riffraff. He would keep open house and entertain like a prince. And he would forget the books he had opened and the world that had proved an illusion. (420–21)[83]

Arbitrary reward, at once material and reputational, haunts the world of fantasy and the world of illusion that Eden here juxtaposes. In his desire to "forget" the bourgeois realm of literary success, Eden turns to another "illusion" (of a paradise in the Marquesas) that, legitimated by book-bound representations and maintaining colonial practice through the accumulation of capital, generates decisively material effects *by means* of its manifest distortions. So understood, the outside envisioned in South Sea fantasy becomes hard to disarticulate from the circuitry of the social and material inside it purports to counter. No wonder, perhaps, that by novel's end Eden, having realized that "[t]he South Seas charmed him no more than did bourgeois civilization" (474), chooses suicide over South Sea travel; the alternative promised him by such travel already circulates within capital's sphere—a commodity inextricable, under American empire, from the material history of bourgeois economics.

If for London's protagonist the South Seas represent the failed promise of escape and of investment, libidinal as well as economic, for London himself that space was at once less contradictory and more complicated in significance. He undertook (at typically ferocious speed) to compose *Martin Eden* while attempting to cruise around the world to escape the constraints of his own fame. The relation of composition to escape is deeply ironic, since London's aim in writing the novel was to produce a source of income with which to reduce his debt—debt incurred in large part to mount the kind of trip not so much afforded as demanded by his reputation. Chronicled in *The Cruise of the Snark*, before its abandonment the voyage saw London through destinations around the Pacific Rim; it evidently originated in tropical fantasies much like those of Martin Eden, and as evidently fell to pieces in face of a number of material, existential, and ideological crises. Most immediately pressing of these was the general failure of London's health. Having begun the adventure with his wife Charmian Kittredge in April 1907, by November 1908 he was laid out in a Sydney hospital, too sick to continue. As he recounts in the postscript of a letter to Richard W. Gilder, the editor of *Century Magazine*, on 22 December 1908:

> P.S.—My sickness is of so serious a nature that I am compelled to abandon the voyage of the *Snark* and to return to my own climate of California. The doctors in Australia can do nothing for me, because they do not know what is the matter with me. My trouble is nervous in origin; and all that I can prescribe for myself is to return to an environment where I maintained a stable nervous equilibrium, in the hope of regaining that equilibrium.[84]

The description of his condition becomes more graphic still in the "Backword" to *The Cruise of the Snark:*

> The mysterious malady that afflicted my hands was too much for the Australian specialists. It was unknown in the literature of medicine. No case like it had ever been reported. It extended from my hands to my feet so that at times I was as helpless as a child. On occasion my hands were twice their natural size, with seven dead and dying skins peeling off at the same time. There were times when my toe-nails, in twenty-four hours, grew as thick as they were long. After filing them off, inside another twenty-four hours they were as thick as before.[85]

Upon his return, London undertook research that convinced him he "had a strong predisposition toward the tissue-destructiveness of tropical light. [On the trip] I was being torn to pieces by the ultra-violet rays just as many experimenters with the X-ray have been torn to pieces."[86] In his introduction to *Martin Eden*, Andrew Sinclair further glosses the problem: "[London's] mental energy seemed to him at times to be mental sickness. He had lamed his splendid body and began to suffer from bowel diseases. The voyage of the *Snark* was meant to reassert his physical dominance, but it ended in his physical collapse" (11). For a self-declaredly strenuous subject the humiliation must have been substantial: London's nervous trouble, only aggravated by an extreme version of the revivifying exaction outlined by Silas Weir

Mitchell in his "West" cure, demanded instead effeminate rest for its repair. The prospect of restoration promised in advance by exotic travel gave way, in the event, to the body's treachery, exposing raw spots marked by failure, entropy, and decay. Shadowed by bowel disease only to be irradiated by the tropical sun, London relinquished the catharsis of escape in a crisis of shit and peeling skin, a traveling experience that recollects, provocatively, his description in "The Tramp" of tramp mobility not as a means of escape but as "one of the safety valves" for the elimination of "the waste of the social organism."

Certainly, such lived crisis suits the brutal materiality regnant in so much of London's writing. At the same time, it signals a failure of the mobile body that provokes, in the narratives inspired by London's South Sea voyages, the ever more desperate reassertion of the brutal manufacture of that body as the relay among cultural production, cultural consumption, and cultural traffic—or indeed among the work of culture, the work of travel, and the work of work. *Martin Eden* provides the backdrop for this reassertion. The emphasis on nervous disorder in the postscript to the Gilder letter insinuates, against London's hope for nervous equilibrium, the feverish body as feverish machine, its motors firing wildly beneath the skin. Disrupting equilibrium's calm, this image figures in shorthand the exacting demands of disciplinary pace. If, in the postscript to the Gilder letter, home sustains where travel only debilitates, nevertheless under the terms of disciplinary pace the contrary actions of sustenance and debilitation become inextricable.

Belied by the brutalities of *Martin Eden*—a novel provoked and, for financial reasons, required by London's South Sea voyage—the forced romanticization of travel in *The Cruise of the Snark* falters more immediately over nearly schizophrenic shifts between idealized glories of traveling escape and ceaselessly realized torments of running sores and rotting flesh. Leprosy on Moloki, South Sea elephantiasis, tuberculosis, Solomon sores: as these come increasingly to dominate *The Cruise of the Snark*, the liberatory power of travel (or what London more prosaically terms its "fun") seems tenable only to the extent that nonwhite flesh decomposes.[87] Writing about the change in the character of life in the Marquesas in the half-century since Melville had published *Typee*, London observes:

> now all this strength and beauty has departed, and the valley of Typee is the abode of some dozen wretched creatures, afflicted by leprosy, elephantiasis, and tuberculosis.... When one considers the situation, one is almost driven to the conclusion that the white race flourishes on impurity and corruption. [But] natural selection... gives the explanation. We of the white race

> are the survivors and the descendants of the thousands of generations of survivors in the war with the microorganisms. Whenever one of us was born with a constitution peculiarly receptive to these minute enemies, such a one promptly died. Only these [sic] of us survived who could withstand them. We who are alive are the immune, the fit—the ones best constituted to live in a world of hostile microorganisms.[88]

Here the prospect of a "white race" that might flourish on "impurity and corruption" gives way to an ideal of that race rendered fit, immune, through the invisible prophylaxis of whiteness itself. Thus protected, London can shift gears into pathos:

> The poor Marquesans had undergone no such selection. They were not immune. And they, who had made a custom of eating their enemies, were now eaten by enemies so microscopic as to be invisible, and against whom no war of dart and javelin was possible. On the other hand, had there been a few hundred thousand Marquesans to begin with, there might have been sufficient survivors to found a new race—a regenerated race, if a plunge into a festering bath of organic poison can be called regeneration.[89]

The concluding image of apocalyptic debasement only underscores the perspective that London presumes from the start: whiteness supplies the standard against which to articulate the childlike fragility of supposedly primitive peoples, here imagined in terms of an evolutionary innocence and its recompense in microbiological cannibalism. In view of London's debilitating and mysterious illness in Australia, however, this account becomes as ironic as it is suspect. By the terms of London's own diagnosis, tropical light supplies the anticolonial X-ray that, by peeling away layer after layer of skin, indicates the instability and unreliability of cutaneous judgment. Disrupting the project of "blond beastly" adventure, the outcome exposes the explanatory failures of imperialist science alongside the constitutional frailties of particular white bodies.

Learning by Accident

This disruptive lesson haunts the politics of mobility at work in *The Cruise of the Snark* and (as decisively, if more obliquely) in *Martin Eden*. In so doing, it intimates something of the volatility of mobility's pedagogy more generally. Although quite disparate in content and focus, the materials addressed in this chapter all emphasize the problems alongside the promise of instruction, returning consistently to entangled issues of habit and conduct as they bear on practices of human movement. This tendency will underscore the importance of the links in the United States during this period among pedagogical ambition, disciplinary method, and material and social mobility. In *Education and the Cult of Efficiency* (a study lending support to my claim), Raymond Callahan argues that "[t]he procedure for bringing about a more businesslike organization and operation of the schools was fairly well standardized from 1900 to 1925. It consisted of making unfavorable comparisons between the schools and business enterprise, of applying business-industrial criteria (e.g., economy and efficiency) to education, and of suggesting that business and industrial practices be adopted by educators."[90] Occurring primarily through an intensive application of the theories of Taylor to the work of schools, the effort to systematize education marked one among a set of allied responses to the unpredictable conditions of mobility and belonging at century's turn, or to what Callahan more matter-of-factly calls "the problems which were a product of rapid industrialization": "the consolidation of industry and the concentration of wealth; the ruthless exploitation of the country's national resources; the corruption and inefficiency of government; the tremendous growth of cities; the flood of immigrants who added to the complexity of the social and political problems in the urban areas; and finally, the fear among the middle class that America would react to these problems in an extreme or radical way."[91] For my purposes here, what matters is the recognition that mobility and its discourses contribute to the work of social and cultural pedagogy by producing, reproducing, yet contesting key forms of common knowledge and belonging: hence the investment of agents in the culture industry in articulating and circulating the terms and conditions of human movement—terms and conditions under which the distribution of mobility as a social resource may have occurred, or for that matter from which the habitus of modern mobility might build. In this light, I find it unsurprising that every author discussed in this chapter doubles, to some degree, as an officer of education. And, though their hegemonic investments vary substantially, for all of them the work of pedagogy submits dynamics of human movement to the action of disciplinary pace. As the lessons at stake underscore the importance of standardization as an issue, so too they raise problems of intimacy and distance that, persistent within modernity's mobility regimes, become increasingly crucial, in the first years of the twentieth century, to emerging forms of modernist cultural authority and epistemology.

The implications of such a claim fall well beyond the scope of my argument here.[92] By raising the matter of pedagogy, I simply wish to emphasize that, in the United States at the turn of the century, workers in the culture industry often use the vocabularies of disciplinary pace to articulate problems of regimental instruction attending the politics of mobility and the politics of social belonging. As a means to imagine and regulate bodies and motion, the use of this discourse undertakes to assess and encompass the shifting lineaments, around 1900, of American geopolitical space, in which migrant, mobile, often alien subjects who would not stay put (the worker, the immigrant) remained indispensable to the industrial, as to the more broadly social and cultural, projects of capitalism.

My aim in this chapter, however, has not been to locate, in disciplinary pace, some overarching logic through which to homogenize mobility's dynamics at the turn of the nineteenth century. What matters instead is the historical contingency of these disciplinary processes, the signs of excess and crisis pressuring any attempt to regulate and occlude struggles over mobility as a social resource. Projects of social regulation and standardization remain haunted by the ragged texture and volatile shock of mobility and movement, travel and traffic, in ways that disciplinary pace, for all its power, fails to prevent or contain. These, I would stress, are the crucial lessons of the politics of mobility, most important because least expected: that, however determined and directed, histories and itineraries of human movement remain contingent, accidental; that the traces of contest legible within these histories and itineraries can teach us to see how they might have been different—and so to imagine how they could now be remade.

Epilogue
Mobilization Time

> But the opacity of the chance thing is precisely what makes history legible as something more than a relation between (or a conflation of) what was and what is. The relation between the underdetermined and the overdetermined . . . allows us to perceive the past, in any one moment, as the struggle between what was and what might have been.
>
> —*Bill Brown*, The Material Unconscious

> It is the time of mobilization, of marching together, and we must go forward in close order, like silver in the veins of the Andes.
>
> —*José Martí, "Our America"*

When marketing executives at Microsoft began asking potential customers in the mid-1990s "Where do you want to go today?" they aimed to capitalize on an orthodox sense of mobility's liberating power, one cherished in the United States since at least the antebellum period. Through the prospect of new technology, Microsoft sold the promise of utmost extension, such that simple keystrokes could conquer time and space in achieving an instantaneous, irrepressible transport. The beauty of the fantasy held not least to the prophylactic on its prosthesis, for by traveling without traveling, one could, for a price, avoid messy forms of contact tainting material movements in the global social sphere.[1]

Nearly a decade later, what seems so striking about the Microsoft campaign has less to do with the insidious force of the fantasy it sold than with the halting failure of that fantasy to occlude volatile contingencies of mobility in an age of global flows. One would struggle today to overestimate the explosive significance of mobility's contest within the neoliberal new world order. Clearly the overdetermined emblem of such contest will remain, for some time, the commercial jet made flying bomb. Yet, if an important symptom of the contemporary politics of mobility, this emblem has nevertheless tended to distract from the larger dynamics determining its emergence, dynamics working, as Neil Smith argues, to conflate American "national self-interest with global universalism" and to reinvent "the national (U.S.) State at the global scale."[2] "No other nation," Smith observes, "has been so immune to and yet so implicated in the terror that made the twentieth century the most deadly in history; nowhere else has a populace had the luxury of deluding themselves that geography is salvation, that geography protects power. With that illusion punctured after 2001, national exceptionalism is reinventing itself as the elixir of a putatively postnational globalism."[3] Claims that "everything changed" on 11 September 2001 presume just such an altered exceptionalism, inscribing ignorance at America's tentacular intimacy with the terror industry so as to mystify, through the prospect of epochal rupture, the messier histories of imperial business as usual.[4] I would argue that such claims not only constitute the dystopian counterpart to Microsoft's utopian tagline—they suffer a comparable fate: the exceptionalist logic of absolute transformation, like the alchemical promise of immediate transport, strives yet fails to solve the crises borne from mobility's contest, crises that command, instead, a fully historical reckoning.[5]

Deeply enmeshed in processes currently understood (whether enthusiastically or skeptically, apologetically or critically) in terms of globalization—market power eclipsing national sovereignty, temporalities and trajectories always accelerating, production and labor deterritorialized, consumption and speculation regnant, commodity culture and mass mediation governing all desire and belonging—the specific issues outlined so provisionally in the paragraphs above provide a way to understand how the global system presumes, as it requires, a politics of mobility through which to work.[6] In their introduction to *Millennial Capitalism and the Culture of Neoliberalism*, Jean and John Comaroff elaborate just this point, emphasizing the productive power of mobility's problematic within the material conditions of globalizing life. As they observe, for many commentators globalization means that "capital has become uncontrollable and keeps moving, at its own velocity, to sites of optimum advantage," that "the global workforce has become ever more mobile as job seekers . . . migrate ever farther in pursuit of even the most menial of jobs, under even the most feudal of conditions," and that "these human flows seem, in varying proportions, to elude surveillance, despite the highly repressive mechanisms often put into place to monitor national frontiers."[7] Although neither entirely new nor conclusively, universally achieved, and although complicated in significance by Smith's argument about the inextricability of globalization from American national interest, nevertheless in a broad sense such developments materialize the conditions of possibility for contests over mobility early in the new millennium. If, as the Comaroffs argue, "[n]eoliberalism aspires, in its ideology and practice, to intensify the abstractions inherent in capitalism itself [by] separat[ing] labor power from its human context, . . . replac[ing] society with the market, . . . [and] build[ing] a universe out of aggregated transactions," then we must also add that it works to realize its aspiration not least through an ever-increasing reliance on traffic, on mobility's mediations.[8]

The point is not simply that, in the present, more people experience more mobility more of the time. Such a mundane insight misses the uncertainties at issue: because the globalizing shift intensifies processes already manifest under capitalism, it will make mobility's contest still more acute, still more volatile. Globalization, Susie O'Brien and Imre Szeman contend, "is nothing if not modernity squared"—and, as such, compounds exponentially one of modernity's prime symptoms: those struggles, uneven and unpredictable, over the determination and distribution of mobility as a material and social resource.[9] In the contemporary American moment, at least, we see (like an uncanny return of Virginia's policy circa 1831) the obsessive will to proscribe the mobility of some and compel the mobility of others. The effect is less pure velocity than lurching rhythm: the strategic deployment of slowness and stasis alongside speed for geopolitical and geoeconomic ends. As Smith observes, the U.S. "'war on terrorism,' pursued to make the world safe for 'our values,' [has] brought with it a whole architecture of 'homeland security' that seriously hinders, prevents, or delays the movement of goods, people, capital, and ideas into and out of the United States."[10] Think, here, of the over six hundred foreign nationals detained since January 2002 by the U.S. government at Guantánamo Bay, an incarceration, violating international law, that reflects the "post-9/11" ideology of epochal rupture, and that counters the threat of volatile movement with brutalizing immobility. For those held without charge or judicial review, first at Camp

X-Ray and, more recently, at Camp Delta, the cruel conjunction of stereotype and stasis regularly reinscribed (as I have argued) in the U.S. nineteenth century has recurred with a vengeance. Or think of the nearly thirty thousand airport baggage screeners fired in 2002 under the draconian terms of the U.S. Transportation Security Act—the majority of them immigrants or ethnic minorities, all of them denied any recourse to collective bargaining on the grounds that, as Admiral James Loy, head of the U.S. Transportation Security Administration, argues, "[f]ighting terrorism demands a flexible workforce that can rapidly respond to threats," where such rapid response "can mean changes in work assignments and other conditions of employment that are not compatible with the duty to bargain with labor unions."[11] Here the words "flexible workforce" veil, as if mere description, an aggressively politicized intervention. With an astounding cynicism, Loy makes grave vulnerabilities in contemporary transport serve brazenly neoliberal ends; the overdetermined prospect of terrorism's arrival in America legitimates an enforced departure of thousands of workers fully consistent with the kinds of downsizing underway long before September 2001. We can detect, within flexibility's demands, a mutated form of vagabondage returning to haunt the scenes of American labor.

Could José Martí have anticipated, without knowing, the insult to his Cuba now installed at Guantánamo Bay? Might we find, damning yet unintended in "Our America," a fractured prophecy of such insult, such violation? Although genuine, these questions neither presume nor settle for the conflation of "what was and what is" (to recall Bill Brown's phrasing); they venture instead to find the uncanny reverberation alongside the "opacity" of chance in history.[12] Understanding the global millennium as what, against the logic of absolute rupture, of complete transformation, Imre Szeman calls "an epochal intensification" of conditions operative at earlier moments in the development of capitalism, gives a way to understand why, with respect to mobility's contest, so many of the processes, practices, and dynamics I have traced in this book seem to animate the present—recognizable yet reconfigured, finding new life in the workings of global capital.[13] When Deputy Defense Secretary Paul Wolfowitz, responding to congressional criticism of the second Bush administration's plea for a further $87 million to finance ongoing military operations in Iraq, can in exasperation contend that "confidence is part of winning," one must suspect that Melville, in anatomizing his age, managed as well to prefigure our own.[14] Globalization spreads illimitably the contagion of confidence. Precisely because what the

Comaroffs term "alchemic techniques" ("casino capitalism" and "occult economics," in their trenchant formulation) can "defy reason in promising unnaturally large profits—to yield wealth without production, value without effort," we know that Melville's con-man still walks among us.[15] Ours too is a moment abandoned to circulation: the catastrophes of speculation and crises of public trust linking 1837 to 1850 to 1857 to 1894 likewise charge the relentlessness yet unpredictability of mobility's contest in the current era. Just as antebellum terrors of subaltern uprising haunt our current moment in refracted, global form, so too the PATRIOT Act, historically particular in significance and astounding in invasiveness, finds conceptual if not legal precedence in the Fugitive Slave Law.[16] And, as I have already implied, the material dynamics of contemporary capitalism mean that vagabondage now returns, only to go global. Although in the millennial economy Fordist manufacture gives way to post-Fordist circuitry, the political project seems entirely familiar: to ensure subjection in stasis through the process of being moved, faster and faster: "Where"—not promise, now, but threat—"do you want to go today?"

What interests me most about the opaque and fractured correspondences I have been tracing has to do with their potential for breakdown or failure—not as correspondences so much as means to ideological and political control. In important respects, any politics of mobility turns on chance, where chance entails both those accidents unforeseen under capitalism and those risks that market governance cannot help (now more than ever) but venture. If mobility has persisted in serving as a key sign of capitalist modernity's progress in America since at least the antebellum period, then historical struggles over the material meanings of mobility as an unevenly distributed resource constitute one cause of rupture within such hegemonic narrative. Thus the recurrence of particular kinds of crisis within histories of mobility's uneven social distribution will underscore and intensify discontinuities and vulnerabilities within progressivist ideology. Here, we must recognize the extent to which any politics of mobility remains, in an irreconcilable tension crucial to its dynamic, overdetermined and underdetermined at once. By analyzing at length mobility's contest as registered and advanced by the traffic in letters in nineteenth-century America, and by emphasizing, much more provisionally, the uncanny reverberation of such contest in the contemporary moment, I hope to have persuasively critiqued naturalizing ideals of human movement—the doxa by which mobility constitutes a common condition, the signature style of supposedly intrinsic American liberty—

while at the same time refusing the lure of an overarching logic and reified understanding of mobility's social, material, and political meanings. At stake is an effort to reckon the disarming unpredictability, and mark the contingent returns, within mobility's contest.

Over a century after Martí wrote "Our America," those troubled by the rapacious advance of American empire, and by the politics of mobility it deploys, must face once more the need to march together. The worldwide demonstrations of 15 February 2003, held to protest U.S. aggression against Iraq and occurring in sequence—from Athens to Caracas, from Brussels to Kuala Lampur, from Sydney to Cairo, from Edmonton to Tel Aviv, from Tokyo to Washington, from Barcelona to Lahore—like so many concussive shocks to the coordinates of global power, set a spectacular standard for the comprehension, and the telling, of mobilization's time. What, by comparison, might cultural criticism possibly hope to contribute?

I hold no illusions about the broad social power of books such as this one—it does not exist. At the same time, though, I like to believe that an historically inflected critical practice matters for the labor and power of mass mobilization in the present, precisely because it can alter and enliven knowledge and belief, even if only incrementally. As Walter Benjamin famously insisted, "[t]o articulate the past historically does not mean to recognize it 'the way it really was.' It means to seize hold of a memory as it flashes up at a moment of danger."[17] The contemporary moment is a gravely dangerous one, not least because it finds collective memory in jeopardy, threatened by what I understand as the operations of selective remembrance or indeed imperial amnesia: memory manipulated in service of a larger forgetting crucial to the aims of empire (to take only one example, the moral case for war against Saddam Hussein's Iraq required that the prior status of his regime as a privileged client of the U.S. government be forgotten).[18] Key, here, is the exceptionalist narrative that relies, so decisively, on a politics of mobility: as a special case, the United States can be in its actions, and can move in its interventions, without precedent—an understanding that works not just to distinguish the United States from other imperial formations but also to separate (or indeed to except) the American imperial present from its imperial history and legacy. At issue is what Tariq Ali calls "[t]he virtual outlawing of history by the dominant culture," which, as he argues, "has reduced the process of democracy to farce."[19] Against imperial amnesia, we must ensure that history's problematic, much like mobility's, stays subject to contest—that politicized resistance works to make memory itself a cause for action. This effort has nothing to do with reflection; understood by analogy to muscle memory, it aims instead to make resistance perpetual, a collective habit.[20] The very possibility of changing history demands nothing less. I hope my book will serve as one small resource in the very large project of making and mobilizing countermemory as counterpower.

Notes

Introduction

1. For the details of this treaty, see the "Indian Affairs: Laws and Treaties (U.S.)" database, at http://digital.library.okstate.edu/kappler/Vol2/tocy2.htm#Y5. In *Indian Nation: Native American Literature and Nineteenth-Century Nationalisms* (Durham: Duke University Press, 1997), Cheryl Walker indicates that Pokagon "opened the fair on Chicago Day by ringing the new Liberty Bell," a reference I take to mean the Columbian Liberty Bell, which had been imagined and produced to evince a renewed patriotism, connecting the Columbian commemorations to the moment of the nation's founding (202). *The Dream City*, a photographic compilation from the fair, observes: "Some time before the opening of the Exposition, it was thought that the unique, popular souvenir of the event should be prepared, and it was suggested that a great bell be cast, material for which should, for the most part, be furnished by people from all parts of the country. Contributions of old coins, precious metal, medals and relics of Colonial and Revolutionary days were called for, and in course of time these began to arrive, and the bell was duly cast in a foundry at Troy, New York. Besides the usual amount of bronze necessary for its proper construction, all these relics were thrown into castings. Since these came from all over the United States, the new bell was as much, or more, a national affair than Old Liberty itself" (*The Dream City: A Portfolio of Photographic Views of the World's Columbian Exposition, with an Introduction by Halsey C. Ives* [St. Louis: N. D. Thompson Company, 1893–94], n.p.; http://columbus.gl.iit.edu). See also the Liberty Bell Virtual Museum website at http://www.libertybellmuseum.com/columbianlibertybell.htm.

2. Brian Dippie, *The Vanishing American: White Attitudes and U.S. Indian Policy* (Middletown, CT: Wesleyan University Press, 1982), 204; emphasis in the original.

3. James Clifton's entry in the *Encyclopedia of North American Indians* (ed. Frederick Hoxie [Cambridge, MA: Houghton Mifflin Company, 1996]) typifies the depiction of Pokagon as an assimilationist fraud: "His [oral] style was a mix of fawning sentimentality and surrender to the inevitable, with just enough of a tinge of anger over paradise lost to titillate but not badly annoy his late nineteenth-century audiences" (494). In "Representing History: Performing the Columbian Exposition" (*Theatre Journal* 54 [4] [2002]: 589–606), Rosemary Banks offers a more nuanced view of Native performance by addressing the inextricability of supposedly ethnographic spectacles from entertainment at the Chicago fair. For Banks, "[p]erformance . . . is live and critiques even the ideas it enacts"—an important reminder about performative undecidability that usefully complicates Clifton's rather simplistic dismissal of Pokagon (596).

4. The 9 October 1893 *New York Times* account of Chicago Day, although silent on the matter of Pokagon's speech, highlights to telling effect the reification at issue: "The first event arranged by the World's Fair Committee of the Chicago Common Council took place at 9 o'clock and was in commemoration of Chicago's birth and early history. The old Pottawatomie chief, Simon Pokaron [sic], whose father, Leopold, deeded the land upon which Chicago is built, had been induced to come from his home in Hartford, Mich., for Chicago Day. He stood beside the Columbian bell with uncovered head in the dress of the white man and received the homage of thousands. He was born sixty-three years ago Sept. 27 last, on the day that the transfer deed was delivered to the agents of the United States Government. By his side stood the most picturesque figure among more than 500,000 people. His dress consisted of a heavy and varied coat of paint on his face, body, and limbs, a headdress of feathers, and a breech clout of beaded buckskin. He wore moccasins and looked a typical Indian on the war path, although he came with a message of peace, standing as a historic figure between the Chicago of yesterday and the Chicago of to-day. He was Chief John Young, sixty years of age, who came from the Pottawattomie Reservation, near Miles, Mich., to tell the people of all nations that his father, who bore the same name, christened the World's Fair city 'Chicago,' which, literally interpreted, means 'where the skunk dwells.' These two old and feeble Pottawattomie chiefs were the idols of the hour" (*New York Times* no. 1857, 10 October 1893, 5). Hubert Howe Bancroft's official *Book of the Fair* manages to efface any sense of participatory agency, replacing reified aboriginal spectacle with the ellipsis of passive action: "At noon the Exposition flag was unfurled in the court of honor above the liberty bell, whose tones were presently heard afar in the grounds. Then was presented to [the city's] mayor the original deed to the site of Chicago, transferred to the government by the chief of the Pottawattomies" (Chicago and San Francisco: The Bancroft Company, 1893, 809; http://columbus.gl.iit.edu).

5. Frederick Ward Putnam, speech to the Committee of Liberal Arts, Chicago, 21 September 1891; quoted in Curtis M. Hinsley, "The World as Marketplace: Commodification of the Exotic at the World's Columbian Exposition, Chicago, 1893," in *Exhibiting Cultures: The Poetics and Politics of Museum Display*, ed. Ivan Karp and Steven Lavine (Washington: Smithsonian, 1991), 347.

6. Ibid.

7. Historians disagree about the date of Pokagon's White City visit, as about the tenor of his speech. Although Frederick Hoxie (in his anthology *Talking Back to Civilization: Indian Voices from the Progressive Era* [Boston: Bedford, 2001]) and James Clifton (in *The Encyclopedia of North American Indians*) assert that Pokagon appeared at the opening ceremonies on 1 May, a *New York Times* story (cited in note 4) corroborates the 9 October date given by Robert Muccigrosso (in *Celebrating the New World: Chicago's Columbian Exposition of 1893* [Chicago: Ivan R. Dee, 1993]), Cheryl Walker (in *Indian Nation*), and Rosemary Banks (in "Representing History"). Hoxie, Muccigrosso, and Banks all argue, however, that Pokagon was explicitly critical in his World's Fair speech, a misperception attributable, as Walker suggests, to the conflation of the speech with the earlier pamphlet. Walker helps to dispel the confusion by noting the concurrent publication of "The Red Man's Rebuke" under the alternate title "The Red Man's Greeting"—the same title Pokagon seems to have given his Chicago Day remarks (209–10). In light of this reuse of the pamphlet's alternate title, I would argue that, even though Pokagon advocated assimilation on 9 October, by using the more biting irony of his pamphlet's two titles to frame his orature, he managed to inject a striking if subtle measure of dissonance into an otherwise constrained performance.

8. Simon Pokagon, "The Red Man's Rebuke," reprinted as an appendix in Walker, *Indian Nation*, 211. The inclusion of Pokagon's pamphlet text in academic books (and particularly in Hoxie's anthology) will reconfigure but not relax the institutionalizing pressures on the "Indian voice" compelled, in 1893, to "talk back to civilization"—a tension, and an irony, likewise attending my use of Pokagon. I am indebted to Pauline Wakeham for this insight.

9. Walker, 213, 212.

10. Ibid., 217.

11. Ibid., 218.

12. Four years later, Pokagon offered a less defensive, more determined assessment of the situation of Native peoples in America. "The Future of the Red Man"(*Forum* 23 [August 1897]: 698–708) marks, as its title suggests, a complex engagement with the well-worn ideology of Indian disappearance by insisting on a form of Native futurity, and so gives a tacit rejoinder to the 1896 biographical sketch of its author, "An Interesting Representative of a Vanishing Race" (*Arena* 80 [July 1896]: 240–50).

13. In the essay from which comes my introduction's epigraph, Doreen Massey invokes this same phrase. Although I arrived independently at the concept of a politics of mobility, beginning to articulate its significance well before I knew of her work, as will become readily apparent her incisive theorizations of space and mobility have profoundly influenced my project. See "A Global Sense of Place," in Massey's book *Place, Space, and Gender* (Cambridge: Polity Press, 1994).

14. The process I am describing here will recall Wai-chee Dimock's marvelous analysis of the spatialization of time in *Empire for Liberty* (Princeton, NJ: Princeton University Press, 1989). For reasons that will become clear in my ensuing discussion of the politics of spatiality, though, I feel uneasy with the implication in her argument that, as space is fundamentally ahistorical, spatialization is, by definition, dehistoricizing.

15. Where to begin? The discourse in question is enormous, eclipsing the will to catalogue it. In fiction, Cooper, Child, and Sedgwick are important early touchstones. Bill Cody's Wild West Show remains the most celebrated traveling materialization of perpetual disappearance. Regardless of form or genre, generalizations of local and cultural belief do predominate, as for instance when Ralph Waldo Emerson supplies the New England view: "We in Massachusetts see the Indians only as a picturesque antiquity" (*The Journals and Miscellaneous Notebooks of Ralph Waldo Emerson*, vol. 9, 1843–1847, ed. Ralph H. Orth and Alfred R. Ferguson [Cambridge, MA: The Belknap Press of Harvard University Press, 1971], 175). More provocative is Margaret Fuller, who finds the book of nature taking its cue from the canons of culture: "Amalgamation would afford the only true and profound means of civilization. But nature seems, like all else, to declare, that this race is fated to perish" (*Summer on the Lakes*, in *The Essential Margaret Fuller*, ed. Jeffrey Steele [New Brunswick, NJ: Rutgers University Press, 1992], 188). Interestingly enough, even in disappearing, "the Indian" supplied, as Nancy Ruttenberg shows, the idealized voice for poetry—and, so, the ideological accents of an "indigenous" American literature. See *Democratic Personality: Popular Voice and the Trials of Authorship* (Stanford: Stanford University Press, 1998), 312–14.

16. Gilles Deleuze, "Mediators," trans. Martin Joughin, in *Incorporations*, ed. Jonathan Crary and Sanford Kwinter (New York: Zone, 1992), 286. Clearly this brief commentary on Native American removal and the discourse of aboriginal disappearance cannot begin to do justice to a fraught, complex history. Brian Dippie's *The Vanishing American* gives a useful overview of the key developments in the long career of this discourse. We will disagree, though, on the larger significance of the progressivist tenor of Pokagon's views.

17. Bill Brown makes a comparable point about the West more generally, observing that, by 1900, "accounts of the West's actual disappearance, the waning of its essential difference, was hardly news; rather, the news had long been part and parcel of the West's appearance in print. . . . In other words, while an authentic West is reported to be absent, its authenticity remains insistently present." See "Reading the West: Cultural and Historical Background," in *Reading the West: An Anthology of Dime Westerns*, ed. Brown (Boston: Bedford Books 1997), 3.

18. Hinsley, "The World as Marketplace," 355. I would note, here, that I take "unmediated" to name its opposite: this fiction marks the very form of ideological mediation.

19. In *The Anarchy of Empire in the Making of U.S. Culture* (Cambridge, MA: Harvard University Press, 2002), Amy Kaplan has demonstrated just how tenuous such acts of veiling could be. Her understanding of U.S. "imperialism as a network of power relations that changes over space and time and is riddled with instability, ambiguity, and disorder, rather than as a monolithic system of domination that the very word 'empire' implies," has been decisive in shaping my own understanding of the imperial dimensions of mobility's contest in nineteenth-century America (13–14).

20. Pierre Bourdieu, "Social Space and Field of Power," trans. Randall Johnson, in *Practical Reason: On the Theory of Action* (London: Polity Press,1998), 32.

21. Neil Smith and Cindi Katz, "Grounding Metaphor: Toward a Spatialized

Politics," in *Place and the Politics of Identity*, ed. Michael Keith and Steve Pile (London: Routledge, 1993), 68.

22. Despite this tendency, for some, travel's discourse remains underappreciated. Within the last decade, Charles Grivel, Michael Kowalewski, and Larzer Ziff have all maintained that, in Grivel's phrasing, "[t]ravel literature is a neglected literature; compared to the samples of canonical genres, it can hardly offer something like 'works'" ("Travel Writing," in *Materialities of Communication*, ed. Hans Gumbrecht and K. Ludwig Pfeiffer, trans. William Whobrey [Stanford: Stanford University Press, 1994], 256). Although I would agree that travel writing has enjoyed an at best uncertain history within traditions of literary criticism, I find that the claims for neglect overlook, or misconceive, the recent rise in the genre's critical fortunes, a rise to which Grivel's, Ziff's, and Kowalewski's projects all contribute. At stake is the cultural turn: where the aestheticizing protocols of an earlier disciplinary moment neglected travel writing, the current demand for cultural critique finds, in that once devalued genre, a rich array of analytic possibilities. See Kowalewski, *Temperamental Journeys: Essays on the Modern Literature of Travel* (Athens: University of Georgia Press, 1994) and Ziff, *Return Passages: Great American Travel Writing 1780–1920* (New Haven, CT: Yale University Press, 2000).

23. Georges Van Den Abbeele, *Travel as Metaphor: From Montaigne to Rousseau* (Minneapolis: University of Minnesota Press, 1992), xiii.

24. Ibid., xxiii.

25. Ibid., xvii.

26. My decision to shift from the singular "structure" invoked by Van Den Abbeele to the plural "structures" will register unease with any generalizing and reductive notion of universal investment. The shifting imbrication of travel with commerce under capitalism alone is a topic of daunting historical complexity.

27. Smith and Katz, "Grounding Metaphor," 75.

28. Van Den Abbeele, *Travel as Metaphor*, xiv.

29. Ibid., xx.

30. Ibid.

31. Van Den Abbeele aims to anticipate such criticisms when he observes (after first anticipating the charge "that such an analysis would in no way be historical") that "[a]nother, perhaps less immediately obvious, centrism is also at work in the economy of travel: the phallocentricism whereby the 'law of the home' *(oikonomia)* organizes a set of gender determinations" (*Travel as Metaphor*, xxv). My worry is that his theory reinscribes, rather than critiques, this "centrism."

32. To different ends, but in ways resonant for my discussion here, Lora Romero offers an incisive analysis of the investments at stake in critical equations of domesticity with normalizing constraint. See chapter 2 in *Home Fronts: Domesticity and Its Critics in the Antebellum United States* (Durham, NC: Duke University Press, 1997). The vein of nineteenth-century thought that worked to *conflate* home and travel, property and mobility (a vein considered later in this introduction) gives another means by which to take up the limitations in Van Den Abbeele's position. Pertinent here is Edward Said's warning in his landmark 1982 essay, "Travelling Theory" (*Raritan* 1 [3] [1982]: 41–67)—itself a key text in the establishment of travel's axial status

within contemporary critical practice, yet *about* travel in only its most conceptual or indeed metaphorical senses—that "a breakthrough can become a trap if it is used uncritically, repetitively, limitlessly," "that once an idea gains currency because it is clearly effective and powerful, there is every likelihood that during its peregrinations it will be reduced, codified, institutionalized" (56).

33. In "Transporting the Subject: Technologies of Mobility and Location in an Era of Globalization" (*PMLA* 117 [1] [2002]: 32–42), Caren Kaplan gives an incisive analysis of the ideology at stake in the etymological relation of travel to theory, one revealing for Van Den Abbeele's investment in the idea of critical distance: "following the concept of the voyage of the Athenian *theor*, foundational to Western culture is the idea that travel produces the self, makes the subject through spectatorship and comparison with others. Thus, in this ideology of subjectivity, distance is the best perspective on and route toward knowledge of self and others. Self-knowledge, standpoint, then requires a point of origin, a location that constitutes the subject as a viewer and a world of objects that can be viewed or surveyed" (36).

34. Hall, "The Problem of Ideology: Marxism without Guarantees," in *Stuart Hall: Critical Dialogues in Cultural Studies*, ed. David Morley and Kuan-Hsing Chen (London: Routledge, 1996), 44.

35. James Buzard, *The Beaten Track: European Tourism, Literature, and the Ways to Culture, 1800–1918* (Oxford: Clarendon Press, 1993); Inderpal Grewal, *Home and Harem: Nation, Gender, Empire, and the Cultures of Travel* (Durham, NC: Duke University Press, 1996); Bruce Harvey, *American Geographics: U.S. National Narratives and the Representation of the Non-European World, 1830–1865* (Stanford: Stanford University Press, 2001); Caren Kaplan, *Questions of Travel: Postmodern Discourses of Displacement* (Durham, NC: Duke University Press, 1996) and "Transporting the Subject"; Mary Louise Pratt, *Imperial Eyes: Travel Writing and Transculturation* (New York: Routledge, 1992); Susan Stewart, *Crimes of Writing: Problems in the Containment of Representation* (New York: Oxford University Press, 1991). Other key texts in what I think of as the materialist constellation of theories of travel and its account include: James Clifford, *Routes: Travel and Translation in the Late Twentieth Century* (Cambridge, MA: Harvard University Press, 1997); David Spurr, *The Rhetoric of Empire: Colonial Discourse in Journalism, Travel Writing, and Imperial Administration* (Durham, NC: Duke University Press, 1993); Ali Behdad, *Belated Travelers: Orientalism in the Age of Colonial Dissolution* (Durham, NC: Duke University Press, 1994); bell hooks, "Representing Whiteness in the Black Imagination," in *Cultural Studies*, ed. Lawrence Grossberg et al. (New York: Routledge, 1992), 338–46; Charles Grivel, "Travel Writing"; Paul Gilroy, *The Black Atlantic: Modernity and Double Consciousness* (Cambridge, MA: Harvard University Press, 1993); Ian MacLaren, "Exploration/Travel Literature and the Evolution of the Author," *International Journal of Canadian Studies* 5 (spring 1992): 39–68; Frances Bartkowski, *Travelers, Immigrants, Inmates: Essays in Estrangement* (Minneapolis: University of Minnesota Press, 1995); John Sears, *Sacred Places: American Tourist Attractions in the Nineteenth Century* (New York: Oxford University Press, 1989); William Stowe, *Going Abroad: European Travel in Nineteenth-Century American Culture* (Princeton, NJ: Princeton University Press, 1994); Dean MacCannell, *The Tourist: A New Theory of the Leisure Class* (New

York: Schocken Books, 1976, 1989); S. Shankar, *Textual Traffic: Colonialism, Modernity, and the Economy of the Text* (Albany: State University of New York Press, 2001).

36. Grewal, *Home and Harem*, 2.

37. Kaplan, *Questions of Travel*, 131.

38. Ibid., 26. In "Representing Whiteness in the Black Imagination," bell hooks makes a similar argument, noting that "[t]ravel is not a word that can be easily evoked to talk about the Middle Passage, the Trail of Tears, the landing of Chinese immigrants at Ellis Island, the forced relocation of Japanese-Americans, the plight of the homeless" (343).

39. Kaplan, *Questions of Travel*, 32.

40. Ibid., 4. I extrapolate my concept of intimate difference from the analysis of intimate distance offered by Susan Stewart in her discussion of the souvenir in *On Longing: Narratives of the Miniature, the Gigantic, the Souvenir, the Collection* (Durham, NC: Duke University Press, 1993).

41. Kaplan, *Questions of Travel*, 155; emphasis in original.

42. Neil Smith, *Uneven Development: Nature, Capital, and the Production of Space* (London: Blackwell, 1984), vii.

43. Doreen Massey, *Space, Place, and Gender* (Cambridge: Polity Press, 1994), 261. Massey argues this case both with reference to gender's problematic, so as to contest the view that traditionally associates time with masculinity and space with femininity, and with reference to contemporary physics, with its understanding of four-dimensional space-time.

44. Ibid., 269.

45. Smith clarifies this point when, in *Uneven Development*, he notes that "in order to produce surplus value it is necessary that vast quantities of productive capital be spatially immobilized for relatively long periods in the form of factories, machinery, transport routes, warehouses, and a host of other facilities . . . [yet i]nsofar as this immobilization process is matched by the mobility of capital, these opposing tendencies throw up not a random but a patterned internal differentiation of world space" (88).

46. Karl Marx, *Capital*, vol. 1, trans. Ben Fowles (New York: Vintage, 1977), 268.

47. Karl Marx, *Grundrisse*, trans. Martin Nicolaus (Harmondsworth, UK: Penguin, 1973, 1993), 546.

48. "The more production comes to rest on exchange value, hence on exchange, the more important do the physical conditions of exchange—the means of communication and transportation—become for the costs of circulation. Capital by its nature drives beyond every spatial barrier. Thus the creation of the physical conditions of exchange–of the means of communication and transport—the annihilation of space by time—becomes an extraordinary necessity for it. . . . while capital must on one side strive to tear down every spatial barrier to intercourse, i.e. to exchange, and conquer the whole earth for its market, it strives on the other side to annihilate this space with time, i.e. to reduce to a minimum the time spent in motion from one place to another" (Marx, *Grundrisse*, 524–39).

49. Régis Debray, *Media Manifestos: On the Technological Transmission of Cultural Forms*, trans. Eric Rauth (London: Verso, 1996), 17.

50. Raymond Williams, *Marxism and Literature* (Oxford: Oxford University Press, 1977), 98. Williams goes on to suggest that, for him, the very sense of the term makes it difficult to employ: "when the process of mediation is seen [in this way] as positive and substantial, as a necessary process of the making of meanings and values, in the necessary form of the general social process of signification and communication, it is really only a hindrance to describe it as 'mediation' at all. For the metaphor takes us back to the very concept of the 'intermediary' which, at its best, this constitutive and constituting sense rejects" (100).

51. Fredric Jameson, *The Political Unconscious: Narrative as a Socially Symbolic Act* (Ithaca, NY: Cornell University Press, 1981), 42.

52. Debray, *Media Manifestos*, 11.

53. Note, here, David Harvey's argument "that each moment [within the circulation of capital—money, commodities, labor power, production, reproduction, and the transitions or metamorphoses between them—] has a different capacity for geographical mobility and that the transitions inevitably entail some kind of spatial movement. . . . [W]hen looked at from the standpoint of exchange, the circulation of capital is a geographical movement in time" (*The Urban Experience* [Baltimore: Johns Hopkins University Press, 1989], 18–19).

54. Debray, *Media Manifestos*, 8.

55. Pierre Bourdieu, *Distinction: A Social Critique of the Judgement of Taste*, trans. Richard Nice (Cambridge, MA: Harvard University Press, 1984), 68.

56. On symbolic capital, see "The Production of Belief: Contribution to an Economy of Symbolic Goods," trans. Richard Nice, in *The Field of Cultural Production*, ed. Randal Johnson (New York: Columbia University Press, 1993), 75; on symbolic violence, see "The Economy of Symbolic Goods," trans. Randal Johnson, in *Practical Reason* (London: Polity Press, 1998), 103.

57. Pierre Bourdieu, *Pascalian Meditations*, trans. Richard Nice (Stanford: Stanford University Press, 2000), 185.

58. See Bourdieu's provocative account of incorporation and belief in chapter 5 of *Pascalian Meditations*, "Symbolic Violence and Political Struggles," where he argues that "the order of *beliefs*" gets produced and maintained "at the deepest level of bodily dispositions" (177). Although indebted to this theorization of embodiment, I find that Bourdieu overstates the case against ideology and representation; the instance of travel, at least, will suggest that bodily habits and representational habits, incorporation and ideology, are everywhere interimplicated in the production of orthodoxy. James Buzard's investigation, in *The Beaten Track*, of the disposition he calls "anti-tourism" provides an exemplary instance of the use of Bourdieu to theorize critical issues in human movement.

59. Terry Eagleton, *Ideology* (London: Verso, 1991), 115. My understanding of hegemony builds as well on Raymond William's theorization in *Marxism and Literature*. See, relatedly, Bourdieu's contention in *Pascalian Mediations* that "[s]ymbolic capital enables forms of domination which imply dependence on those who can be dominated by it, since it can only exist through the esteem, recognition, belief, credit, confidence of others, and can only be perpetuated so long as it succeeds in

obtaining belief in its existence," an argument that complements the understanding of hegemony (or what Bourdieu calls *doxa*) as dependent for its power not least on those gaps that mark its vulnerability (166).

60. Robert Rydell, *All the World's a Fair: Visions of Empire at American International Expositions, 1876–1916* (Chicago: University of Chicago Press, 1984), 46.

61. Henry van Brunt, "The Columbian Exposition and American Civilization," *The Atlantic Monthly* 71 (427) (May 1893): 579–80.

62. David Lloyd and Paul Thomas, *Culture and the State* (New York: Routledge, 1998), 3.

63. Ibid., 7. Through the sort of training Lloyd and Thomas describe, "aimed not so much at particular objects of knowledge as at forming an ethical disposition," "[c]ulture produces the consensual ground for the state form of representative democracy" precisely "by drawing the formal or representative disposition in every individual out of each person's concrete particularity. . . . Culture mediates the shift from self-representation to being represented by developing in each that 'indifferent' disposition of the Subject in which material differences are annulled. While allowing representational politics to take place by formalizing political subjects, it simultaneously allows that politics to take place as if material conditions were a matter of indifference" (15). Although Lloyd and Thomas specify aesthetic culture, I maintain that the ethnographic turn at the end of the nineteenth century exemplified by the World's Columbian Exposition serves a closely related project, both in its tendency to aestheticize the exotic and in its capacity to educe indifference from difference and, thus, to represent representability.

64. Amy Schrager Lang, *The Syntax of Class: Writing Inequality in America* (Princeton, NJ: Princeton University Press, 2003), 2.

65. Agnes Repplier, "Terra Incognita," *Cosmopolitan* 20 (April 1896): 661.

66. Article 19, "Sketches of Naval Life," *American Journal of Science* 16 (2) (1829): 321.

67. Dimock, *Empire for Liberty: Melville and the Poetics of Individualism* (Princeton, NJ: Princeton University Press, 1989), 14.

68. In view of the general formulation of hegemony supplied by Lloyd and Thomas—"[h]egemony depends exactly, not on direct control (domination), but on dispersion"—we note the striking redundancy of the hegemonic process I am describing, dependent as it was on materialities of dispersion (the apparatuses and practices of mobility) to maintain hegemonic dispersion (*Culture and the State*, 19). James Jasper's recent book, *Restless Nation: Starting Over in America* (Chicago: University of Chicago Press, 2000), will begin to indicate the resilience of the common sense I am describing. Although filled with engaging historical insight, Jasper's account seems only to hold American restlessness as a given, and so to reinscribe its orthodoxy: "Our famous American individualism arises from movement. That restless motion begins with immigration, but it affects all of us—even those who stay put. . . . Here's my recipe for the United States. Take an enormous territory, rich with deep forests, the blackest soil, every manner of animal, vegetable, and mineral, and endless navigable rivers and coasts. Exterminate most of its native people. Then, over four hundred years, repopulate it with immensely diverse folk, from all around the globe, whose only common feature is their restlessness"(3–4).

69. Kaplan, *The Anarchy of Empire in the Making of U.S. Culture*, 46.

70. Robert Tomes, "The Americans on Their Travels," *Harper's New Monthly Magazine* 31 (181) (June 1865): 57.

71. Ibid.

72. Ibid.

73. Ibid.

74. Ibid.; emphasis added.

75. Kaplan, *The Anarchy of Empire in the Making of U.S. Culture*, 23–50. Exemplifying perfectly what Kaplan calls "a mobile and often unstable discourse that can expand or contract the boundaries of home and nation" (26), in its concern over the security and stability of the distinction between 'home' and 'abroad' Tomes's essay likewise exemplifies her analysis of the exceptionalist ideology in the American tradition: "American exceptionalism is in part an argument for boundless expansion, where national particularism and international universalism converge. . . . If the fantasy of American imperialism aspires to a borderless world where it finds its own reflection everywhere, then the fruition of this dream shatters the coherence of national identity, as the boundaries that distinguish it from the outside world promise to collapse" (16). Although not explicit in Tomes's essay, the second aspect of Kaplan's concept of "Manifest Domesticity," that the "interdependency [of home and nation] relies on racial conceptions of the foreign" (26), remains what I would call a spectral presence haunting his argument from the margins.

76. Alexis de Tocqueville, *The Republic of the United States of America, and Its Political Institutions, Reviewed and Examined* (New York: A. S. Barnes and Co., 1851), pt. 2: 170.

77. Harriet Jacobs, *Incidents in the Life of a Slave Girl: Written by Herself*, ed. Valerie Smith (Oxford: Oxford University Press, 1988), 224.

78. Ronald Takaki, *Iron Cages: Race and Culture in Nineteenth-Century America* (New York: Knopf, 1979), 148–49.

79. Harvey's superb study, which analyzes how "U.S. national ideologies, as embodied in the U.S. traveler-citizen, are literally put into circulation," remains an indispensable touchstone for my own project (*American Geographics*, 3).

80. Kaplan, *The Anarchy of Empire in the Making of U.S. Culture*, 16, 26; Romero, *Home Fronts*.

1. Nat Turner's Restlessness

1. In *The Southampton Slave Revolt of 1831: A Compilation of Source Material* (Amherst: University of Massachusetts Press, 1971), Henry Irving Tragle argues that "since [by legal precedent] 'insurrection' implied treason, and since under Virginia law a slave could not be charged with treason, the proper designation of the event must be 'revolt'" (23). Although I grant the importance of the distinction, what seems most telling in its light is the widespread use of "insurrection" in the literature produced in the wake of the revolt, not least in the text of Turner's confession itself—a use, and a contradiction, exemplary for the problems of will that I discuss subsequently. Tragle also observes that the "basic difference between 'rebellion' and 're-

volt'" involves the "order of magnitude of the action": rebellion is bigger than revolt (23). Like the previous one, this distinction makes sense, but I wonder if the question of magnitude in the case of the Southampton uprising can be settled so easily: the threat of this insurgence resides not least in its epistemological instability. Given such messiness, I prefer, unlike Tragle, to suspend the propriety of naming and use all three terms.

2. In *Of Grammatology*, translated by Gayatri Chakravorty Spivak (Baltimore: Johns Hopkins University Press, 1976), Jacques Derrida theorizes this sense of the supplement—addition yet substitution, addition as displacement—in detail. His treatment shapes my use of the term throughout this project. See also the provocative materialist account of supplementation in the discussion by Lloyd and Thomas of "culture as supplement to the state," in *Culture and the State*, 46ff.

3. On dissection, see the Ayer edition of *The Confessions of Nat Turner* (Salem, NH: Ayer Company Publishers, 1991), 12. On souvenirs, see Eric Foner, *Nat Turner* (Englewood Cliffs, NJ: Prentice Hall, 1971), 6. In *On Longing: Narratives of the Miniature, the Gigantic, the Souvenir, the Collection*, Susan Stewart contends that "souvenirs of death . . . mark the horrible transformation of meaning into materiality more than they mark, as other souvenirs do, the transformation of materiality into meaning. If the function of the souvenir proper is to create a continuous and personal narrative of the past the function of such souvenirs of death is to disrupt and disclaim that continuity. Souvenirs of the mortal body are not so much a nostalgic celebration of the past as they are an erasure of the significance of history" (140). Hence the important use of such souvenirs of death within ritual spectacles of slavery's regime; hence the paradox of a *mnemotechnics* aimed at cultural amnesia.

4. One should note that open revolt was unusual in the U.S. context precisely because, as Eugene Genovese argues in *From Rebellion to Revolution: Afro-American Slave Revolts in the Making of the Modern World* (Baton Rouge: Louisiana State University Press, 1979), "the slaves of the United States faced a highly unfavorable relationship of forces, which shifted them away from revolt and toward other forms of resistance" (49). In her brilliant *Scenes of Subjection: Terror, Slavery, and Self-Making in Nineteenth-Century America* (New York: Oxford University Press, 1997), Saidiya Hartman elaborates the complexity of the issues at stake: "The everyday practices of the enslaved encompassed an array of tactics such as work slowdowns, feigned illness, unlicensed travel, the destruction of property, theft, self-mutilation, dissimulation, physical confrontation with owners and overseers that document the resistance to slavery. These small-scale and everyday forms of resistance interrupted, reelaborated, and defied the constraints of everyday life under slavery and exploited openings in the system for the use of the enslaved. What unites these varied tactics is the effort to redress the condition of the enslaved, restore the disrupted affiliations of the socially dead, challenge the authority and dominion of the slaveholder, and alleviate the pained state of the captive body. However, these acts of redress are undertaken with the acknowledgment that conditions will most likely remain the same. This acknowledgment implies neither resignation nor fatalism but a recognition of the enormity of the breach instituted by slavery and the magnitude of domination" (51). I analyze in detail one form of "unlicensed travel," fugitivity, in chapter 3.

5. Kenneth S. Greenberg, "*The Confessions of Nat Turner*: Text and Context," in *The Confessions of Nat Turner and Related Documents*, ed. Greenberg (Boston: Bedford, 1996), 2.

6. William Lloyd Garrison, *The Liberator*, 3 September 1831, reproduced in Greenberg, ed., *The Confessions of Nat Turner and Related Documents*, 70.

7. Greenberg, ed., *The Confessions of Nat Turner and Related Documents*, 48. All subsequent citations of the text of Turner's confession refer to this edition.

8. Ibid., 110.

9. Ibid., 110–11.

10. Ibid., 111.

11. As Greenberg observes, "[t]ransportation out of state was a brutal punishment involving permanent separation from family and friends, but the white authorities saw it as a merciful alternative to execution. . . . [Yet] the goal is to understand how 'mercy' strengthened a slave society. Masters liked to think of themselves as caring and humane in dealing with their slaves. The brutality generated by the initial reaction to the rebellion exposed the ugly force and violence which lay behind the power of the ruling group. The trials should be seen as an attempt to recover from that exposure. Masters were most powerful and most dangerous not when they cut off heads, but when they commuted the death sentences of fifteen-year-old children; not when their power was displayed in its most brutal form, but when their 'decency' was displayed in its most benevolent form" (21–22).

12. One has a hard time not asking: which is it, a bit of variation or none at all? The point here is to indicate how Turner's confession is rendered public, sent out into the world, on the premise of a vacillation intended, ironically enough, to stabilize and reassure. Note that already Gray has recourse to the concept of insurrection—and so to the crime of treason for which Turner, legally, could not be tried. See note 1 above.

13. Richard Brodhead, *Cultures of Letters: Scenes of Reading and Writing in Nineteenth-Century America* (Chicago: University of Chicago Press, 1993), 109. With this concept Brodhead aims to understand "by what means and by virtue of what circumstances different potential authors have been able to lay claim to different powers in the literary realm" (110).

14. Eric Sundquist, *To Wake the Nations: Race in the Making of American Literature* (Cambridge, MA: The Belknap Press of Harvard University Press, 1993), 29, 40. Sundquist's argument, to which I am indebted, outlines incisively the problems posed by Turner's collaboration in the work of authorship for the disciplinary methods (confession, but also copyright) used in the attempt to fix him. My argument differs from Sundquist's in foregrounding the problem of movement in Turner's insurgence.

15. Ibid., 39.

16. David Saunders and Ian Hunter, "Lessons from the 'Literatory': How to Historicize Authorship," *Critical Inquiry* 17 (spring 1991): 483.

17. Ibid.

18. James Clifford argues that "[o]nce dialogism and polyphony are recognized as modes of textual production, monophonic authority is questioned, revealed to be characteristic of a science that has claimed to *represent* cultures. The tendency to

specify discourses—historically and intersubjectively—recasts this authority, and in the process alters the questions we put to cultural descriptions" (*Writing Culture: The Poetics and Politics of Ethnography*, ed. Clifford and George E. Marcus [Berkeley and Los Angeles: University of California Press, 1986], 15). What seems most brilliant in Turner's specifying intervention is that it comes, ironically enough, on the back of a throwaway phrase ("as you call it") seemingly superfluous to the content of his speech.

19. Larzer Ziff, *Great American Travel Writing 1780–1920* (New Haven, CT: Yale University Press, 2000), 7.

20. Susan Stewart, *Crimes of Writing: Problems in the Containment of Representation* (Oxford: Oxford University Press, 1992), 177.

21. Note Stewart's provocative complication of the paradigm in question: "The function of the tour is the estrangement of objects—to make what is visible, what is surface, reveal a profound interiority through narrative. This interiority is that of the perceiving subject; it is gained at the expense of risking *contamination* . . . and the dissolution of the boundary of that subject" (*Crimes of Writing*, 146–47).

22. Lauren Berlant, *The Anatomy of National Fantasy: Hawthorne, Utopia, and Everyday Life* (Chicago: University of Chicago Press, 1991); Dimock, *Empire for Liberty*, 8.

23. Dimock, *Empire for Liberty*, 8.

24. Kaplan, *The Anarchy of Empire in the Making of U.S. Culture*, 26.

25. Bruce Greenfield, *Narrating Discovery: The Romantic Explorer in American Literature 1790–1855* (New York: Columbia University Press, 1992), 83. Terry Caesar makes a similar point in *Forgiving the Boundaries: Home as Abroad in American Travel Writing* (Athens: University of Georgia Press, 1995): "[e]xactly because American identity lacked stability, travel writing proved to be an especially suitable textual practice for expressing, if not empowering, some confidence about why, away from home, it might be important to have a home" (36). I would emphasize that, as my book means to show, the collective category of "American identity" is as fraught as it is suspect.

26. The classic text here is C. B. MacPherson's *The Political Theory of Possessive Individualism: Hobbes to Locke* (Oxford: Oxford University Press, 1962), which analyzes the historical "conception of the individual as essentially the proprietor of his own person or capacities, owing nothing to society for them. . . . The relation of ownership, having become for more and more men the critically important relation determining their actual freedom and actual prospect of realizing their full potentialities, was read back into the nature of the individual. The individual, it was thought, is free inasmuch as he is proprietor of his person and capacities" (3). See also Eric Cheyfitz's argument in *The Poetics of Imperialism: Translation and Colonization from "The Tempest" to "Tarzan"* (New York: Oxford University Press, 1991): "[i]n the West, property, in that tangled space where the physical and the metaphysical mix, is the very mark of identity, of that which is identical to itself: what we typically call a 'self' or an 'individual,' indicating the absolute boundaries that are predicated on this entity. The *self*, like *property*, has its history, or, rather, histories (and, of course, I am suggesting that the histories of *self* and *property* are inseparable)" (50).

27. I borrow the homonymic pun roots/routes from Paul Gilroy, who in *The Black Atlantic* analyzes "the interplay between . . . two dimensions of racial ontology," one

that understands identity in terms of its stability, or roots, and one that understands identity in terms of its mobility, or routes (19).

28. Michel Foucault, *The History of Sexuality*, vol. 1: *An Introduction*, trans. Robert Hurley (New York: Vintage, 1990), 58–59.

29. Stewart, *Crimes of Writing*, 57; emphasis added.

30. Foucault, *History of Sexuality*, vol. 1, 60.

31. Hartman, *Scenes of Subjection*, 82. Hartman's insight can help to make sense of the conundrum surrounding the concept of insurrection as it gets used in public discourse to characterize Turner's revolt: Turner comes into the subjectivity necessary for the charge of insurrection—of treason—to stick only at the moment of its prohibition and punishment.

32. I return to this problem in chapter 3, with respect to the case of the fugitive Henry Bibb.

33. As Michael Warner notes in *The Letters of the Republic: Publication and the Public Sphere in Eighteenth-Century America* (Cambridge, MA: Harvard University Press, 1990), "[l]etters could have a prominent role even in the lives of the illiterate and semiliterate. The extreme case was that of slaves, since a slave was required to carry a letter written by his owner simply in order to travel" (27).

34. Well back in its history, this project bore the working title "Between Panic and Rapture." A dynamic such as the one I have been analyzing supplies a means with which to focus and specify these two terms, even as it seems to require their reversal: the significance of the Southampton rebellion consists not least in between Turner's rapture and the panic it inspires in Virginia's planter class.

35. Sundquist, *To Wake the Nations*, 29, 32.

36. In all its considerable indeterminacy, Gray's production of Nat Turner's confession holds a telling, albeit complex, significance for the historical process by which stories of illicit slave movement served, in Lisa Brawley's formulation, "to code slavery's landscape as alternatively haunted and exotic . . . [and] to code the shifting meaning of mobility itself at a time when mobility was a 'brand new fact' of American life" ("Frederick Douglass's My *Bondage and* My *Freedom* and the Fugitive Tourist Industry," *Novel: A Forum on Fiction* 30 [1] [fall 1996]: 2). Brawley's concern, in advancing this argument, is what she terms "the fugitive tourist industry," a means of conceptualizing social and cultural problematics of enslaved fugitivity that bears tellingly on the argument I advance in chapter 3.

37. Not coincidentally, two of these three adjectives recollect racist typifications of slaves as idle and mischievous. Thus can Gray yoke together rumor and revolt, managing to diminish yet intensify their correlation—and, with it, their threat.

38. Quoted in Tragle, *The Southampton Slave Revolt*, 35.

39. Ibid., 38, 40.

40. Ibid., 38.

41. Ibid., 58, 62.

42. Ibid., 91; emphasis added. Although acknowledging the account's authority, critics cannot agree on who wrote it. Tragle argues for John Hampden Pleasants, editor of the *Constitutional Whig*, though Foner and Greenberg argue for Thomas Gray himself. What matters here is less who "really" wrote the piece than the way anonymity

and authority conspire in the attempt to quell another kind of compelling, sourceless discourse (but sourceless and insurgent, rather than authoritative in the narrow sense). We may infer that authority comes not simply from anonymity (since rumor is also anonymous) but, more particularly, from the means of informational transmission. Thus, while you may believe what you hear, you can *trust* what you read—a view making clear how anxiety about rumor is not least anxiety about rival forms of news.

43. The significance of "country" in media accounts is admittedly unclear: does it mean nation or region? I take the uncertainty to indicate a synecdochic slippage between the geographical part and the geopolitical whole.

44. As Greenberg observes, "Gray must have understood the economic value of the Nat Turner story. He joined the procession of those who hoped to profit by writing about the suffering of others" (*The Confessions of Nat Turner and Related Documents*, 8).

45. Sundquist, *To Wake the Nations*, 50.

46. On the significance of this ideology, see Michael Warner's argument in "The Mass Public and the Mass Subject" (*The Phantom Public Sphere*, ed. Bruce Robbins [Minneapolis: University of Minnesota Press, 1993]): "In the bourgeois public sphere, . . . a principle of negativity was axiomatic: the validity of what you say in public bears a negative relation to your person. What you say will carry force not because of who you are but despite who you are. . . . [Yet] the ability to abstract oneself in public discussion has always been an unequally available resource. . . . The subject who could master this rhetoric in the bourgeois public sphere was implicitly—even explicitly—white, male, literate, and propertied. These traits could go unmarked, even grammatically, while other features of bodies could only be acknowledged in discourse as the humiliating positivity of the particular" (239). See also Lauren Berlant's important reminder that the privilege of disembodiment, if fully national in the abstract, tended in practice to vary (with the franchise) from state to state, and so to be unequally available even among white men (*The Anatomy of National Fantasy*, 14–15).

47. Thus rumor will complicate the distinction that, in Warner's formulation, divides "both media and news along the same axis" so as to classify "the spoken with the local and the printed with the exotic" (*The Letters of the Republic*, 17). For rumor is all at once insistently local and irreducibly exotic: as a kind of disembodied speech, it remains entirely proximate, vertiginous; coming from nowhere—sourceless, strange, exotic—it nevertheless will tend to throw down roots.

48. Here we need to bear in mind Mark Rose's contention, in *Authors and Owners: The Invention of Copyright* (Cambridge, MA: Harvard University Press, 1993), that "[c]opyright is founded on the concept of the unique individual who creates something original and is entitled to reap a profit from those labors. Until recently, the dominant modes of aesthetic thinking have shared the romantic and individualistic assumptions inscribed in copyright. But these assumptions obscure important truths about the processes of cultural production," truths measured in Gray's case by the necessary yet troublesome place of Turner's collaboration in the act of authorship protected by copyright (2).

49. Sundquist, *To Wake the Nations*, 45.

50. Note here the suggestive link between rumor's poison and what, in his 1831 pamphlet on the revolt, Samuel Warner calls the "noxious vapors" issuing from Dismal Swamp, believed in Virginia lore to be the scene of the rebels' concealment and plotting (*The Southampton Slave Revolt*, 297). By way of such association, rebellion and rumor come to enjoy the same, poisonous origin.

51. On the significance of vocality in the early American context, see Christopher Looby's *Voicing America: Language, Literary Form, and the Origins of the United States* (Chicago: University of Chicago Press, 1996).

52. According to Tragle, "Gray's work was reprinted at least twice. Thomas Wentworth Higginson estimated, in 1861, that 50,000 had been distributed. It is sometimes claimed that *The Confessions* was proscribed in the Southern States, but this seems unlikely. There may have been localities where it was not permitted to be sold, because of its presumed incendiary character, but its republication by a Richmond printer in 1832 suggests that it was bought and read by many Southerners" (*The Southampton Slave Revolt*, 279).

53. Avital Ronell, "Street Talk," in *Finitude's Score: Essays for the End of the Millenium* (Lincoln: University of Nebraska Press, 1994), 95. Less convincing than Ronell's provocative analysis of rumor is her claim that "gossip has something to do with assuring a community's stasis" (90). My point is not so much that gossip is inherently enabling as that its energies seem less predictably consistent with the status quo than Ronell would allow. For a more nuanced view of gossip, see Eve Kosofsky Sedgwick's arguments in *Epistemology of the Closet* (Berkeley and Los Angeles: University of California Press, 1990).

2. Abandoned to Circulation

1. John Rollin Ridge, *Poems* (San Francisco: Henry Payot and Company, 1868), 17–21.

2. Cheryl Walker has glossed Ridge's investment as a belief "that the nation of the United States as an 'imagined community' transcended the experiential polity whose actions at both the federal and the state levels were deeply unjust" (*Indian Nation: Native American Literature and Nineteenth-Century Nationalisms* [Durham, NC: Duke University Press, 1997], 233).

3. See James W. Parins, *John Rollin Ridge: His Life and Works* (Lincoln: University of Nebraska Press, 1991), 21–28; William G. McLoughlin, *After the Trail of Tears: The Cherokees' Struggle for Sovereignty, 1839–1880* (Chapel Hill: University of North Carolina Press, 1993), 7. Most commentators agree that the rationale for removal held most immediately to the discovery of gold in the Cherokee's Georgia lands and, more generally, to the intense race hatred fostered under Jacksonian ideology. Yet, as Priscilla Wald contends, the prospect of Cherokee sovereignty also exerted a terrifying because uncanny force: "the threat that the [sovereignty-seeking] indigenous tribespeople [came by 1830] . . . to pose to the anxious confederation inhere[d] at least as much in their resemblance to as in their differences from other cultural subjects. . . . The Cherokee's becoming like but not of the United States' political entity, mirroring without acceding to its claims, seem[ed] to threaten the terms of

[collective] identity" ("Terms of Assimilation: Legislating Subjectivity in the Emerging Nation," in *Cultures of United States Imperialism*, ed. Amy Kaplan and Donald E. Pease [Durham, NC: Duke University Press, 1993], 61–67). I would stress that the threat of this "mirroring" reflection consists in the incommensurability of part to whole. The particular terms of synecdochic relation, joining part with whole through the paradox of independent or separated membership, jeopardize the integrity of the national body—and with it the modes of representation key to the modern workings of state power.

4. Walker, *Indian Nation*, 116. Most accounts of this period in Cherokee history tend not just to reflect but to endorse this contempt, condemning as treacherous the capitulations of the Ridge-Boudinot party while praising the entrenched resistance of the Ross party. Such judgments will risk obscuring a larger point about the relentless capacity of the genocidal policies of Jackson's government; as Mary Young argues, "Political oppression—the sustained cooperative effort of the United States and the sovereign state of Georgia to destroy first the unity and then the existence of the Cherokee Nation East—created . . . [the crises of] faction" in Cherokee society ("The Cherokee Nation: Mirror of the Republic," *American Quarterly* 33 [1981]: 523).

5. Young, "The Cherokee Nation," 520. The fallout from these executions, most historians agree, played a role in driving John Rollin to California. The immediate circumstances surrounding his westward flight likewise involved unpredictable violence: in May 1849, he was accosted by David Kell, a member of the Ross party, in a disagreement over one of Ridge's horses; Kell died in the ensuing exchange and Ridge, fearing political intrigue, fled to California to escape the charge of murder and the uncertainties of factional justice. See the discussions of these events in Parins, *John Rollin Ridge*, and in David Farmer and Rennard Strickland, eds., *A Trumpet of Our Own: Yellow Bird's Essays on the North American Indian* (San Francisco: Book Club of California, 1981).

6. Ridge, *Poems*, 7–8.

7. Ridge, *The Life and Adventures of Joaquín Murieta, the Celebrated California Bandit* (Norman: University of Oklahoma Press, 1955), 9.

8. E. J. Hobsbawm, *Bandits*, revised edition (New York: Pantheon, 1981), 65.

9. Ridge, *Murieta*, 34.

10. Ibid., 22.

11. Edgar Allan Poe, "Prospectus of *The Stylus*," *Edgar Allan Poe: Essays and Reviews*, ed. G. R. Thompson (New York: Library of America, 1984), 1033.

12. *The Letters of Edgar Allan Poe*, vol. I, ed. John Ward Ostrom (New York: Gordian Press, 1966), 210.

13. See Joseph V. Ridgely, "The Growth of the Text," in *Edgar Allan Poe: The Imaginary Voyages*, ed. Burton R. Pollin (Boston: Twayne, 1981), 29–35.

14. Travel writing was evidently Harper and Brothers's most marketable commodity. As Eugene Exman, the firm's historian, relates, when James Harper was asked by John Stephens, the celebrated antebellum traveler, about the salability of genres, he replied: "Travels sell about the best of anything we get ahold of. . . . They don't always go with a rush, like a novel by a celebrated author, but they sell longer, and in the end, pay better.'" According to Exman, Harper then "urged Stephens to write

up his experiences, but Stephens replied that he had gone to out-of-the-way places, had traveled very fast, and made no notes that could now be useful." In response, Harper counseled plagiarism—advice that, as will become clear, has real resonance for Poe's case: 'That's no matter... [y]ou went through and saw the signs. We have got plenty of books about those countries. You just pick out as many as you want, and I will send them home for you; you can dish up something'" (*The Brothers Harper: A Unique Publishing Partnership and Its Impact upon the Cultural Life of America from 1817 to 1853* [New York: Harper and Row, 1965], 94–95). The confidence expressed by the Harpers about the viability of travel writing is certainly borne out by William Lenz's "representative but not exhaustive list" of nearly one hundred travelogues published between 1815 and 1840. See *The Poetics of the Antarctic: A Study in Nineteenth-Century American Cultural Perceptions* (New York: Garland, 1995), 10–15.

15. Poe, *The Narrative of Arthur Gordon Pym of Nantucket*, in *Edgar Allan Poe: The Imaginary Voyages*, 57–58. All subsequent citations refer to this edition.

16. Eve Kosofsky Sedgwick, *Between Men: English Literature and Male Homosocial Desire* (New York: Columbia University Press, 1985), 73.

17. Pym's near-fatal fall on the cliff face in Tsalal, where he is saved by his biracial companion Dirk Peters, will exemplify this dynamic (196–98). Situating vertiginously the crisis of interracial eroticism (as thrill but also threat), Pym's swoon draws him, and with him the text's readers, into the fantasmatic space of same-sex miscegenation. On the significance of racial difference in *Pym*, see Jonathan Elmer's *Reading at the Limit: Affect, Mass Culture, and Edgar Allan Poe* (Stanford: Stanford University Press, 1995) and Dana Nelson's *The Word in Black and White: Reading "Race" in American Literature 1638–1867* (New York: Oxford University Press, 1992).

18. I would note here that I take "immediacy"—the unmediated exchange of stories—to name a fully ideological impossibility.

19. "Poe, Literary Nationalism, and Authorial Identity," in *The American Face of Edgar Allan Poe*, ed. Shawn Rosenheim and Stephen Rachman (Baltimore: Johns Hopkins University Press, 1995), 282. Hence the considerable irony of Poe's defense, while editor of *The Southern Literary Messenger*, against the charge of "indiscriminate cutting and slashing," a practice that, in his view, proceeds "only from the vilest passions of our nature." Given the determining conditions of the reprint process, moral outrage seems immaterial, not least because editorial agency (to slash or not to slash) was redundant, superfluous. See Poe's letter to the editor of the Richmond "Courier and Daily Compiler," written before 2 September 1836, *The Letters of Edgar Allan Poe*, vol. 1, 100–103.

20. McGill, "Poe, Literary Nationalism, and Authorial Identity," 283.

21. I mean by invoking *The Confidence-Man* here to underscore a striking tension: the idealization early on in *Pym* of intimate narrative exchange, antithetical to the treatment of comparable exchanges in Melville's narrative, exists in conflict as well with Poe's own narrative practice, a practice determined by the overriding unpredictabilities of the antebellum literary field.

22. Michael Newbury, *Figuring Authorship in Antebellum America* (Stanford: Stanford University Press, 1997), 179.

23. Not surprisingly, in his history of Harper and Brothers, Eugene Exman takes a much kinder view of the role of the firm, and of antebellum publishing houses

more generally, in the business of literary piracy. Reflecting on "[t]he refusal [in 1837] of Congress to pass the Clay bill" on international copyright—"a deplorable failure to recognize the property rights of authors in what they published"—Exman strikes a note of caution: granting that "[t]he lack of an international copyright was... for authors in both [England and America] unfair and often onerous," he is quick to add that "[e]ven so, claims to that effect made then, and often repeated today, may easily be overstated.... A contemporary generalization made by a man who was both a writer and a publisher is more accurate historically. Horace Greeley knew that 'scarcely a handful' of publishers 'could survive at all' during the two depression periods of the thirties." I would only note that the claim manages to gloss over whether or not the House of Harper was among that handful (for reasons that seem rather more than less transparent, given the status of Exman's history as an in-house production). See *The Brothers Harper*, 117–18.

24. Whalen, *Edgar Allan Poe and the Masses: The Political Economy of Literature in Antebellum America* (Princeton, NJ: Princeton University Press, 1999), 160.

25. *The Narrative of Arthur Gordon Pym of Nantucket*, ed. J. Gerald Kennedy (Oxford: Oxford University Press, 1994), 287.

26. Whalen gives a brilliant materialist analysis of the significance of Poe's borrowing from these earlier travels. See *Edgar Allan Poe and the Masses*, 147–92.

27. *The Narrative of Arthur Gordon Pym of Nantucket*, ed. Kennedy, 287.

28. As Marx argues in the *Grundrisse*, "indifference and equal worthiness are expressly contained in the form of the thing. The particular natural difference which was contained in the commodity is extinguished, and constantly becomes extinguished by circulation" (246).

29. Recall Poe's reference, in the previously quoted excerpt from the 1843 "Prospectus of *The Stylus*," to "the universal *disgust*" at "the *cheap* literature of the day." The bathos of filberts as the culmination of anguishing sensational trials will, in this reading, reflect as it satirizes the indigestion occasioned by the consumption of cheap literature.

30. Poe, "Frederick Maryatt," *Edgar Allan Poe: Essays and Reviews*, 325.

31. In her study of accident theory in nineteenth-century American literary and legal discourse, Nan Goodman makes an observation that suggests another way of reading the excess of sensational effects in *Pym*. The narrative, she rightly notes, "serves to reinforce a connection between recklessness... and the process of storytelling." Could recklessness and accidentalism in narrative answer, even in capitulating to, the illogic of capital's market demands? See Goodman, *Shifting the Blame: Literature, Law, and the Theory of Accident in Nineteenth-Century America* (New York: Routledge, 2000), 48.

32. Reynolds had argued in his address that "*liberality* is *economy*." In his glowing review in the January 1837 *Southern Literary Messenger* of the published version of this address (a review I discuss subsequently), Poe excerpted the phrase directly (*Edgar Allan Poe: Essays and Reviews*, 1245).

33. Ibid., 1230–31; emphasis added.

34. Ibid., 1231–32.

35. Ibid., 1235.

36. Ibid., 1236.

37. The term "Manifest Destiny" was coined in 1845 by John Louis O'Sullivan, the editor of the *United States Magazine and Democratic Revue*—but as Bruce Harvey notes, its "tenets had become commonplaces at least four decades before [the term itself] came into prominence." Harvey observes, rather wryly, that it remains "one of the few ideologies, in the history of nations, that in its own time became so reified as to garner initial capitals in its name" (*American Geographics: U.S. National Narratives and the Representation of the Non-European World, 1830–1865* [Stanford: Stanford University Press, 2001], 6–7). See also Reginald Horsman, *Race and Manifest Destiny: The Origins of American Racial Anglo-Saxonism* (Cambridge, MA: Harvard University Press, 1981), 219–20.

38. *Edgar Allan Poe: Essays and Reviews*, 1244; emphasis added.

39. Given the material contingencies and investments I have been tracing, I find it hard to agree with Bruce Greenfield's assessment of Poe's endeavor in *Pym*: "Poe construes exploratory travel as an act of transcendent insubordination in which the voyager sloughs off the ties of family and nation so that travel may signify in relation to the soul. Geographic discovery is virtually equated with self-discovery, and the discovery narrative is reorganized as a quest for self-knowledge" (*Narrating Discovery*, 167). Likewise, I hesitate to accept Bruce Harvey's contention that, in a "fabular" narrative such as *Pym*, "both the traveler's body and the other's body hold only a distant, spectral relation" to what Harvey understands as "American geographics"; if what I am arguing is right, Poe aims precisely to capitalize on the potential for interimplication between "fabular" narrative and material "geographics," a potential realized not least through human bodies in motion (*American Geographics*, 24).

40. Whalen, *Edgar Allan Poe and the Masses*, 18.

41. Teresa Goddu, *Gothic America: Narrative, History, and Nation* (New York: Columbia University Press, 1997), 82.

42. Ibid., 82, 84, 85.

43. Ibid., 88.

44. See chapter 2, "The Horrid Laws of Political Economy," and chapter 5, "Average Racism: Poe, Slavery, and the Wages of Literary Nationalism," in Whalen, *Edgar Allan Poe and the Masses*.

45. At stake here is the perilous intimacy of science and commerce: the recognition that the power of science, in charting new territories, to underwrite rapacious commercial expansion—its power to invent new markets—will belie the interestedness of supposedly disinterested speculation.

46. *The Writings of Herman Melville*, vol. 14: *Correspondence*, ed. Harrison Hayford et al. (Chicago: Northwestern University Press and the Newberry Library, 1993), 193.

47. Ibid., 343.

48. In *The Division of Literature, or The University in Deconstruction* (Chicago: University of Chicago Press, 1997), Peggy Kamuf characterizes *Typee* and *Omoo* as "titles serving in sum as letters of reference or credit" against which "Melville would seek a writing whose credit was undecidable, . . . a writing that could cause a failure of the determination, according to the values in place, of what 'to succeed' or 'to fail' *could mean* in literature" (180). To the extent that this reading attributes textual indeterminacy to authorial determination (Melville's seeking), it misses what I take

to be Melville's more conflicted, even anguished relation to the material and aesthetic pressures determining the evaluation (not to mention the profit) of literary production.

49. Quoted in Watson Branch et al., "Historical Note," *The Writings of Herman Melville*, vol. 10: *The Confidence-Man: His Masquerade*, ed. Harrison Hayford et al. (Chicago: Northwestern University Press and the Newberry Library, 1984), 272.

50. Watson Branch et al., "Historical Note," 273.

51. Philip Fisher, "Democratic Social Space: Whitman, Melville, and the Promise of American Transparency," *Representations* 24 (fall 1988): 88.

52. Ibid.

53. Eric Sundquist, *To Wake the Nations: Race in the Making of American Literature* (Cambridge, MA: The Belknap Press of Harvard University Press, 1993), 146.

54. Ibid., 154.

55. As John Blassingame argues, "[w]ith Nat perenially in the wings, the creation of Sambo was almost mandatory for the Southerner's emotional security. . . . The more fear whites had of Nat, the more firmly they tried to believe in Sambo in order to escape paranoia" (*The Slave Community: Plantation Life in the Antebellum South* [New York: Oxford University Press, 1979], 230–33). Ronald Takaki concurs: "Here was a society which was almost hysterically fearful of slave rebellions and which needed Sambos, even imagined ones" (*Iron Cages*, 121).

56. Herman Melville, "Benito Cereno," in *The Writings of Herman Melville*, vol. 9: *The Piazza Tales and Other Prose Pieces, 1839–1860*, ed. Harrison Hayford et al. (Chicago: Northwestern University Press and the Newberry Library, 1987), 47, 116.

57. Ibid., 116.

58. Here I would disagree with Kamuf's view that "Benito Cereno" "has essentially the structure of a credit account open and closed, however misleading or finally impossible this closure proves to be" (*The Division of Literature*, 200) since for me the crisis of closure in the story has less to do with structure than with history.

59. "Benito Cereno," 116.

60. See Takaki's discussion of "The New Body" in *Iron Cages* (148–54) for an account of the confident celebration after 1830 of those new forms of technology, especially the steam engine and the telegraph, ideally suited, in the eyes of their celebrants, to a society like that of the United States, "where people were in constant motion, socially and geographically" (149).

61. Hugh Rockoff, "Banking and Finance, 1789–1914," in *The Cambridge Economic History of the United States*, vol. 2: *The Long Nineteenth Century*, ed. Stanley L. Engerman and Robert E. Gallman (Cambridge: Cambridge University Press, 2000), 667.

62. Karl Marx, "Comments on James Mill, *Éléments D'économie Politique*," *Paris Notebooks* no. 4–5 (1844), http://www.marxists.org/archive/marx/works/1844/james-mill/index.htm#026 (accessed 9 January 2003).

63. *The Writings of Herman Melville*, vol. 10: *The Confidence-Man: His Masquerade*, 105. All subsequent citations refer to this edition. *Webster's Dictionary* states that "to clip" is "to take money from unfairly or dishonestly esp. by overcharging" but also "to travel or pass rapidly"; "sweat," meanwhile, means "to extract something valuable from by unfair or dishonest means" and "to remove particles of metal from

(a coin) by abrasion," but also "to heat (as solder) so as to melt and cause to run esp. between surfaces to unite them." Melville's invocation of suspect currency recalls Hawthorne's figure of "the bad half-penny" (12) in the "Custom-House" preface to *The Scarlet Letter,* corrupt currency that, because it unsettles the secure division of foreign from familiar, will not stay away. The destabilizing trickery of suspect currency in such examples bears comparison to William Wells Brown's account, in the preface to *Clotel,* of his daredevil turn using corrupt currency ("shinplasters") to generate sound currency. Here the circulation of phony money glosses to devastatingly ironic effect the passing that, for the fugitive slave, threatened to carry mortal cost (29–31). Contrast, in this context, Emerson's audacious assertion in the 1860 essay "Wealth" (*The Conduct of Life* [Boston: Ticknor and Fields, 1860]) that "[a] man in debt is so far a slave" (90–91), or for that matter his equally provocative claim in the 1870 essay "Domestic Life" (*Society and Solitude* [New York: Routledge, 1887]) that "[m]y expenditure is me" (107).

64. Wai-chee Dimock, *Empire for Liberty,* 189.

65. Dimock, *Empire for Liberty,* 190.

66. Lendol Calder, *Financing the American Dream* (Princeton, NJ: Princeton University Press, 1999), 98.

67. Ibid., 100.

68. Ibid., 76.

69. Ibid., 79.

70. Ibid., 84.

71. Ibid., 88. In his 1844 notes on Mill, Marx punctures the common sense of the historical view that Calder describes, exposing as a cruel fraud the notion of character as capital's substitute for the poor: "[m]utual dissimulation, hypocrisy and sanctimoniousness are carried to extreme lengths [in the credit relationship], so that on the man without credit is pronounced not only the simple judgment that he is poor, but in addition a pejorative moral judgment that he possesses no trust, no recognition, and therefore is a social pariah, a bad man, and in addition to his privation, the poor man undergoes this humiliation and the humiliating necessity of having to *ask* the rich man for credit" ("Comments on James Mill," *Paris Notebooks* no. 4–5).

72. Quoted in Calder, 93.

73. When David Harvey contends that, "[alt]hough the movement of commodities is constrained by the cost and time of transportation, credit money now moves as fast and with as few spatial constraints as information," he gives one way of imagining the inextricability of credit, movement, and discourse—an inextricability key to meaning in Melville's 1857 novel (*The Urban Experience,* 19).

74. To the extent that the simile excavates the history of colonial conquest in the Americas, it also serves to initiate (in admittedly oblique fashion) the complex interrelation of confidence trickery with aboriginal decimation central to the section on Indian-hating (and so to the narrative as a whole). Interestingly, the narrative effect at issue here recalls what, in chapter 1, I argued is a key tendency of travel writing as a genre: the imaginative and affective collapsing of those distances in space and time it draws into view (or indeed produces in the very process of collapsing). And in turn this capacity bears provocatively on Georg Simmel's theorization

of credit: "[i]n credit transactions the immediacy of value exchange is replaced by a distance whose poles are held together by trust"(*The Philosophy of Money*, 2nd ed., trans. Tom Bottomore and David Frisby [London: Routledge, 1990], 480). When understood as inextricable from crises of confidence, the problem of credit thus becomes, much like that of travel's discourse, a problem in the modulation of intimacy with distance.

75. Calder, *Financing the American Dream*, 78.

76. In *Subversive Genealogy: The Politics and Art of Herman Melville* (New York: Knopf, 1983), Michael Rogin locates in the story of China Aster the autobiographical core of *The Confidence-Man*—"the bankruptcy, madness, and death of Allan Melvill" (249).

77. In "Citizens of a World to Come: Melville and the Millennial Cosmopolitanite" (*American Literature* 59 [1] [March 1987]: 20–36), John Bryant makes a convincing argument about both the sociocultural resonance of cosmopolitanism in 1850s America and the concept's significance for anxieties of confidence in Melville's text.

78. The first chapter of Charles MacKay's 1841 classic, *Extraordinary Popular Delusions and the Madness of Crowds* (London: R. Bentley, 1841), examines in detail the career of this capitalist visionary. Although I have no evidence to suggest that Melville knew of or had read the account, in *Delusions*, of what MacKay calls "the Mississippi madness," his reading habits coupled with the book's impact make speculation impossible to resist (1).

79. Michael Warner, "The Mass Public and the Mass Subject," in *The Phantom Public Sphere*, ed. Bruce Robbins (Minneapolis: University of Minnesota Press, 1993), 396–97. Note, too, with respect to the sort of absence I am describing, Rogin's telling contention in *Subversive Genealogy* that "[t]he confidence man exposes the absent core of marketplace reality itself" (238).

80. Helen Trimpi, *Melville's Confidence Men and American Politics in the 1850s*, in *Transactions: The Connecticut Academy of Arts and Sciences* 49 (June 1987): 1–339 (Hamden, CT: Archon Books, 1987).

81. For an argument that plays out such undecidability into a deconstruction of the literary institution, see Peggy Kamuf's analysis, in *The Division of Literature* (167–222) of the "radical credit operation" of Melville's novel.

82. Bill Brown, *The Material Unconscious: American Amusement, Stephen Crane, and the Economies of Play* (Cambridge, MA: Harvard University Press, 1996), 98. Brown invokes this dialectic in the course of critiquing Walter Benn Michaels's reification of the market, through which both causation and accident "must be bracketed" (98). As I hope my discussion indicates, Melville's last novel, in no sense romantic about the prospect of escaping economic determinations, nevertheless demonstrates to spectacular effect the vertiginous power of accident as a material force in commercial exchange.

83. "In credit, the *man* himself, instead of metal or paper, has become the *mediator* of exchange, not however as a man, but as the *mode of existence of capital* and interest. . . . Within the credit relationship, it is not the case that money is transcended in man, but that man himself is turned into *money*, or money is *incorporated* in him. *Human individuality*, human *morality* itself, has become both an object of

commerce and the material in which money exists. Instead of money, or paper, it is my own personal existence, my flesh and blood, my social virtue and importance, which constitutes the material, corporeal form of the *spirit of money*. Credit no longer resolves the value of money into money but into human flesh and the human heart" (Karl Marx, "Comments on James Mill," *Paris Notebooks* no. 4–5).

84. Karl Marx, *Capital*, vol. 1, 255.

85. Ibid.

86. Ibid.

87. Ibid., 253–55. In *Textual Traffic*, S. Shankar offers a comparable analysis with respect to capital's mobile tendencies: "the processes of capitalism are reiteratively characterized . . . by [the] feature of circular but transformative travel. . . . Commodities in capitalism *must* describe such circular and transformative journeys so that value may be appropriated by the capitalist. Does not this represent a capitalist travel narrative, the travel account of a commodity? Is not the commodity then a kind of traveler?" (9). Likewise pertinent is David Harvey's understanding of mobility within capital's dynamic (see note 53 in my introduction).

88. Herman Melville, *Correspondence*, 148.

89. Ibid., 332.

90. For contextualizing analysis of these lectures, see Merton M. Sealts Jr.'s "Historical Note," 514–30, and the editors's textual notes, 723–81, in *The Writings of Herman Melville*, vol. 9.

91. *The Writings of Herman Melville*, vol. 9, 421.

92. Ibid.

93. Ibid.

94. Marx, "Comments on James Mill," *Paris Notebooks* no. 4–5.

95. *The Writings of Herman Melville*, vol. 9, 422–23.

96. Ibid., 423.

97. Ibid.

98. Ibid., 422.

99. Ibid.

3. Secret Circuits, Fugitive Moves

1. Warner, "The Mass Public and the Mass Subject," 239. The sort of disembodied subjectivity analyzed by Warner thrives well past the Republican moment. Note, for instance, its manifestation in the split of "soul" from "nature" in Emerson's "Nature." As Jeannine DeLombard argues, "Emerson . . . provides a transcendentalist version of the implicitly white, implicitly male, implicitly bourgeois universal subject that had only recently become consolidated in Western culture; here the Kantian disinterested subject lives on as the disembodied Emersonian Soul" ("'Eye-Witness to Cruelty': Southern Violence and Northern Testimony in Frederick Douglass's 1845 *Narrative*," *American Literature* 73 (2) (2001): 247.

2. Herman Melville, *The Writings of Herman Melville* vol. 10, 10. Melville here returns to the canine trope he had likewise used in "Benito Cereno" to register the assaultingly casual brutality of supposedly benevolent racism.

3. Ibid.

4. Ibid., 16.
5. Ibid., 17.
6. Ibid.
7. Ibid., 18.
8. Ibid., 18, 19.
9. Hartman, *Scenes of Subjection*, 32.
10. Melville, *The Confidence-Man*, 17.
11. Recall, here, Homi Bhabha's theorization of the stereotype, a theorization focused on colonial discourse but immensely suggestive in other historical contexts: "it is the force of ambivalence that gives the colonial stereotype its currency: ensures its repeatability in changing historical and discursive conjunctures; informs its strategies of individuation and marginalization; produces that effect of probabilistic truth and predictability which, for the stereotype, must always be in *excess* of what can be empirically proved or logically construed" (*The Location of Culture* [London: Routledge, 1994], 66).
12. Hartman, *Scenes of Subjection*, 32.
13. Ibid., 38.
14. Ibid., 37.
15. Ibid., 31. Benjamin Reiss's marvelous cultural history of Joice Heth and P. T. Barnum, *The Showman and the Slave: Race, Death, and Memory in Barnum's America* (Cambridge, MA: Harvard University Press, 2001), offers an extended case study with which to work through the implications of Hartman's point. Although not speaking directly to minstrelsy's dynamic, the rice planter Louis Manigault's 1867 meditation on "the sad reality of affairs" on his Savannah River plantation exemplifies, to striking effect, another version of the white endeavor to retool black subjection in face of emancipation's rupture—and the importance of mobility to that work. A lament, the passage rings out with accents of loss and melancholy: "I imagined myself for the moment a Planter once more, followed by Overseer and Driver.... These were only passing momentary thoughts... soon dispelled by the sad reality of affairs.... In my conversation with these Negroes, now free, and in beholding them my thoughts turned to other Countries, and I almost imagined myself with Chinese, Malays, or even the Indians in the interior of the Philippine islands. That mutual and pleasant feeling of Master toward Slave and vice versa is now as a dream of the past" ("Visit to Cowrie and East Hermitage Plantations, March 22, 1867"; quoted in Eric Foner, *Politics and Ideology in the Age of the Civil War* [New York: Oxford University Press, 1980], 98–99). Although the former "Master" now styles himself a stranger, nevertheless the newly discovered foreignness of freed slaves is every bit as disciplinary as the intimate familiarity—that "dream of the past"—it supplants. Made persons through emancipation, Manigault's ex-slaves still cannot be people in his eyes: instead, they get subjected to the exoticizing otherness previously reserved for the inhabitants of the imperial periphery. The melancholic fantasy was hardly pure fantasy: Manigault had toured China and the Philippines in 1850–51. Thus the repertoires of imperial travel, its politics of mobility, make possible this homebound shift in racist subjection. At stake is what Amy Kaplan, in *The Anarchy of Empire in the Making of U.S. Culture*, calls "the entanglement of the domestic and the foreign" through the routes of modern mobility (1). When we recognize the strong

possibility that some of these once familiar, now foreign ex-slaves are Manigault's children, the complexity of the passage becomes still more acute.

16. Shirley Samuels, "Introduction," *The Culture of Sentiment: Race, Gender, and Sentimentality in Nineteenth-Century America*, ed. Samuels (Oxford: Oxford University Press, 1992), 4.

17. Quoted in William Still, *The Underground Railroad* (New York: Arno Press, 1968), 344.

18. Ibid., 346.

19. For intensive discussion of the passage, enforcement, and reception of the law, see Stanley W. Campbell, *The Slave Catchers: Enforcement of the Fugitive Slave Law 1850–1860* (New York: Norton, 1972).

20. Eber Pettit, *Sketches in the History of the Underground Railroad* (Freeport, NY: Books for Libraries Press, 1971), 116.

21. In a horrifying anecdote included in his *Reminiscences* (New York: Arno Press, 1968), Levi Coffin, the rumored president of the underground railroad, gives a more visceral measure of movement's volatility. He recounts witnessing a recaptured runaway punished for fugitivity and forgery (an event inspirational for Coffin's subsequent career as an abolitionist). The slave, who cannot write, will not divulge the secret of who forged his pass even after his hand has been broken with a hammer, so his owner fastens "[o]ne end of the chain, riveted to the negro's neck . . . to the axle of his . . . buggy" and drives "off at a sweeping trot, compelling the slave to run at full speed or fall and be dragged by his neck" (20). "I watched them till they disappeared in the distance," writes Coffin, "and as long as I could see them, the slave was running" (20). As compensatory as retributive, the punishment here rewards the crime with itself ("You want to run? So run"). By thus insinuating the entanglement of illicit and punitive motion, this harrowing account limns the conflicted centrality of mobility to slavery's system.

22. James Beniger, *The Control Revolution: Technological and Economic Origins of the Information Society* (Cambridge, MA: Harvard University Press, 1986), 219.

23. Lawrence Buell, "American Decolonization," in *Melville's Evermoving Dawn: Centennial Essays*, ed. John Bryant and Robert Milder (Kent, OH: Kent State University Press, 1997), 91. Amy Kaplan's argument in *The Anarchy of Empire in the Making of U.S. Culture* indicates, as well, the importance of understanding the interpenetration of debates about slavery (to which the 1850 Compromise was key) with debates about territorial expansion and continental conquest.

24. Alongside Hartman's *Scenes of Subjection*, see Kawash's *Dislocating the Color Line: Identity, Hybridity, and Singularity in African-American Narrative* (Stanford: Stanford University Press, 1997). Marcus Wood's stunning analysis of woodcuts on slave advertisements usefully complements the argument I am making here. As Wood contends, "[t]he icon of the runaway . . . is an image of appalling force, a statement that in the eyes of the law, and the eyes of the slave power, one runaway is the same as every runaway, while the act of running away always takes the same literal form. The image is part of a commercial nexus in which the North was as deeply implicated as the South." In the icon for the male runaway, we see "the strange effects latent in the depiction of frozen motion. . . . He will be perpetually running, until he is re-instated in his legal position as a slave. This is the *locus classicus* for the slave-

holder's view of the runaway. In its literalisation of the concept of 'run-away' it is a negation of the slave's most radical anti-slavery gesture. The slave does not guilefully depart under shade of night, but stands out bold and stupid on the bleak white background of the printed page. . . . Comic, trivial, pathetic, and always the same, with his bundle of goods and one foot eternally raised, he proclaims his inadequacy for the task he has set himself" (*Blind Memory: Visual Representations of Slavery in England and America 1780–1865* [New York: Routledge, 2000], 87, 93. In note 64 of this chapter, I engage with Wood's reading of Bibb's narrative.

25. At the same time, we need to recognize the potential tenuousness of the difference between open secrecy and publicity. Frederick Douglass's 1845 perspective is relevant here: "I have never approved of the very public manner in which some of our western friends have conducted what they call the *underground railroad*, but which I think, by their open declarations, has been made most emphatically the *upperground railroad*" (*Narrative of the Life of Frederick Douglass, an American Slave*, ed. Benjamin Quarles [Cambridge, MA: The Belknap Press of Harvard University Press, 1960, 1988], 136–37).

26. Still, *The Underground Railroad*, 5.

27. Ibid., 1.

28. Ibid.

29. Ibid., 2.

30. We recall here the valuable papers that Black Guinea does not possess. Intriguing in Still's account is the intimation that fugitives hold an uncommon degree of literacy.

31. Joseph Roach gives a brilliant analysis of the performativity of these rituals in his "Slave Spectacles and Tragic Octoroons: A Cultural Genealogy of Antebellum Performance," *Theatre Survey* 33 (2) (November 1992): 167–93.

32. Pettit, *Sketches in the History of the Underground Railroad*, 114.

33. With this phrase, I echo Judith Halberstam's trenchant characterization of the dynamics of difference written into the gothic mode. See *Skin Shows: Gothic Horror and the Technology of Monsters* (Durham, NC: Duke University Press, 1995).

34. Coffin, *Reminiscences of Levi Coffin*, vi. Coffin gives a notably humorous version of such rhetorical naming in the entry "Collecting Funds for the Road," 320–23.

35. *Sketches*, 34–35.

36. Larry Gara, *The Liberty Line: The Legend of the Underground Railroad* (Lexington: University of Kentucky Press, 1961), 2.

37. *The Black Abolitionist Papers*, vol. 2: *Canada*, 1830–1865, ed. C. Peter Ripley (Chapel Hill: University of North Carolina Press, 1986), 176.

38. I would recall, here, Lisa Brawley's incisive observation that narratives of the underground railroad served to link an idealized version of northern freedom with the supposedly liberating power of train technology: "as the railroad to freedom, the rhetoric of the underground railroad helped to align freedom with the railroad: going from Maryland to Massachusetts could transform a thing into a man—what more convincing testimony could one find of the humanizing power of the train and, by association, of the industrial revolution the train quite literally motored across the continent?" ("Frederick Douglass's My *Bondage and* My *Freedom* and the Fugitive Tourist Industry," *Novel: A Forum on Fiction* 30, [1] [fall 1996]: 100).

39. William Wells Brown, *Clotel; or, the President's Daughter*, ed. Henry Louis Gates Jr. (New York: Vintage, 1990), 24.

40. Recall C. B. MacPherson's argument, outlined in chapter 1, note 26, about the ideology of self-possession under liberalism: "The individual, it was thought, is free inasmuch as he is proprietor of his person and capacities" (*The Political Theory of Possessive Individualism: Hobbes to Locke*, 3). In *Dislocating the Color Line*, Kawash gives a brilliant reading of the fissures in this ideology as exposed by Bibb's text.

41. Henry Bibb, *Narrative of the Life and Adventures of Henry Bibb, an American Slave*, ed. Charles J. Heglar (Madison: University of Wisconsin Press, 2001), xiii. All subsequent citations refer to this edition.

42. *The Black Abolitionist Papers*, vol. 2, 171.

43. Gilroy, *The Black Atlantic*, 19.

44. Thus the passage may be said to bear out Philip Fisher's axiom, "[t]he climatic act that asserts the full possession of an individual self is the act of disappearing," in ways unexplored by Fisher himself ("Appearing and Disappearing in Public: Social Space in Late-Nineteenth-Century Literature and Culture," in *Reconstructing American Literary History*, ed. Sacvan Bercovitch [Cambridge, MA: Harvard University Press, 1986], 178). All the same, as I have already observed with respect to *Clotel* and will go on to analyze with respect to Bibb's *Narrative*, the ideal of self-possession key to liberalism (and assumed by Fisher) holds fraught significance for fugitives from slavery. Interestingly, in the preface to the narrative, Bibb represents its writing as occurring "during irregular intervals, while I have been travelling and laboring for the emancipation of my enslaved countrymen," thereby suggesting that travel and abolition, but not writing, remain his prime trades (11).

45. Mary Louise Pratt, "Scratches on the Face of the Country; or, What Mr. Barrow Saw in the Land of the Bushmen," in *"Race," Writing, and Difference*, ed. Henry Louis Gates Jr. (Chicago: University of Chicago Press, 1986), 143.

46. W. E. B. Dubois, *The Souls of Black Folk*, ed. Candace Ward (New York: Dover, 1994), 2. Pertinent, here, is Hartman's gloss on "'stealing away'"—a phrase that "designated a wide range of activities, from praise meetings, quilting parties, and dances to illicit visits with lovers and family on neighboring plantations. It encompassed an assortment of popular illegalities focused on contesting the authority of the slave-owning class and contravening the status of the enslaved as possession. The very phrase 'stealing away' played upon the paradox of property's agency and the idea of property as theft, thus alluding to the captive's condition as a legal form of unlawful or amoral seizure, what Hortense Spillers describes as 'the violent seizing of the captive body from its motive will, its active desire.' Echoing Proudhon's 'property is theft,' Henry Bibb put the matter simply: 'Property can't steal property'" (*Scenes of Subjection*, 66).

47. W. T. J. Mitchell, "Imperial Landscape," in *Landscape and Power*, ed. Mitchell (Chicago: University of Chicago Press, 1994), 15.

48. Ralph Waldo Emerson, *Nature*, in *Emerson's Complete Works*, vol. 1: *Nature, Addresses, and Lectures* (London: Routledge, 1886), 69. Jeannine DeLombard underscores how the Emersonian conception serves literary ends, envisioning a "potentially unifying national literature . . . [through which] to transcend the property relations that subdivide the U.S. countryside" ("'Eye-Witness to Cruelty,'" 247).

49. Read in this way, Bibb's apostrophe instances the differential production of space outlined in my introduction. It likewise gestures toward what Hartman calls "the disavowed transactions between slavery and freedom as modes of production and subjection," and so toward the grave limitations of the liberal concept of self-possession as a means to articulate human freedom—what Hartman calls "the new forms of bondage enabled by proprietorial notions of the self" (*Scenes of Subjection*, 13, 6). The apostrophic tendency in the passage will recall comparable moments in other slave narratives (for instance the famous apostrophe to the tall ships in Frederick Douglass's 1845 *Narrative*), and as such will intimate the generic pressures to produce such discursively spontaneous expressions of anguish.

50. A medicalizing term for the desire of the enslaved to run away, "drapetomania" was first coined by Samuel Cartwright in an article in *The Georgia Blister and Critic* 1 (7) (September 1854) by combining the Greek for "runaway slave" and "mad or crazy." As Kawash observes dryly, "[d]rapetomania was a curious condition, in which the symptom (running away) was completely equivalent to the disease" (*Dislocating the Color Line*, 59). The concept will supply an exemplary instance of the purely social force of medical diagnosis, generating an order of pathology it claims merely to discover (and, as Kawash goes on to argue, "the need to invent a pathology to account for the running away of slaves points to how widespread and disruptive such running away must have been" [59–60]). The irony of the ascription is considerable, since it turns the concept emergent in the period as key to national character, restless mobility, into the pathological condition of the noncitizen fugitive within the nation's space. Evidently, the fugitive's mobile practice troubled the hegemony of spatial as of social and national relations in midcentury America.

51. See Eve Kosofsky Sedgwick's analysis of "the deadly system of double binds where an assertion that one can act freely is always read in the damning light of the 'open secret' that the behavior in question is utterly compelled—while one's assertion that one was, after all, compelled, shrivels in the equally stark light of the 'open secret' that one might at any given moment have chosen differently" ("Epidemics of the Will," in *Tendencies* [Durham, NC: Duke University Press, 1993], 133–35).

52. Here, then, we may say that Bibb's narrative anticipates the crises of confidence grimly anatomized by Melville.

53. Kawash, *Dislocating the Color Line*, 60.

54. Hortense Spillers, "Mama's Baby, Papa's Maybe: An American Grammar Book," *Diacritics* 17 (2) (summer 1987): 67.

55. Thus slave bodies on the auction block can *tell* in ways not incommensurate with the laboratory truth-claims of comparative anatomy.

56. When, in his *Sketches*, Eber Pettit typifies "[t]he 'fugitives from labor' who took passage on the U.G.R.R.," he appeals—alarmingly enough—to an association of pigment with intellect comparable to that attributed by Bibb to slaveholders: "[they] were generally of the most intelligent class, and but for their use of certain words and phrases common to both master and servant in the slave States, . . . would often have been rejected as having no claim to accommodations on our line" (27). By implication, a lack of intelligence announces the slave. Read this way, Pettit's generalization transposes the racist habit of linking intellect to skin pigmentation, with darkness signaling dumbness and lightness (or whiteness) signaling brightness.

Thus the passage hides a twofold secret: either the dark-skinned, intelligent African-American cannot possibly be a slave, or else (and also?) "most intelligent class" is code for light-skinned. By limning miscegenation's unspeakability in the concept of "certain words and phrases," Pettit does not just gloss a means of fugitive escape—he reveals a stain of racist belief.

57. *Dislocating the Color Line*, 62.

58. Ibid., 59.

59. See Hartman's analysis of this strategy in *Scenes of Subjection*: "The sexual exploitation of the enslaved female [by slavers], incredulously, served as evidence of her collusion with the master class and as evidence of her power, the power both to render the master weak and, implicitly, to be the mistress of her own subjection. The slave woman not only suffered the responsibility for her sexual (ab)use but also was blameworthy because of her purported ability to render the powerful weak" (87). My point, I would stress, is only to remark on troubling rhetorical resonance, not to hint at the possibility of abuse in Bibb's relationship with Malinda.

60. *Dislocating the Color Line*, 38.

61. Russ Castronovo, *Necro Citizenship: Death, Eroticism, and the Public Sphere in the Nineteenth-Century United States* (Durham, NC: Duke University Press, 2001), 43. Hence Castronovo's telling insight into Bibb's later admission that he regards Malinda as effectively dead to him: "the social death of these other bodies"—slavery's "abjected populations"—"leaves the citizen free" (44).

62. Lora Romero, *Home Fronts*, 59.

63. Ibid., 53.

64. As Marcus Wood has shown in his dazzling interpretation of the numerous woodcut illustrations in Bibb's narrative, much the same seems true of the production and circulation of fugitivity as a *visual* commodity. Reprinted from a whole host of antebellum sources, these woodcuts "testify that there is no pictorial language to do justice to the horror of slave-life, only a series of well-circulated, well-digested stereotypes." The frontispiece, with its realistic portraiture, constitutes for Wood the exception, countering "the ability of the image of the runaway slave to depersonalize its subject." Yet in so doing it cannot overcome "the dismaying truth that the atrocity suffered by slaves can only be recounted according to a set of technical and imaginative lowest common denominators. [The woodcut] images reduce slave experience to a set of repeated scenes; they constitute an essentialist base for the depiction of slave life within abolition semiotics" (*Blind Memory*, 120, 130, 133).

65. *Dislocating the Color Line*, 61.

66. Ibid., 62.

67. Carla Kaplan, "Narrative Contracts and Emancipatory Readers," *Yale Journal of Criticism* 6 (1) (1993): 108. See also Kaplan's analysis, in *The Erotics of Talk: Women's Writing and Feminist Paradigms*, of the problematics of narrative contract in Harriet Jacobs's *Incidents in the Life of a Slave Girl*; William Andrew's analysis, in *To Tell a Free Story: The First Century of Afro-American Autobiography, 1760–1865* (Chicago: University of Illinois Press, 1988), of tensions within the genre more generally; and C. Peter Ripley's commentary, in *The Black Abolitionist Papers* vol. 3: *The United States, 1830–1846* (Chapel Hill: University of North Carolina, 1991), on white

efforts to restrict black agency in the production and dissemination of antislavery materials (26–30). Clearly I am not the first to suggest that the conventions of the slave narrative could constrain those subjects whose struggles for freedom were recounted. The emphasis I aim to make falls particularly on the issue of circulation as it contributes to the conflicted, contestatory significance of mobility recorded in Bibb's narrative.

68. The claim here does not discount the political potential within affect, potential demonstrated again and again in the antebellum moment. My point is rather about the conflicted status of readerly enticement in the prefatory apparatus to Bibb's text. Others might want to link such enticement, as a market strategy, much more directly and decisively to the political work of abolition.

69. *The Black Abolitionist Papers*, vol. 3, 460; spellings are presumably Bibb's.

70. "Slave Spectacles and Tragic Octaroons," 170. As the foregoing discussion begins to suggest, I am less likely to concur with Dickson Bruce Jr. when, in *The Origins of African-American Literature, 1680–1865* (Charlottesville: University Press of Virginia, 2001), he contends that interpretations of testimonials "as creating a white control over the black author and his voice . . . should not obscure what was, within abolitionism, the more important concern" (241) than I am with Hartman when, in *Scenes of Subjection*, she argues that "[s]lave narrators were literally and figuratively forced to display themselves in order to tell their stories" and that "[s]ince the veracity of black testimony is in doubt, the crimes of slavery must not only be confirmed by unquestionable authorities and other white observers but also must be made visible, whether by revealing the scarred back of the slave—in short, making the body speak—or through authenticating devices, or, better yet, by enabling reader and audience member to experience vicariously the 'tragical scenes of cruelty'" (209, 22).

71. Richard Hall, *Patriots in Disguise: Women Warriors of the Civil War* (New York: Paragon House, 1993), 83.

72. Elizabeth Young, *Disarming the Nation: Women's Writing and the American Civil War* (Chicago: University of Chicago Press, 1999), 154–55.

73. Karen Sánchez-Eppler, *Touching Liberty: Abolition, Feminism, and the Politics of the Body* (Berkeley and Los Angeles: University of California Press, 1993), 15–19. In *American Anatomies: Theorizing Race and Gender* (Durham, NC: Duke University Press, 1995), Robyn Wiegman delineates the complex problematic in striking terms: "To be excluded from the public sphere of citizenship was not to be uniformly cast as inhuman, and it was this difference in human status between the white woman and the enslaved—both female and male—that became crucial to articulating the relationship between gender and modern social and political subjectivity. In the incompatible convergence between the white woman's excision from the public domain of enlightened citizenship and the slave's corporealization as the inhuman, we approach one of the most powerful and consequential asymmetries through which the coupling of 'blacks and women' has been historically framed" (45).

74. Young, *Disarming the Nation*, 152.

75. Ibid.

76. Ibid., 156. One might in fact suspect that what, at the level of autobiographical history, serves as a kind of counterfeit—the suppression of the framing

masquerade as a man—functions at the level of narrative inscription to clarify by making as starkly schematic as possible the homology woman/slave.

77. Stowe, *Going Abroad*, 107.

78. Sarah Emma E. Edmonds, *Nurse and Spy in the Union Army: Comprising the Adventures and Experiences of a Woman in Hospitals, Camps, and Battle-Fields* (Hartford: W. S. Williams and Co., 1865), 6. All subsequent citations refer to this edition.

79. Hence the considerable irony of Edmonds's subsequent condemnation of military dandies (237) and clerical fops (279), and her approving account of rebel women who shame their men into joining the army by giving them "skirts and crinoline" (332). Such moments find in the dimensions of male costume a normative expression of masculinity.

80. Young, *Disarming the Nation*, 154.

81. Here I mean to invoke what Sánchez-Eppler takes to be the constant problem of miscegenation, that it offers "a bodily challenge to the conventions of reading the body, thus simultaneously insisting that the body is a sign of identity and undermining the assurance with which that sign can be read" (*Touching Liberty*, 104).

82. To the extent that, as Robyn Wiegman observes, "the visible, progressive 'whitening' of the slave body throughout the century... mark[ed] in particular and urgent ways the crisis of race in nineteenth century America" (*American Anatomies*, 47), Edmonds's pigment "problem" limns the occluded history of a century's racial transformation and racialized anxiety.

83. Young, *Disarming the Nation*, 151.

84. Ibid., 150.

85. We might well take the risks in question to exemplify what, in *Crimes of Writing*, Susan Stewart argues will characterize travel's practice more generally: "the problems of coming too close or going too far, the problems of staying too long or leaving too quickly, the problems of rigidity and provinciality on the one hand and promiscuousness and contamination on the other" (177–78).

86. Hartman, *Scenes of Subjection*, 6.

87. The passage continues so as to teach its readers a troublesome lesson in the aesthetics of benevolent racism: "'Some of them are whiter and prettier than most of our northern ladies. There is a family here, all of whom have blue eyes, light hair, fair skin and rosy cheeks; yet they are contrabands, and have been slaves. But why should blue eyes and golden hair be the distinction between bond and free?'"

88. The analysis of such stasis is the project of the next chapter. I would note that the dynamic at play here will exemplify what Jenny Franchot calls the "recreation [of religious belief] as visual memory, or more precisely as souvenir and entertainment, one fit for visual scrutiny and memorial appropriation as the 'seen'" ("Unseemly Commemoration: Religion, Fragment, and the Icon," *American Literary History* 9 [3] [fall 1997], 502).

89. *The Black Abolitionist Papers*, vol. 5: *The United States, 1859–1865*, ed. C. Peter Ripley (Chapel Hill: The University of North Carolina Press, 1992), 220.

90. Ibid., 221.

91. Ibid.

92. Nell Irvin Painter, "Sojourner Truth in Feminist Abolitionism," in *The Abolitionist Sisterhood: Women's Political Culture in Antebellum America*, ed. Jean Fagan Yellin and John C. Van Horne (Ithaca, NY: Cornell University Press in cooperation with the Library Company of Philadelphia, 1994), 140.

93. Jean Humez, "In Search of Harriet Tubman's Spiritual Autobiography," *NWSA Journal* 5 (2) (summer 1993): 163.

94. Relevant, here, is Lauren Berlant's more general therorization of the social circulation of minority subjects such as Tubman: "the minority subject who circulates in a majoritarian public sphere occupies a specific contradiction: insofar as she is exemplary, she has distinguished herself from the collective stereotype; and, at the same time, she is also read as a kind of foreign national, an exotic representative of her alien 'people' who reports to the dominant culture about collective life in the crevices of national existence" ("The Queen of America Goes to Washington City: Harriet Jacobs, Frances Harper, Anita Hill," in *Subjects and Citizens: Nation, Race, and Gender from "Oroonoko" to Anita Hill*, ed. Michael Moon and Cathy N. Davidson [Durham, NC: Duke University Press, 1995], 457). Although Tubman struggled for the rest of her life to secure any sort of government support in recognition of her wartime service, Edmonds, despite defecting from the army (an episode misrepresented in *Nurse and Spy*), managed successfully to appeal for an army pension. Both women had access to the market in slave stories still so popular in the postbellum period, but where for Edmonds such literary production apparently only amplified the emancipatory benefits of cross-racial masquerade, for Tubman it seems to have been measurable instead through its costs.

4. Mobility's Disciplines

1. This date is contested. In "Hale's Tours: Ultrarealism in the Pre-1910 Motion Picture" (*Cinema before Griffith*, ed. John L. Fell [Berkeley and Los Angeles: University of California Press, 1983]), Raymond Fielding puts its first appearance in 1904 at the St. Louis Exposition; however, in the more recent *The Emergence of Cinema: The American Screen to 1907* (New York: Scribner's, 1990), Charles Musser cites ads and promotional material as evidence that the attraction did not debut until 1905, in Kansas City. See Lynn Kirby's discussion of this debate in *Parallel Tracks: The Railroad and Silent Cinema* (Durham, NC: Duke University Press, 1997), 266, n. 144. The Ford epigraph comes from *Today and Tomorrow* (New York: Doubleday, Page, and Company, 1926), 4.

2. Miriam Hansen, *Babel and Babylon: Spectatorship in American Silent Film* (Cambridge, MA: Harvard University Press, 1991), 32.

3. Recall Walter Benjamin's celebrated formulation in "The Work of Art in the Age of Mechanical Reproduction" (*Illuminations*, ed. Hannah Arendt, trans. Harry Zohn [New York: Schocken Books, 1969]): "[o]ur taverns and our metropolitan streets, our offices and our furnished rooms, our railroad stations and our factories appeared to have us locked up hopelessly. Then came the film and burst this prison-world asunder by the dynamite of the tenth of a second, so that now, in the midst of its far-flung ruins and debris, we calmly and adventurously go traveling" (232).

4. As Kirby notes, "[t]he apparatus was modeled on turn-of-the-century fairground and amusement park entertainments that seated 'passengers' in railway cars while painted scenery rolled past the windows. Hale's Tours used filmed panoramic views shot from the fronts of locomotives, which gave the viewer the illusion of being on a train—an illusion reinforced by the rocking back and forth of the train car and often by the blowing of a whistle. . . . At its most popular moment in 1906–7, Hale's Tours theaters numbered more than five hundred around the United States" (*Parallel Tracks*, 46).

5. In *Bodies and Machines* (New York: Routledge, 1992), Seltzer argues that, in the United States at the turn of the nineteenth century, persons become individuals through the double logic of system and individuation. In Seltzer's account, machine culture does this work because it extends yet suspends human agency. In thus regulating human unpredictability, machine culture, and especially the body/machine complex, helps to render individuation systematic, disciplinary.

6. What I call the strategic potential of inertia indicates the mobilization of *slowness* as a political mode. Here slowness has nothing to do with nostalgia: it gives a way to defend hegemonic interests, working not least to counter labor's resistant use of the slowdown (what, in *The Principles of Scientific Management* [New York: Norton, 1967], Frederick Winslow Taylor calls "systemic soldiering" [20ff]). Resonant, here, is Paul Virilio's argument, in *Speed and Politics*, trans. Mark Polizzotti (New York: Semiotext(e), 1986), about the late-twentieth-century moment: "In a social configuration whose precarious equilibrium is threatened by any ill-considered initiative, security can henceforth be likened to the absence of movement" (125). I return to the contemporary power of strategic stasis in this book's epilogue.

7. Kirby, *Parallel Tracks*, 3.

8. In *Doing the Town: The Rise of Urban Tourism in the United States, 1850–1914* (Berkeley and Los Angeles: University of California Press, 2001), Cocks argues that "[t]he extra-fare cars constituted a space at once genteel and transient, distinct from a particular community yet fostering a national community of the refined . . . [and thereby] eased mid-nineteenth century fears about public spaces and social interactions" (55). Cocks's analysis makes evident how such material differentiations helped to advance a concept of "democratic luxury" in travel, a recognizably American ideology of *social* mobility working to occlude class differences through the premise that anyone could rise into luxury simply by making money.

9. Recall, here, the "we" in the epigraph from Ford's *Today and Tomorrow*—haunted as it is, when read to name an exclusive elite, by the prospect of the loss of authority and agency in face of unpredictabilities of social movement.

10. Martha Banta, *Barbaric Intercourse: Caricature and the Culture of Conduct, 1841–1936* (Chicago: University of Chicago Press, 2003), 1.

11. Florence Howe Hall, *The Correct Thing in Good Society* (Boston: Dana Estes and Company, 1902).

12. Julia Dewey, *Lessons on Manners, Arranged for Grammar Schools, High Schools and Academies* (New York: Hines and Noble, 1899), 5.

13. The fact that manners discourse is no more "about" industrial relations than, say, *The Red Badge of Courage* is "about" football will seem to bring us close, here, to what Bill Brown calls "the material unconscious" (*The Material Unconscious*). One

might speculate that in this regard a useful means of measuring the impact of what I call disciplinary pace will be to read for its traces in genres and discourses that would seem farthest removed from the immediate scenes of technological contest—although, of course, the absent presence of industrial conflict at the end of the century is absolutely crucial in understanding the urgency of manners instruction for the rising entrepreneurial classes.

14. Mary Louis Pratt, "Scratches on the Face of the Country; or, What Mr. Barrow Saw in the Land of the Bushmen," in *"Race," Writing, and Difference*, ed. Henry Louis Gates Jr. (Chicago: University of Chicago Press, 1986), 140.

15. Margaret E. Sangster (Elizabeth Munson), *Good Manners for All Occasions* (New York: The Christian Herald/Louis Klopsch, 1904), 3.

16. Mrs. John Sherwood (Mary Elizabeth Wilson), *Manners and Social Usages* (New York: Harper and Brothers, 1888), 5–6.

17. Ibid., 6.

18. Ibid., 7.

19. Amy Kaplan, *The Anarchy of Empire in the Making of U.S. Culture*. Her argument that "'Manifest Domesticity' turns an imperial nation into a home by producing and colonizing specters of the foreign that lurk inside and outside its ever-shifting borders" bears suggestively on the materials I am addressing here (50).

20. Pierre Bourdieu, *Distinction: A Social Critique of the Judgement of Taste*, trans. Richard Nice (Cambridge, MA: Harvard University Press, 1984), 68.

21. Sangster, *Good Manners for All Occasions*, 23. On American restlessness as common sense, see my introduction.

22. Sherwood, *Manners and Social Usages*, 4.

23. Ralph Waldo Emerson, "Self-Reliance," in *The Collected Works*, vol. 2: *Essays: First Series*, ed. Joseph Slater et al. (Cambridge, MA: The Belknap Press of Harvard University Press, 1979), 46–47. In the late essay "Culture," Emerson revisits his theme, noting that "I am not much an advocate for travelling, and I observe that men run away to other countries, because they are not good in their own, and run back to their own, because they pass for nothing in the new places. . . . Who are you that have no task to keep you at home?" Subsequently, though, he tempers his critique: "But let us not be pedantic, but allow to travel its full effect. . . . No doubt, to a man of sense, travel offers advantages. . . . A foreign country is a point of comparison, wherefrom to judge his own" (*The Conduct of Life*, 125–27).

24. Emerson, *The Journals and Miscellaneous Notebooks of Ralph Waldo Emerson*, vol. 8, ed. William H. Gilman and J. E. Parsons (Cambridge, MA: The Belknap Press of Harvard University Press, 1970), 251. Such traveling lessons will begin to intimate the curiously contradictory status of travel not just in the discourse on manners but in the social formation to which that discourse spoke: at once an inclusive social practice and a mode of pointed social discrimination. As Richard Brodhead observes in *Cultures of Letters*: "[e]volved *at* this time, elite vacation habits also took on a heavily symbolic function *in* this time in dramatizing [upper class] social superiority. . . . The better-off of this time invested themselves in vacation travel not only because they liked to or were free to but because such travel was a chief means to establish elite social standing. . . . In distinction from other contemporaneous formations, the postbellum elite and its adherents made other *ways of life* the object of

their admiration and desire, objects which they then felt free to annex: the upper class vacation, thus, entails crossing out of one's own culture into another culture (not just place) to the end of living another way of life" (125–33).

25. Florence Hartley, *The Ladies' Book of Etiquette and Manual of Politeness* (New York: Salvation Press, 1882), 40.

26. Sangster, *Good Manners for All Occasions*, 31. The sort of nerve-wear Sangster attributes to modern transit exemplifies Kirby's insight into metropolitan modernity: "Living by the clock in a dense urban world electrified by a skein of traffic, the vulnerable urbanite succumbed to a host of nervous disorders" (*Parallel Tracks*, 63). Such disorders reference neurasthenia, or what in 1881 George Beard termed "Americanitis," a condition capacious in its symptomology and suggestive through its cures ("rest" and "camp" or "West") for the politics of mobility at issue here.

27. Hartley, *The Ladies' Book of Etiquette*, 34.

28. Dewey, *Lessons on Manners*, 95. Against this conception of betrayal into impropriety, consider Bourdieu's theorization, in *Pascalian Meditations*, trans. Richard Nice (Stanford: Stanford University Press, 2000), of habitus or disposition as "the inscription of a relation of domination into the body" that "often takes the form of *bodily emotion* (shame, timidity, anxiety, guilt) . . . betrayed in visible manifestations, such as blushing, inarticulacy, clumsiness, trembling, all ways of submitting, however reluctantly, to the dominant judgement" (169).

29. Theodore Roosevelt to Stephen Crane, in *The Western Writings of Stephen Crane*, ed. Frank Bergon (New York: The New American Library, 1979), 227.

30. I would add that in this effort Crane will recall Mark Twain, who, as Amy Kaplan makes clear with respect to his Hawaiian travels in 1866, labored "to dissociate his position as a traveler and writer from . . . overt assertions of imperial force" (*The Anarchy of Empire in the Making of U.S. Culture*, 62).

31. Bill Brown, *The Material Unconscious*, 74.

32. Ibid., 73, 74.

33. Ibid., 74.

34. *The University of Virginia Edition of the Works of Stephen Crane*, vol. 8: *Tales, Sketches, and Reports*, ed. Fredson Bowers (Charlottesville: The University Press of Virginia, 1973), 431. All subsequent citations refer to this edition.

35. Brown, *The Material Unconscious*, 79.

36. Tacit in the tourist's frustration at the lack of profit is a submerged fantasy that Mexican travel will enable and legitimate exploitation, a fantasy realizable on an *individual* basis to the extent that the tourist steers clear of imported things, of those items and services that give to a place such as Mexico City its "American aspect."

37. In this sense Crane models a dissonant version of the standard travel posture identified by Mary Louise Pratt: "protagonists . . . everywhere on the margins of their own story, present not as heroes but as effaced information-producers gazing in from a periphery" ("Scratches on the Face of the Country," 146). We may also see, in Crane's narrative posture and performance, one trace of the imperial discourse he seems otherwise to be critiquing—what Kaplan in *The Anarchy of Empire in the Making of U.S. Culture* calls "disincarnation," an imperial style in which "[d]isembodiment . . . [indicates a] cultural fantasy underlying what historians have called the

economically determined 'informal empire,' the desire for total control disentangled from direct political annexation" (96).

38. This critique resonates with David Spurr's assessment, in *The Rhetoric of Empire*, of "the complexity and ambiguity" of Crane's "role in the colonial situation": "Crane writes as if, recognizing the dilemma of the colonial writer, he could escape from the obligations of power by cultivating a purely aesthetic view, by reducing everything to 'form and color.' . . . [Yet this] aesthetic functions as a form of colonization in itself, relegating Mexico to the status of an object to be appreciated for its beauty, pathos, and passion. Simultaneously, however, this cultivation of an aesthetic ideal opens up a space for domination in the realm of concrete practice" (56–57).

39. Brown, *The Material Unconscious*, 94. Brown's brilliant reading of Crane's Mexican travel dispatches has greatly influenced my own—but I would note, here, that his account of "The Mexican Lower Classes," by implying that Crane fails to return in the piece to "the horror of Mexican indigence," effaces the specificity of the horror in question, the indigeneity of indigence in Mexico.

40. Ibid.

41. Michael Denning, *Mechanic Accents: Dime Novels and Working-Class Culture in America* (London: Verso, 1987), 149.

42. Brown, *The Material Unconscious*, 100. In *Stephen Crane in the West and Mexico* (Kent, OH: Kent State University Press, 1970), Joseph Katz suggests that the short story "Billy Atkins Went to Omaha," also published under the title "An American Tramp's Excursion," will indicate Crane's ongoing imaginative engagement with the trip he would subsequently take, and accordingly his identification with the tramp as a figure (xi). More interesting to me than these autobiographical speculations are the material fissures of history. As Bergon notes, the West through which Crane traveled in 1895 bore undeniable signs of the labor violence at stake in tramp discourse: "[t]he actual West of Crane's visit had seen sixty thousand Western members of the American Railway Union walk out during a series of strikes in 1893 and 1894. . . . During these same years thousands of unemployed Westerners followed the lead of Coxey's Army [of tramps and migrants] and began marches to Washington, D.C., from Texas and California" (*The Western Writings of Stephen Crane*, 7). The point is precisely that the nascent hegemony of north-south tourism submitted to such critical scrutiny by Crane in his Bacheller dispatches emerged in interimplication with, not isolation from, these other, less predictable itineraries and mobilities.

43. Quoted by Almont Lindsey, *The Pullman Strike: The Story of a Unique Experiment and of a Great Labor Upheaval* (Chicago: University of Chicago Press, 1942), 13.

44. Jonathan Auerbach, *Male Call: Becoming Jack London* (Durham, NC: Duke University Press, 1996), 134.

45. Ibid., 8. London's tramp writing occupies a place within a burgeoning discourse on tramping at the turn of the nineteenth century, one generated as part of the new sociology devoted to the study of urban problems. For some commentators tramping was pathological, what they termed wanderlust or dromomania, diagnoses recalling the medical comprehension of slave fugitivity (see chapter 3, note 50). Heather Tapley's Ph.D. thesis, "The American Hobo-Sexual: A Connective History in Material Queer Culture" (University of Alberta, 2003), gives an excellent overview of disciplinary and resistant forms of tramp knowledge. As she makes clear,

commentators in the period around 1900 hotly debated the correspondences and differences between the terms "tramp" and "hobo." I choose to use the former because, as Denning argues, it captures the sense of "ideological naming" at stake. And I should note, here, that Tapley and I disagree on the resistant significance of London's interventions into the tramp debates.

46. Jack London, "The Road," in *Jack London on the Road: The Tramp Diary and Other Hobo Writings*, ed. Richard W. Etulain (Logan: Utah State University Press, 1979), 70.

47. Auerbach, *Male Call*, 135; London, "The Road," 71.

48. Richard Brodhead, *Cultures of Letters*, 133. The grimness of the mimicry here has not least to do with the fact that, as Brodhead makes clear, regionalism as a "reading of regions" evolves alongside elite vacation habits—alongside leisured luxury, not (as we see in London's case) laboring misery. Pertinent on this question is Keith Gandal's provocative analysis, in *The Virtues of the Vicious: Jacob Riis, Stephen Crane, and the Spectacle of the Slum* (New York: Oxford University Press, 1997), of what I would call the touristic supplement to Progressive-era reform discourse.

49. London, "Rods and Gunnels," in *Jack London on the Road*, 94; italics in original.

50. Ibid., 89.

51. Ibid., 90.

52. Ibid., 91.

53. Ibid., 91, 92.

54. As indicated in the introduction, I derive my understanding of the concept of intimate distance, and extrapolate my concept of intimate difference, from Susan Stewart's analysis of the effect of souvenirs in *On Longing*.

55. London, "Rods and Gunnels," 95. Indicative of a problematic crucial to London's tramp writing, the fitness and fittedness of tramp aristocrats and their investigators here invoked recalls, to dissonant effect, the comparable understanding of placement within the social machine emphasized by Julia Dewey in her 1899 *Lessons on Manners* (see earlier discussion).

56. London, "The Road," 71.

57. London, "How I Became a Socialist," in *Jack London on the Road*, 100.

58. The project becomes more striking still when we note that, as Tapley makes clear in her thesis, tramp discourse typically advanced a countervailing view, abjecting in racist and xenophobic terms the tramp population.

59. London, "The Tramp," in *Jack London on the Road*, 135–36.

60. Ibid., 135.

61. Ibid., 129–30.

62. Ibid., 134.

63. Ibid., 135.

64. Auerbach, *Male Call*, 9. I should note that I differ with Auerbach with respect to the issue of determinism in this essay, which in my view builds on traces of determinist thinking—not least in its misrecognition, as capitalism's logic, of the *illogic* of capitialism.

65. London, "The Apostate," in *Jack London on the Road*, 161.

66. Seltzer, *Bodies and Machines*, 13.

67. I am indebted to Seltzer's theorization of such coupling, both in London's story and in the era more generally. See *Bodies and Machines*, especially the section "Bodies in Motion" (12–16).

68. London, "The Apostate," 152.

69. Ibid., 160.

70. Ibid., 151, 158.

71. See Brown's discussion of the "uncanniness" of automata, an uncanniness intimately involved in the entrancing hesitations of automatic things ("Science Fiction, the World's Fair, and the Prosthetics of Empire," in *Cultures of United States Imperialism*, 135).

72. To the extent that trampland offers to the apostate at least the fantasy of release from the neurasthenic ordeal of industrial life, I am tempted to read the story's conclusion as, among other things, a hybrid fusion of Silas Weir Mitchell's "rest" and "West" cures parodically envisioned for the underclass.

73. *The Portable Jack London*, ed. Earle Labor (New York: Penguin, 1994), 462, 463.

74. Auerbach, *Male Call*, 44.

75. Ibid., 136.

76. London, *Martin Eden* (New York: Penguin, 1984), 115. Subsequent citations refer to this edition.

77. Eden's first topic is his new project: writing about "the voyage of the treasure-hunters" is manifestly a hunt for treasure. "[D]runk with unguessed power," he sees in writing a means to "master" the world: "He was invincible. He knew how to work, and the citadels would go down before him. He would not have to go to sea again—as a sailor; and for the instant he caught a vision of a steam yacht. There were other writers who possessed steam yachts" (115). Thus in this fantasy a knowledge of travel coupled with a practice of writing promises to transform travel's experience, its materiality.

78. The concept gets invoked by Eden's lover Ruth, to exemplify the "chimeras" that "eccentric inventors" seek while "starving their families" (329). Evidently the narrative aims to dispel the notion that perpetual motion is merely ephemeral, by documenting its exactions.

79. Loren Glass, "Nobody's Renown: Plagiarism and Publicity in the Career of Jack London," *American Literature* 71 (3) (September 1999), 537.

80. "The Tramp," in *Jack London on the Road*, 135.

81. The emergence of exoticizing fantasy from "a long horizontal line of white" will recall the earlier "white heat" of Eden's authorial endeavors (as, more obliquely, the bleaching effects of laundry work), and as such will intimate the racialist cast of dynamics of labor and leisure in London's novel.

82. The reading will recall Eve Kosofsky Sedgwick's argument, cited in chapter 2, about the requisitioning of "whole societies in the service of fantasy needs . . . [especially] sexual fantasy" (*Between Men: English Literature and Male Homosocial Desire*, 73).

83. One might speculate that, with this vision of a prince surrounded by "dark-skinned servitors" and entertaining "all the best of the South Pacific riffraff," London has Eden place himself in intimate association with what London calls "the

lords and masters" of trampland—"the aggressive men, the primordial noble men, the *blond beasts* of Neitzsche [sic], lustfully roving and conquering through sheer superiority and strength" ("Rods and Gunnels," 95).

84. *Portable Jack London*, 544.

85. London, *The Cruise of the Snark* (New York: The Macmillan Company, 1936), 338.

86. Ibid., 339. It seems telling that, in solving the mystery of his body's "nervous" dissolution, London ends up entangling solar or "natural" and technological or "cultural" ravages.

87. Ibid., 338.

88. Ibid., 170.

89. Ibid., 171.

90. Raymond Callahan, *Education and the Cult of Efficiency* (Chicago: University of Chicago Press, 1962), 6.

91. Ibid., 3.

92. For an incisive analysis of the significance of Taylorization for the cultural projects and productions of the several, interimplicated modernisms, see Martha Banta, *Taylored Lives: Narrative Productions in the Age of Taylor, Veblen, and Ford* (Chicago: University of Chicago Press, 1993).

Epilogue

1. Greg Boozell's "Commemorative Postage Stamp Series," a politicized online installation, includes an image entitled "Where Do You Want to Go Today?" that juxtaposes the phrase "job security" with the charge "prison labor packages software" (www.mayweek.ab.ca/md1948/contest/greg12.html; accessed 18 September 2003). The ironies of immobility underscored by Boozell's satire bear on my analysis of strategic stasis in the contemporary moment.

2. Neil Smith, *American Empire: Roosevelt's Geographer and the Prelude to Globalization* (Berkeley and Los Angeles: University of California Press, 2003), xi, xii.

3. Ibid, xiii. What I would call the *ambidexterity* of American exceptionalism, advancing both nationalism and globalism, likewise preoccupies Amy Kaplan in her incisive account of "the anarchy of empire" in the U.S. nineteenth century: "American exceptionalism is in part an argument for boundless expansion, where national particularism and international universalism converge" (*The Anarchy of Empire in the Making of U.S. Culture*, 16). For a related argument, see also Thomas Peyser, *Utopia and Cosmopolis: Globalization in the Era of American Literary Realism* (Durham, NC: Duke University Press, 1998). Focused on nineteenth-century moments, the arguments of Kaplan and Peyser will trouble claims for globalization's utter *newness*—an issue I address later in this epilogue.

4. By contrast, an engagement with these messier histories would, for a start, need to take seriously the overdetermined, potentially recompensatory correspondence between 11 September 2001 and 11 September 1973, when a U.S.–sponsored coup in Chile led to the overthrow of Salvador Allende's government and to years of fascist terror under Pinochet.

5. Mike Davis makes a provocative argument that the atrocities of "9/11" mark "the end of American exceptionalism"—precisely because on that day the United States could no longer maintain delusions of geographical invincibility: "The walled subdivision on End of History Lane turned out to be only one subway stop from The War of the Worlds." Given the strikingly exceptionalist character of U.S. domestic and foreign policy since the attacks, however, I find Smith's concept of a reinvented exceptionalism more convincing. See *Dead Cities and Other Tales* (New York: The New Press, 2002), 3–4.

6. Tending toward caricature, my five-part list of processes flattens the complex contradictoriness of the contemporary moment, as a sustained reading of the critical literature on globalization will show. This literature is too vast to summarize adequately here. For an excellent introduction to the often conflicting meanings of the term, and to the debates it has inspired, see Imre Szeman's entries in the *Encyclopedia of Postcolonial Studies*, ed. John Hawley (Westport, CT: Greenwood Press, 2001), 209–17, and *The Johns Hopkins Guide to Literary Theory and Criticism*, 2nd ed., ed. Michael Groden, Martin Kreiswirth, and Imre Szeman (Baltimore: Johns Hopkins University Press, 2005).

7. Jean and John M. Comaroff, "Millennial Capitalism: First Thoughts on a Second Coming," in *Millennial Capitalism and the Culture of Neoliberalism*, ed. Comaroff and Comaroff (Durham, NC: Duke University Press, 2001), 28.

8. Ibid., 14.

9. Susie O'Brien and Imre Szeman, "'Content Providers of the World Unite!,'" Institute on Globalization and the Human Condition Working Papers Series (March 2003), www.humanities.mcmaster.ca/~szeman/cv.htm (accessed 15 September 2003).

10. Smith, *American Empire*, xvi.

11. 9 January 2003; quoted by David Bacon in "Using National Security to Bash Workers," *ZMag* 12 May 2003, www.zmag.org/content/showarticle.cfm?SectionID=19&ItemID=3606 (accessed 27 August 2003).

12. On the "global" Martí, see the dossier of essays, "'Our Americanism' in the Age of 'Globalization': Contemporary Frontiers," in *José Martí's "Our America": From National to Hemispheric Cultural Studies*, ed. Jeffrey Belnap and Raúl Fernández (Durham, NC: Duke University Press, 1998).

13. Imre Szeman, "Culture and Globalization, or, The Humanities in Ruins," *CR: The New Centennial Review*, 3 (2) (2003), 96.

14. CBC Radio 2, World Report, 10 September 2003. In the same news story, Senator Robert Byrd, Democratic Representative from West Virginia, observed that "Congress is not an ATM."

15. Jean and John M. Comaroff, "Millennial Capitalism," 23.

16. My point about antebellum terrors haunting the present is not at all intended to equate Nat Turner with Osama Bin Laden. The latter is in no sense subaltern; he represents instead the counterpart of and complement to the capitalist elites driving globalization. Pertinent, here, is what Smith calls "the prospect of a neoliberal global economy cross-cut and always potentially disrupted by a contest between the private-market terror of the al Qaeda sort on one side and state-sponsored terror of the U.S., British, Israeli, or Iraqi sort on the other" (*American Empire*, xv).

17. Walter Benjamin, "Theses on the Philosophy of History," in *Illuminations*, ed. Hannah Arendt, trans. Harry Zohn (New York: Schocken Books, 1969), 255.

18. My concept of imperial amnesia draws on Michael Rogin's bracing theorization of political amnesia in "'Make My Day': Spectacle as Amnesia in Imperial Politics," *Representations* 29 (winter 1990): 99–123.

19. Tariq Ali, *Clash of Fundamentalisms* (London: Verso, 2002), 281.

20. For a provocative counterpart to my sense of memory as an embodied, active habit, see Pierre Bourdieu's argument about the incorporation of habitus in *Pascalian Meditations*.

Index

Mark Simpson is associate professor of English at the University of Alberta.